THE GLORIOUS
REVOLUTION OF
1688

THE GLORIOUS
REVOLUTION OF
1688

by
MAURICE ASHLEY

CHARLES SCRIBNER'S SONS
New York

Acknowledgements

I am indebted to Professor G. H. Jones of Eastern Illinois University for reading this book in manuscript and to Ivan Roots of the University of Wales for reading it in proof and for their valuable suggestions. I am also obliged to Professor E. H. Kossmann for reading Chapter I. I am grateful to the Librarian of Nottingham University for allowing me to look at the Portland MSS. and for the unfailing courtesy of the officials of the British Museum and of the higher officials of the Public Record Office. It is a pity that for forty years the services and comfort of the Record Office have not been up to the standard set by the Museum, but, I am told, on good authority, that one day they will improve.

I regret that I have not had the time or opportunity to examine the Dutch archives, but I understand these may not be very important. With regard to published works I should like to express my debt to Professor J. P. Kenyon of the University of Hull whose ideas are always original and stimulating; I understand that he is engaged on a comprehensive and important study of the Revolution which will not appear for some years.

I should also like to take this opportunity to pay my heartfelt tribute to the memory of David Ogg, my former tutor, who died last year and first aroused my interest in the subject. Ogg, like my friend Dr. Esmond de Beer (whose chapter on this subject in the *New Cambridge Modern History* will appear some day), was an admirer of Lord Macaulay's account in his *History of England*. While recognizing Macaulay's genius I do not admire him to the same extent. But of course my aim is modest compared with that of the works I have mentioned. I simply want to retell and reappraise a remarkable historical episode in the light of modern research. I hope I have succeeded in that aim.

MAURICE ASHLEY

Ruislip, January, 1967.

Contents

Documentation

CHAPTER I

Portraits of Two Princes

THE 'Glorious Revolution' of 1688 was a decisive event in the history of modern Europe and also of the English-speaking world; for it changed the character of English government, gave meaning to a political philosophy and contributed to the working out of a balance of power among nations. Its hero was Prince William III of Orange, who was to become King William III of England; its villain—or victim—was King James II of England who was also King James VII of Scots. James was not only the uncle but also was the father-in-law of William who, as a result of the Revolution, replaced him on the thrones of England and Scotland.

The causes of the Revolution stretch far back into English history, at least as far as the Protestant Reformation; its consequences have endured until present times. Traditionally it has been presented as a triumph for the purity of constitutional law over a blatant and outrageous attempt at its perversion, a reaffirmation of the liberties of the English people after the exercise by a monarch of unbridled arbitrary power. That has been called 'the Whig interpretation' which extends from those who wrote about the Revolution soon after it took place to the late Dr. G. M. Trevelyan whose popular account was published in 1938.

But to other twentieth-century historians it has appeared as a 'respectable revolution', an upper-class revolution, which left the integrity of the Stuart monarchy almost unimpaired: a slow and sober development of the inevitable forces of history, following accepted lines and scarcely deserving the title of a revolution at all. Yet history is, after all, the story of human beings, of individuals, as well as of the classes and the masses. These two princes, nephew and uncle, who were the leading actors in the drama, were both men of ideals as well as of human weaknesses, and both were politicians, though one was clever and the other rather stupid. Let us take a look at them first before examining the background and telling the story of the Revolution of 1688.

9

William of Orange[1] was the great-grandson of William the Silent, Prince of Orange and Count of Nassau, who fought for the political independence of the Netherlands against the tyranny of Spain. But in his blood too was mingled that of the Stuarts, the Scottish kings who succeeded Elizabeth Tudor on the English throne. William III's mother was a daughter of King Charles I of England, a princess who never adapted herself, or tried to adapt herself, to Dutch ways. The principality of Orange that he inherited was merely a small enclave in southern France, of little territorial or economic significance. But the Nassau inheritance was a rich one. Thus the princes of Orange enjoyed a title that gave them honour and a property that afforded them wealth. All of them indeed were cosmopolitan figures and William III especially so. William the Silent had been the protégé and servant of the Spanish King Charles I. As a boy William III himself had at times been the personal concern both of the King of England, his uncle, and of the King of France, his self-appointed 'tutor' for the principality of Orange. William's grandmother was a strong-minded German princess, Amalia of Solms-Braunfelt. Her nephew, another of William's uncles, was Frederick William, the 'Great Elector' of Brandenburg, the forefather of the Hohenzollern dynasty of Prussian kings. Through his mother William was descended also from King Henry IV of France.

But though he was of mixed descent, he was a Dutchman by birth, through his father's line, and because of his upbringing. His father, William II of Orange, and his grandfather, Prince Frederick Henry, had both been Stadholders or executive officers of Holland and other Dutch Provinces as well as Captains-General and Admirals of the Dutch Union. But they had been the servants, not the masters of the Dutch republic. Neither the Stadholderate nor the Captain-Generalship was a hereditary office.

Both William's grandfather and father had been extremely ambitious statesmen, who, because of the latter's marriage to Princess Mary of England in 1641, were committed to the cause of the Stuarts. Prince William II had done everything he could to help his father-in-law, the unfortunate King Charles I, who lost both his throne and his head as a result of the civil wars in England. William II had been opposed in his political schemes by the Regents of Holland, the single-minded bourgeois class of oligarchs whose aim was, above all, national peace and prosperity, not international glory or foreign wars. In support of his plans William II had in August 1650 seized six leading Dutch Regents, including Jacob de Witt, the Pensionary of Dordrecht, and imprisoned them in Loevestein castle. But the *coup d'état* failed and soon afterwards he died.

So William III, who was born a posthumous son on November 4, 1650, eight days after his father's death, inherited his father's acquired unpopularity with the Regent class or 'Loevestein party'. These oligarchs professed themselves afraid of one-man rule by yet another member of the princely family that recently had proved itself far too attached to its own interests and those of the Stuarts. Indeed William's widowed mother, who had never cared for the Dutch, threw herself wholeheartedly into the support of her exiled brother, the future Charles II of England. She sold all she could spare to obtain money for his purposes. She entertained him, and followed him around Europe. In a famous letter she said—light-heartedly perhaps—that she loved this brother more than she did her only son.

Thus in the early years of his life Prince William III had no father and rarely saw his mother. Moreover he was without honours in his own country. Under pressure from the Lord Protector Oliver Cromwell, who feared the Oranges' aid to the royal Stuarts, he was banned from election to the Stadholderate or Captain-Generalship of the State of Holland by an Act of Seclusion. For his education he was given into the hands of his grandmother's secretary and a Dutch Calvinist pastor. But he was at least not encumbered with the all-embracing classical education so acceptable to the English upper classes. Instead he received instruction in modern history and military science. He learned French, German and English as well as Dutch. He read Italian and Spanish. Mathematics, geography and Latin were also inculcated. For a time he pursued these studies in the university town of Leiden. It was a broad and useful education. His amusements included tennis, fencing and hunting, which he adored, like all the Stuarts.

As he was to confess later, William was a lonely youth. In 1660, after Charles II had been restored to his throne, his mother hastened over to England to see her favourite brother and collect her debts, to be struck down with small-pox and to die there. Though in her will Charles II was asked to take responsibility for this ten-year-old orphan, the Dutch Regents would not acquiesce in that and for a time his guardianship in effect devolved upon his grandmother, the Dowager Princess Amalia, while an illegitimate uncle was appointed to be his governor; but finally in 1666, as William approached manhood, the State of Holland decided to make itself directly responsible for the upbringing of the Prince of Orange and he became a 'Child of State'. Thenceforward John de Witt, the Grand Pensionary of Holland, son of the Regent who had been imprisoned in Loevestein castle by William's father, took a personal interest in the completion of the young man's education. Perhaps he hoped to make a better Dutchman of him than his parents had been. By now William had been fully instructed in the Reformed or Calvinist religion, the official religion of the Dutch republic, which conferred on him a melancholy outlook tempered by a glowing belief in Providence. But from De Witt he received political and constitutional lessons, though, unlike Cardinal Mazarin in France, from whom King Louis XIV had been receiving lessons in the mysteries of government, De Witt did not dream that one day his pupil would supplant him. It was a curious relationship. Yet can it be doubted that De Witt's teaching took root?

A striking portrait of Prince William at the age of eleven exists in Haarlem attributed to his drawing master. It shows him to have been slim, dark, pale and handsome with a thoughtful look on his face: he is pictured, appropriately enough, in ceremonial armour. His large and brilliant eyes and aquiline or hooked nose were noted by all observers. At fifteen he was described as vigorous and tall, though in fact he was never much over five feet six inches high. In his twenties he was struck down with small-pox, the scourge of his times. According to Dr. Gilbert Burnet, who came to know him well, he was always asthmatical 'and the dregs of the small-pox falling on his lungs, he had a constant deep cough'.[2] Others have thought him to have been tubercular. One foreigner observed that 'his life always hung by a thread'.[3]

As to William's character, Sir William Temple, for a time the English ambassador at The Hague, commended his 'good plain sense',[4] but unquestionably he was a self-possessed and passionate young man, with a formidable will-power. He told the Marquis of Halifax in later life that he had 'a great jealousy of being thought to be governed'.[5] But at an early age he taught himself to control his temper and conceal his emotions. Far from insensitive to what went on around him, he was normally withdrawn and grave, and rarely gay. Yet he relaxed among his own intimates. Dr. Burnet, who did not find him very affable (but then William thought Burnet was a tedious busybody), admitted the Prince could be cheerful 'with a few',[6] while the Prince himself confessed that he had 'naturally an aversion to talk with many together . . . he loveth single conversations'.[7] With his favourites, William Bentinck, his boyhood page, with Elizabeth Villiers, his only known mistress, and with Arnold Joost van Keppel, the handsome substitute-son of his widowerhood, he was more open and friendly: at least that may be inferred from some of his letters.

The qualities that built William into a statesman were his immense self-control and self-assurance, his aptitude for hard and thorough work, his strength of character, fired by an inner passion, his amazing memory, his power to concentrate on essentials, and his consciousness of his destiny, derived from a Presbyterian upbringing. It was complained that he was slow in reaching decisions, but once he had taken them, he stuck to them. Always he was eager to learn. That was what prompted his first visit to England when he was twenty. He was anxious to see for himself the land of his mother and of his own country's enemies and trade rivals. His uncle, Charles II, then hoped to mould the Prince according to his own wishes. He made, it was said,[8] 'uncommon much of his nephew' and later hints came William's way that he might be a welcome suitor for his cousin, the Princess Mary, James's daughter, who was still a child. William kept his thoughts on this subject to himself. The French ambassador then in London noted that 'he was of a humour naturally solitary and retiring'.[9] His family still had too many critics in Holland to permit him to drop his guard. For a young man he was supremely cautious.

When William paid his first visit to England in November 1670, King Charles II had already concluded with King Louis XIV a secret treaty at Dover whereby he pledged himself to take part in a joint attack on the United Netherlands and to divide the spoils with France. The French King sought revenge for the Dutch diplomatic intervention against him earlier; the English King anticipated some profitable pickings. To pave the way for this piece of highway robbery of the Protestant Dutch, Charles had told the French King and also confided to his brother James that he was ready to declare himself a Roman Catholic and lead his kingdom back into the papal fold. The French King at the time was more eager for the use of Charles's navy than for the salvation of his soul. Part of the original scheme of these two royal conspirators was that Prince William should be bribed to agree to their military plot with the offer of the 'sovereignty' over such Dutch territory as remained after its partition. That, it was believed, would be an overwhelming temptation to a young Prince whose ancestors had never before enjoyed supreme power or indeed held higher office than that of Captain-General or Stadholder.

Once the assault by French troops and English warships came in 1672, the Dutch citizens—in spite of all the precautions taken by John de Witt and the Loevestein or Republican party—called upon Prince William, who, they hoped, was stamped with the genius of his ancestors, to head their resistance to the Anglo-French invasion. The orthodox ministers of the Reformed Church gave him their blessing: he was their predestined leader. Captain-General at last, William then revealed his ruthlessness as a statesman. The Orangist partisans who had continued to exist and to drink William's health in secret ever since he was a child now broke into the open. De Witt, who had for so long tried to exclude the Prince from office, was held up to obloquy. William published a letter in which his uncle had squarely placed the blame for the outbreak of what was in fact an unprovoked war on John de Witt. Thus the Prince deliberately allowed public indignation to be worked up against this loyal servant of the republic; when, soon afterwards, De Witt and his brother were murdered, the assassins were not prosecuted and indeed some of those who were implicated were rewarded and promoted. It may well be, however, that William honestly considered that the De Witts had betrayed their country by the former alliance they had made with the French. He himself was to prove single-minded in his patriotism and in his distrust of France. He loved the Dutch and was true to the example of independence set by his ancestors.

William the Silent, like his great-grandson, had been the subject of temptations. But when he had been offered terms by Spain for his own benefit if he would abandon the fight for Dutch independence he had declared himself to be 'the servant and elected defender of the Estates of Holland'.[10] In the same way when, 100 years later, after the first disastrous campaign of this war of 1672, Charles II of England had sent a delegation to offer his nephew personal sovereignty as the price of surrender, William answered that 'he liked better the condition of Stadholder which they had given him, and that he believed himself obliged in conscience and honour not to prefer his interest before his obligation'.[11] Temple tells us that he spoke even more clearly and simply: 'I will never betray the trust that I was given nor sell the liberties of my country that my ancestors have so long defended.'[12]

Yet the methods that William used to achieve his high aims were frequently unscrupulous. Outwardly reserved, austere, taciturn, aloof, William employed every devious weapon in the politician's armoury, intrigue, bribery, party jobbery. He was no democrat. At home he was ready to allow the existing political system to continue so long as his own direction of military and foreign affairs was accepted. Abroad he worked ceaselessly for the security of his country. He had his network of agents and spies both in the Netherlands and in England. He once declared that he 'would think no more of doing things popular but doing what was right';[13] yet, at the same time, he cynically confessed that 'the world is a beast that must be cozened before it is tamed'.[14]

His period of tutelage during the Stadholderless period had lasted for twenty-two years and taught him ingenuity and restraint in his political dealings. After his call to power in 1672, like William the Silent before him, William III of Orange defended his country heroically from behind the water line. He was not to become an outstanding soldier, but, like George Washington later, he never knew when he was beaten. The French retreated: the English withdrew from the contest; German allies were acquired. The war continued with many changes of fortune. Gradually European opinion was marshalled on the side of the victims of French aggression. But the Dutch Regents—the oligarchic rulers of Holland and other States who gathered in the States-General to determine foreign policy—did not want the war to be prolonged indefinitely. Their aim was a quiet and cultured life in their richly-furnished houses, not war *à l'outrance* for some distant and obscure ideal. Even Prince William's most intimate advisers, like Caspar Fagel, who succeeded the murdered De Witt as Grand Pensionary of Holland, turned against him. Stiffly and bitterly William went on fighting to the end. He had said in 1673 that he would be the enemy of France as long as he lived. Fifteen years later, after he had successfully invaded England to achieve the Glorious Revolution, that concept remained the driving force behind all his policies. As to war with France, Halifax was to observe after the Revolution had been completed, 'his eagerness that way never ceased; it was a question whether that thought was not the greatest inducement to his undertaking'.[15]

. . . . .

James, Duke of York,[16] was seventeen years older than his nephew: the second son of King Charles I and his French wife, Queen Henrietta Maria, he was exactly nine when, together with his elder brother, he became in 1642 a spectator at the first big battle of the English civil war, fought at Edgehill. He spent the formative years of his boyhood in the city of Oxford, then less a university town of dreaming spires and intellectual aspirations than the royalist military headquarters. When his father had fled in disguise and the city surrendered to the Roundheads in 1646, James became a prisoner in honourable captivity at St. James's Palace in London. Thence after various attempts to escape he finally got away disguised as a girl, to join his sister, the mother of Prince William of Orange, at The Hague.

Thus the Prince was 'much neglected in his childhood'.[17] Nor can he have enjoyed a very thorough education in war-scarred Oxford. His relations with his mother, whom he later joined in Paris, were ambivalent: at any rate they did not get along well together. Disobediently he left her side, but was forced by his elder brother to return. Nobody wanted a penniless and exiled prince. Eventually when he was eighteen he enlisted in the French Army as a volunteer and the happiest years of his life were those which he passed fighting under the famous Marshal Turenne. Whether, as Dr. Burnet asserts, Turenne really 'said often of him, "There was the greatest prince, and like to be the best general of his time" ' must be doubted; but he certainly praised the young prince. And James learned something of the science of warfare, as one can see by reading his dull and detailed memoirs of those campaigns.

After the Paris Government broke with King Charles II of

16

England, James reluctantly left the French Army and joined the Spanish. On his return to England with his restored brother in 1660 James actively assumed the position of Lord High Admiral of England, which he had held since he was a baby, and actually fought at sea in critical battles at the beginning of each of two wars against the Dutch. James has not lacked his modern admirers. 'He was a prince of firm integrity,' writes Sir Arthur Bryant,[18] 'a strong religious faith, a loyal master and friend and . . . a fine administrator, especially in naval and military matters in which from his earliest years he had had much experience.' But Samuel Pepys, who served him in the Admiralty after the Restoration, was not impressed by his capabilities, and though he later became more assiduous in his administrative duties, he never acquired much technical naval knowledge except perhaps as a navigator. And if he achieved more fighting experience than most modern English monarchs, he revealed little evidence of skill as a commander.

The truth was that after years of penury and exile James on his return to England set out to make up for lost time by enjoying himself in his own rather narrow way. His two passions were women and hunting. King Charles once said to a French ambassador, Courtin:[19] 'I do not believe that there are two men who love women more than you and I do, but my brother, devout as he is, loves them more.' On the eve of the Restoration he fell in love with Anne Hyde, the daughter of the Lord Chancellor, whose qualities, James wrote in his memoirs, were 'capable of surprising a heart less inclinable to Sex than was that of his Royal Highness in the first warmth of his youth'.[20] Just before she gave birth to their child, James married her, whether at his own wish or on his brother's insistence is not clear. At any rate his marriage did not interrupt his other sexual activities. Lord Ailesbury, who knew him well, wrote long afterwards that 'in former days he had been very amorous more out of a natural temper than for the genteel part of making love which he was much a stranger to'.[21] 'Quickly,' noted Dr. Burnet severely,[22] he 'ran into amours and vice.'

Prince James is said to have been one of the first English exponents of fox-hunting. During the interval between being a soldier and a sailor, he occupied much of his time in the hunting field or the bedchamber. All that would have been unimportant if he had not allowed his 'vices' to prey on his mind. Attracted to the Roman Catholic religion when he and his first wife were in Brussels before their marriage, he finally became 'a hearty penitent'. When he was in his middle thirties he was converted. First he gave up taking the sacraments according to the rites of the Church of England; then he ceased attending its services altogether. His new faith became common knowledge when he resigned the post of Lord High Admiral after the first Test Act, forbidding Roman Catholics to hold public office, was passed in 1673. He came to believe that the only road to forgiveness and salvation was through his Church. His policy as King, as we shall observe later, was determined by his desire to obtain equal rights for his fellow-religionists. One of his intimates then wrote, 'If he had the empire of the whole world, he would venture the loss of it, for his ambition is to shine in a red letter after he is dead.'[23]

James therefore took his pleasures sadly and grew increasingly conscious of the wrath of God. Whereas William of Orange felt that Providence guided his every footstep, James thought that Providence inspected his and sometimes disapproved. He could only hope, not blithely as his elder brother did, but mournfully that his sins would be forgiven him. When he was a boy he was said to have been 'fair and handsome', rather dashing, speaking fluent French, and not without admirers at his mother's Court. He had a long jaw and a narrow nose. The contrast between his youthful and later portraits is noticeable. He became increasingly more arrogant and disagreeable-looking as he grew older. Unlike his brother, he was rarely light-hearted or good-humoured or able to laugh things off. He treated himself and his offices with gravity. And he was exceptionally obstinate.

His stubbornness was remarked upon by all who discussed him. 'He suffers very impatiently the least contradiction,' wrote a French ambassador in London,[24] 'he is very pleased at being complimented on bold displays of power'; another noted that he was 'firm to the point of pig-headedness'.[25] As King he was to be haughty, lacking in self-control, proud, quick to punish, though capable of showing mercy less out of a sense of justice than as a noble demonstration of his own might. But whether, as some said, he was a strong man is questionable. Obstinacy is not strength. Certainly he learned again and again to obey his brother. Even before Charles II got back his throne, he insisted on James doing what he was told: for example, to rejoin his mother when he was a boy, to leave the French Army when he was twenty-two, to dismiss servants and advisers of whom his brother disapproved. Later he was twice obliged by the King to give up his active command at sea even when he was 'master of our whole sea force'. In theory, it is true, he did not approve of showing weakness. In his memoirs he condemned his father, taking his mother's side in the belief that the civil war would never have come about, or been lost by the royalists when it did, if a tough policy had been followed. Inevitably, in view of the impressions garnered in his youthful and formative years, James disliked Parliament and distrusted puritans. 'I know the English,' he told the French ambassador immediately after he became King, 'you must not show them any fear in the beginning.'[26]

The attempts that were made in Parliament, after his known conversion to Roman Catholicism, to exclude Prince James from the succession to the throne merely sharpened his dislike of the institution as such. 'The Exclusion Bill,' he wrote in July 1679, 'destroys the very being of the monarchy, which, I thank God, yet has had no dependency on parliaments nor on nothing but God alone, nor never can, and be a monarchy.'[27] These exclusionist Parliaments, he thought, aimed at nothing less than the destruction of monarchy and 'to set England aflame again'. Like his grandfather, he clung to the divine right of kings. Like Queen Elizabeth I, he believed that Parliaments should be obedient and be kept in order.

But if, theoretically, James wanted to act as a strong man and a strong king, hard yet wise, if he was anxious to show himself capable of 'bold displays of power' and to be the master of his Parliaments, he was lacking in those absolute requisites of statesmanship: resilience, adaptability, tact. He possessed qualities which for a time commanded respect. He was accessible. Unlike most of the Stuarts, he was pretty loyal to his advisers and servants. He did not penalize men who failed him. As a king he was methodical, diligent and conscientious over reading papers, seeing ambassadors, inspecting troops. Genuinely proud of his country, he wryly praised the prowess of English soldiers or sailors who defeated his side in battle. He had, it was said, 'a true English spirit'.[28] Indeed Lord Ailesbury, the author of this tribute, thought he had 'all the moral virtues', was 'a most sober prince' and 'a great and good Englishman'. Certainly his innate stubbornness would never have permitted him to become the mere officer of either the Pope or the French King.

Yet with all his patriotism, all his pride, all his obstinacy, James was a lath painted to look like iron. William of Orange might be slow to make up his mind, but once decided he acted ruthlessly and effectively. James turned from one set of advisers to another; he looked for counsel, for support, for consolation. Largely he depended on his wives. His first wife, whom he commended in his memoirs, managed his private business affairs and probably took him into the Roman Catholic Church. An Italian envoy noted of his young and beautiful second wife, Mary Beatrice of Modena, whom he married in 1673, that 'the Duke loves her tenderly, and does nothing without informing her'.[29] Indeed he was not a little afraid of her. When they were in exile together after the Revolution, it was she who tried to incite him to regain his throne.

James long enjoyed excellent health. He hunted until the end of his days. He outlived his elder daughter and nearly succeeded in surviving her husband. The idea that has been put forward in explanation of his failure as a king that he suffered from some obscure mental disease is hard to prove or accept. What he lacked, like so many of his family, was moral courage and intellectual ability. An astute French observer wrote in December 1687, on the very eve of the Revolution: '*les lumières de son esprit ne sont pas fort étendues*'.[30] That perhaps best sums up the character of King James II.

. . . . .

In the autumn of 1677 Prince William sought the hand of his cousin Mary, Prince James's elder daughter, in marriage. As has been noted, the first suggestion of this alliance had come from the English side. King Charles II's motives were clear: he hoped to bind his nephew to his interests and at the same time impress upon his Parliament, which had sat ever since his accession, that he was neither the sycophant of France nor, as had naturally been rumoured since the signature of the treaty of Dover, a Roman Catholic in disguise. For his part William had heard good reports of his cousin, who was in fact to grow into a beautiful woman and a devoted wife, but he had also hoped to wean his royal uncle from his former ties with France. When he visited England for a second time, in 1677, in pursuit of marriage, William was utterly determined that it should be a marriage without conditions. He was still fighting against France and had no intention of being forced into accepting Louis XIV's peace terms as the price of a dynastic alliance with the English Crown. Under pressure Charles II yielded the point. No sooner had the wedding been celebrated (November 4) than Prince William quickly took his fifteen-year-old bride back home. The doubtful party to this transaction was the bride's father, James, Duke of York. For James had even hoped at one time that Mary might marry the Dauphin, heir to the French throne. Even if she could not acquire so splendid a prospect, surely she might have been found a Roman Catholic husband and thus be wedded to the true faith? But, as usual, James did as his brother ordered and indeed boasted that he thus was setting a good example of obedience to the King's less exalted subjects. It was not because James was in any sense a French client or agent that he hesitated over agreeing to the marriage; on the contrary. He had, or thought he had, the best interests of his daughter at heart. In the following year he even hoped that Charles might place him in command of an English expeditionary army to be sent over to the United Netherlands to fight alongside his son-in-law and compel the mighty Louis XIV to accept peace in Europe. That was not to be. But for the eleven years that were to follow, the paths of William of Orange and his father-in-law were intertwined and not to be finally distinguished until the Revolution of 1688.

NOTES TO CHAPTER I

1. The best biographies in Dutch are by N. Japikse (1930) and J. K. Oudendijk (1954). That by Stephen B. Baxter appeared since this book went to press.
2. Burnet, iv, 548.
3. De la Tour in Krämer, *Archives*, 3rd series, i (1907), xxviii *seq.*
4. T. P. Courtenay, *Memoirs . . . of Sir William Temple Bart*, i (1836), 285.
5. Foxcroft, ii, 203.
6. Burnet, iv, 508.
7. Foxcroft, ii, 202.
8. Cit. Nesca Robb, *William of Orange, etc.*, i (1962), 181.
9. Dalrymple, ii, 70.
10. Cit. C. V. Wedgwood, *William the Silent* (1944), 139.
11. Cf. P. Geyl, *History of the Low Countries* (1964), 119.
12. *Works* (1770), ii, 259.
13. Foxcroft, ii, 219.
14. *Ibid.*, 211.
15. *Ibid.*, 210.

16. The best biography is by F. C. Turner (1948).
17. Burnet, iii, 3.
18. *Memoirs of James II* (1962), i.
19. Cit. Turner, 61.
20. Clarke, i, 387.
21. Ailesbury, 132.
22. Burnet, iii, 5.
23. Kenyon, 112.
24. Cit. Turner, 235.
25. 'Memoir on the State of England', Dec. (?) 1687 in Baschet.
26. C. J. Fox, xviii.
27. *H. M. C. Savile Foljambe*, 133–4.
28. Ailesbury, 103.
29. Cit. Martin Haile, *Queen Mary of Modena* (1905), 54.
30. 'Memoir on the State of England', *ut supra*.

CHAPTER II

The Last Years of Charles II: (i) 1678-81

AFTER Prince William of Orange and Princess Mary of England had married in 1677, the English Government tried to help bring to an end the long war between the United Netherlands and France into which Spain and much of Germany as well as Sweden had been drawn. At that time King Charles II, supported emphatically by his brother James, was anxious to prove to the English Parliament and to his more influential subjects that he was no longer subservient to France or wished automatically to range himself on the side of the most powerful of Roman Catholic kings.

For feelings against 'popery' had been running high in England for the past hundred years. The memories of 'Bloody Mary' and her execution of Protestants were handed down from generation to generation. It was remembered too that the Pope had published a Bull excommunicating Queen Elizabeth I and that Jesuits had encouraged attempts to murder her. So had her cousin, Mary, Queen of Scots, who, when she was in honourable captivity in England, plotted to rally English Roman Catholics to her cause. Every year Queen Elizabeth I's Accession Day, November 17, was celebrated by the burning of dummy popes. Then it was recalled also how Queen Elizabeth's successor, James I, who had been willing enough to show tolerance to English Catholics, had, together with his leading subjects, been menaced by the Guy Fawkes plot, concerted by Roman Catholics, to blow up the Houses of Parliament in 1605. Charles I's Queen, the mother of Charles II and James II, was known to have been a zealous Roman Catholic propagandist; Archbishop Laud, Charles I's choice for Canterbury, was widely believed to have been a disguised papist; and a so-called massacre of English in Ireland by wild Irish papists had contributed to the revolt of Parliament against the monarchy in 1642.

In spite of the progress being made towards modern science, notably by the foundation of the Royal Society at the beginning of Charles II's reign, this was still a credulous age. As much importance was attached to astrology and alchemy as to astronomy and chemistry. Even educated Englishmen were genuinely and persistently afraid of the black and evil intentions of the papists, the dedicated servants of Anti-Christ. The Great Fire of London, which took place in 1666, was popularly attributed to them. In so far as witchcraft lingered on in rural areas it was associated in people's minds with popery.

It was also thought that insidious Roman Catholic influences prevailed at the Court of Whitehall and were responsible for the unsuccessful wars against the Protestant Dutch. There was an element of truth in that. According to the sole evidence of James II's memoirs (not a sound or reliable historical source) Charles II had declared himself privately to be a Roman Catholic as early as 1668. It may be doubted if he was ever a practising Catholic, but he certainly sympathized with the Catholic approach to religion and morality; and unquestionably James was a sincere convert. A Catholic camarilla had signed and approved the secret treaty of Dover which envisaged Charles II leading his people back into the Roman Catholic Church if a suitable opportunity presented itself. That was a diplomatic mirage; the King was far too realistic to push through such a policy. Unfortunately he had committed himself to it in black-and-white. And such projects have a habit of becoming known; there are no sustained secrets in political life. The King did not want to provoke his Parliament by being permanently labelled pro-French; and James believed that his only chance of retaining his position at the centre of affairs (having given up all his offices in consequence of the Test Act of 1673) was by directing a movement against France.

Thus immediately after Prince William's marriage Charles II sent an envoy to the French Court to try to persuade King Louis XIV to end the war on terms favourable to the Dutch. After the attempt failed plans were discussed both for an offensive treaty with the Dutch and for a long-term defensive alliance. Parliament was recalled in January 1678 and invited to vote money so that an army and navy might be made ready to give teeth to an Anglo-Dutch alliance. James talked about forcing the French King to see reason: Charles II's leading minister, the Earl of Danby, had told William of Orange at the end of November 1677 that James had said 'very briskly' that if the French did not agree to the English proposals the King of France should be told that he would not hinder England from coming into the war against him. In February 1678, English troops were actually landed at Ostend and in the same month the House of Commons voted the King a million pounds, carefully appropriating it to the cost of a war with France.

These were brave words and deeds. But in fact they got nowhere, for three reasons. In the first place, the French King had no intention of allowing himself to be intimidated by England. He launched an early campaign in Flanders and captured Ghent and Ypres, compelling the Dutch States-General, which was tiring of the war, to think seriously of peace. Secondly, the House of Commons had suspicions of the royal government that went deep. Members muttered about 'popery' and 'arbitrary power'. They were slow and difficult over giving effect to their money votes; they were dubious about the use the King might make of an army. Lastly Charles II himself did not have his heart in the plan. He had always admired the 'Sun King' and shown himself willing to be bribed to join his side with relatively small sums of money that were judiciously applied by the French ambassadors in London. So the proposed Anglo-Dutch treaties were never ratified. By May a secret agreement had been reached with France. At the same time the French ambassador distributed bribes among Members of Parliament, thus paralysing effective intervention.

So the hopes of William of Orange, nurtured by his English marriage and by the martial ambitions of his father-in-law, were blasted. Much to his indignation the States-General insisted on concluding peace with France. 'He withdrew to his estate at Dieren to find distraction in solitary hunting' (Geyl). A treaty was signed at Nymegen on July 31, 1678, which was of some value both to the Dutch and the French. The French granted important economic concessions, but acquired fortresses in the Spanish Netherlands. The Dutch burghers were thus able to return to their comforts and their commerce, while King Louis XIV, having successfully overcome the resistance of much of the rest of Europe, and having strengthened his north-east frontier, was in a position, after a short interval of deceptive quiet, to embark on fresh acts of aggression, this time against Germany. William of Orange watched all these developments with attention. He had made friends in England who kept him informed. He understood the temper of Parliament; he was also aware that the thirst for conquest in King Louis XIV was unquenched.

But England was little disturbed by any approaching storm

over Europe. Indeed the last seven years of Charles II's reign were rent by internal dissensions which brought fears of a renewed civil war and almost rehearsed the Glorious Revolution. The landmarks were two plots, the Popish Plot of 1678, epitomizing the fears of a Roman Catholic king of England, and the Rye House Plot of 1683, suggesting that if James's enemies could not secure their ends constitutionally they would do so by revolutionary means. Neither of these plots was completely genuine; both were largely the inventions or embroideries of lying informers. The clouds of smoke that enveloped the kingdom started from quite small fires. Yet the fires were real.

The original version of the Popish Plot as presented by the informers was that a group of Roman Catholics had been planning to murder the King in order to put his brother on the throne and hand over the kingdom to the papacy. It was first revealed to Danby in August. The King himself never believed in it, but as it gathered momentum, it endangered his brother's chances of succeeding peacefully to the throne. In a sense the plot stemmed from the pro-French and pro-Catholic atmosphere of the Court, and yet for a time Danby, a bold Yorkshire politician who owed his position to his financial gifts, hoped that it would actually strengthen him by weaning the King from his French affections and by rallying Parliament and people around the Church and Crown. Two events gave weight to the stories invented by the chief informer, Titus Oates: one was that incriminating letters were discovered written by a Roman Catholic who had been at one time secretary to James; the other was that the London magistrate before whom Oates swore depositions was found apparently murdered—of course by Catholics—on Primrose Hill in London. The King retreated before the consequent outcry and general excitement; the alleged plotters were arrested and put to death; Parliament was hastily recalled. One of its first decisions was to pass a second Test Act excluding Roman Catholics from both Houses of Parliament (though James himself was excepted from the Act by a majority of two votes). Articles of impeachment were prepared against Danby because of his secret dealings with France, dealings undertaken at the King's own orders, that were revealed by a disgruntled ambassador. Under these pressures Charles II realized that he might be obliged to accept limitations on the rights of the Crown if James were to succeed him without a civil war.

In an attempt to save Danby from impeachment the King dissolved Parliament, which had sat for eighteen years and had long ceased to be eagerly royalist, as it had been in its salad days, though it was still rigidly Anglican. Charles had one of his sudden fits of political energy. To spike the guns of those who wanted to replace James by the Duke of Monmouth, his eldest illegitimate son, known as 'the Protestant Duke', Charles II swore in public that he had not married Monmouth's mother; he ordered James to leave the country; he accepted the resignation of Danby, who was imprisoned in the Tower of London; and he established a new Privy Council whose members included such opposition critics as the Earl of Shaftesbury. The King again made known his willingness to agree to limitations on the Crown's prerogative if James were to become his successor. But the new House of Commons, which met in March 1679, insisted on introducing a Bill to exclude James completely from the throne, which passed its second reading by 207 votes to 128. To prevent it becoming law the King was compelled to prorogue and later to dissolve Parliament.

Before another Parliament met, the virulence of the anti-popery movement began to subside. The Queen's doctor was actually acquitted of planning the King's murder. Inquiries were made of the King of France whether he were willing to help preserve the integrity of the Stuart monarchy. James, in his enforced exile abroad, tried to steel his brother to stand up for the divine right of kings. Monarchy, he asserted, need not depend on the institution of Parliament: 'I hope his Majesty will be of this mind,' he wrote in July 1679,[1] 'and never let this House of Commons sit again.' Meanwhile William of Orange was perturbed about the unsettled state of England, about the threats to the future of the monarchy, about the danger that his wife's chances of succeeding to the throne might be impaired. He offered to provide the King with the English regiments which were in Dutch service. But he suspected and feared Charles II's negotiations with France and was opposed to any decision that would permanently dispense with Parliaments, as James wanted, since the last two Parliaments had proved themselves to be hostile to France. But William's own position at home was shaky and remained so for several years; for the States-General had come to regard him as a warmonger eager to renew the struggle with France. When Charles II actually suggested a kind of quadruple or even sextuple alliance should be formed in collaboration with the Dutch as a counter-weight to French ambitions, William was obliged to inform him that the States-General would not in its present mood contemplate such a proposal. William in fact was delicately placed in relation to England. On the one hand, Dutch suspicions of England after two wars fought against them by Charles II were still profound; on the other hand, the only way in which William himself could hope to keep the French in check was by means of an Anglo-Dutch alliance, the idea that had been toyed with, but not fulfilled, in the previous year.

Meanwhile James had ceased to be pro-Dutch and become pro-French because he thought that his own chances of succeeding to the throne with his rights unaltered now depended largely on French support. In the late summer of 1679 Charles II was taken seriously ill and James without permission hastened home; the King recovered, and James propped him up. Charles agreed to exile the Duke of Monmouth and to dismiss the Earl of Shaftes-bury, Monmouth's patron and the principal architect of the Exclusion Bill. A new Parliament, which had been elected that year and was due to meet in October, was at once prorogued until the following summer. Three 'middle-of-the-road' politi-cians, the second Earl of Sunderland, Laurence Hyde, later Earl of Rochester, and Sidney Godolphin took over as the King's chief ministers. James himself was allowed to retire to Scotland with a promise that he might soon come back to England.

But the long intermission in Parliaments—none met for eigh-teen months—a revival of anti-popery demonstrations, the publi-cation of numerous pamphlets, the widespread petitioning of the Crown to recall Parliament all combined to create a state of fear and uncertainty. Some of the more moderate advocates of exclusion urged William to come over to England to sustain and support his wife's claims as the next heir presumptive to the throne, should James be banned from the succession. But the Prince felt that[2] 'would do him hurt and the King no good and that he and the Dutch shall enter into disputes that may make them worse than they are now'. James's influence was reduced during his stay in Scotland and even after his return to England in February 1680. Indeed he actually seems to have hoped for a civil war which he thought this time the royalists would win and the Whigs, as the exclusionists were coming to be called, be crushed for ever. As for the French, on whom so many royal hopes were pinned, they were happy enough to see England neutralized by dissensions and threats of civil war. They knew that the English King was evasive and unstable, that his word was rarely his bond. In order to confuse matters further, they held out to the States-General the possibility of a Franco-Dutch alliance. That did alarm Charles II, who saw himself faced with isolation in Europe as well as with discord at home. He and his ministers put the boldest face they could on the matter. If the French should attack the Dutch, he assured Prince William, he would immediately declare war and at the same time call his Parliament. (That was a safe bet since the French King was not intending to attack the Dutch.) Schemes for defensive alliances were taken off the shelf and dusted. All that came of these manoeuvres was an Anglo-Spanish treaty which was signed in June. But Spain was a declining power; no one imagined her alliance was worth very much. These anti-French gestures, lighting up the Stuart monarchy with a glow of independence and a tinge of Protestantism, however, made the King feel that he would be able to dish the exclusionists. Schemes for legitimizing the Protestant Duke of Monmouth or getting the King to divorce his barren Portuguese Queen and produce a suitable Protestant offspring (as he was known from his adventures with his mistresses to be capable of doing) were firmly rejected. It looked as if Shaftesbury and the extreme Whigs must beat a retreat.

But the exclusionists had not yet shot their bolt. In June Shaftesbury had the audacity to appear before the Middlesex Grand Jury to indict James as a popish recusant and Charles II's mistress, the Frenchwoman Louise de Kéroualle, Duchess of Portsmouth, as a common prostitute. A quiet word was spoken to the Lord Chief Justice and the case was suppressed. But tempers were still boiling. In July James had informed his son-in-law that 'factious people grow very insolent'. Whig sheriffs, who controlled the choice of juries, were elected to the City of London. The differences between James and William of Orange were beginning to come into the open. On September 3 James, writing to tell his son-in-law that he thought there were some who intended to impeach him when at last Parliament met and adding that he would prepare for the worst, none the less insisted that he did not think, as William thought, that it would have a 'bad effect' if the King decided to dissolve the second exclusionist Parliament.[3] A month later in another letter James wrote to

William that the real design of the Whigs was 'to destroy the monarchy and all our family'.[4] He put his trust, as he was to do again later, in the loyal 'Church of England men' since 'all the fanatical dissenters were for a commonwealth'.

William of Orange had other sources of information besides his father-in-law's letters. Henry Sidney, who was the English ambassador to the United Netherlands but was on leave in England, told him rather disloyally that James 'has so exasperated the people they can scarce hear his name with patience'.[5] 'The King,' he added, 'is persuaded that it is impossible to agree with parliament and stick to his brother.' Before Parliament was at last called together in October 1680, James was packed off to Scotland. Undoubtedly a genuine fear prevailed among the well-to-do, 'the rich, sober men', that unless the Exclusion Bill were passed a republic would be established. James, sitting in more amenable Edinburgh, certainly thought so himself: 'For my part,' he wrote to William on November 5, 'I fear a rebellion or something worse, for everything almost goes after the same manner as it did in the year [16]40; only this country, God be thanked, is quiet, which it was not then.'[6]

The Whigs—and these included Robert, Earl of Sunderland, one of Charles II's Secretaries of State—had decided that the exclusion of James from the succession to the throne was inevitable, if only to prevent another civil war. To avert such a catastrophe they wanted William of Orange to come over to England so as to be a steadying influence among them once the Exclusion Bill was passed. For his wife, after all, was the next legitimate heiress in the royal line, while the Duke of Monmouth, the other Whig candidate, might become a mere tool of republicans. On November 5, the same day that James was writing mournfully from Scotland about the likelihood of civil war, Sunderland's wife was telling Henry Sidney, who was Sunderland's uncle, now back in Holland, 'if the Prince will not come, he must never think of anything here . . . his part is only to come and prevent the confusion which we must of necessity fall into'. Otherwise, she warned, Monmouth must be King. 'If the Prince thinks it not worth going over a threshold for three kingdoms, I know not why he should expect anybody else should for him.'[7] Though Sidney was reputed to be her lover, she must surely have been speaking for her husband. Sidney Godolphin added his pleas to those of his colleague's wife. Urging William to come over while Parliament was still sitting, he wrote that it was[8] 'absolutely necessary to the supporting of your own particular interests here which . . . stand at present upon very nice terms'.

What in fact was William's attitude to the proposal to exclude his uncle from the succession? As was his habit, he thought over the matter carefully, determined not to be hurried into making up his mind. Clearly he realized from the outset that if James were excluded by law from the throne, and if the movement in favour of Monmouth collapsed, then he himself would become a force in England. It was true that he had treated his wife badly; within a year of their marriage he had taken one of her ladies-in-waiting, Elizabeth Villiers, as his mistress, and his unfaithfulness had made Princess Mary ill. But she was a young and loyal wife. If she were called to the throne of England, she was bound to convey the executive power into his hands. Indeed later she promised as much. On the other hand, a practical alternative to excluding James from the throne that had been contemplated by Charles II from an early stage was to accept statutory limitations on the powers of the monarchy. And William did not like the idea of that alternative in the least. Still, if the exclusionist movement failed, and James later became King, the open support of William for the exclusionists would ruin any influence he might have at Whitehall. So in all his correspondence with his friends in England William maintained an attitude of caution and diplomacy. On November 11, after Parliament met, he informed one of Charles II's Secretaries of State, Sir Leoline Jenkins,[9] that he was 'vexed at the animosity against the Duke', that he hoped that Charles II and Parliament would now come to an agreement, and that all business in Holland was suspended while the results of the session were awaited. He feared that both the Stuart family and the future of Europe would be in grave danger if the meeting of the new Parliament did not have a satisfactory outcome.

In fact the House of Commons quickly passed the Exclusion Bill without a division; but it never looked like getting through the House of Lords. The King exerted his considerable influence with the peers, who on November 14 rejected the Bill by sixty-three votes to thirty. Speaking again and again, the Earl of Halifax, known to history as the Trimmer, put the arguments against the Bill and refuted the extreme Whig leader, the Earl of Shaftesbury. But the following day he introduced an alternative

Bill proposing strict limitations on the rights of the monarchy if a Roman Catholic should come to the throne. The Whigs, however, were not appeased and petitioned Charles II to dismiss the Earl of Halifax and even named him 'an enemy of the people'.

The defeat of the Exclusion Bill in the Lords and the limitations on the Crown proposed by Halifax came as a shock to Prince William. He at once made it clear that he was dead against limitations which he was convinced would undermine the very fabric of monarchy. For even if nominally they were imposed merely on a Roman Catholic king, they might not, he thought, be removed if a Protestant monarch succeeded. He had to decide whether he should openly exert his influence in favour of excluding his father-in-law from the succession, which he fancied might well be agreed at the next parliamentary session and be accepted by Charles II. His friend Sir William Temple told William that three courses were available to him:[10] he could come over at once and press for exclusion, he could stay where he was and see what happened, or he could wait until Parliament were dissolved and then cross to England to express his own views. But it hardly needed to be explained to him, as it was, that if he adopted the first course it would arouse unpleasant comment. Clearly a visit to England demanded the most delicate timing.

William seems to have decided that exclusion sooner or later was certain and was at any rate infinitely to be preferred to limitations upon the Crown he might one day wear. The States-General now sent over a memorandum through Henry Sidney pressing Charles II to come to an agreement with his Parliament for the sake of Europe as a whole. That meant, in effect, that they were advising him to accept exclusion. There can be little doubt that William approved the memorandum, although he wrote to James denying that it was so. The memorandum was evidently a mistake of judgment. Nothing infuriates a government more than to have its domestic policy dictated to it from abroad. James was enraged. Either limitations or exclusion, he thundered from Edinburgh, would destroy the monarchy, as it had once been destroyed before. But it was at this very time, around Christmas 1680, that William told Sidney that if in the next session of Parliament the Bill were passed and the King accepted it, he was ready to come over to England. He even asked if a yacht could be sent for him.[11]

Charles II, however, was not convinced that in order to avoid civil war he must abandon his brother, though many people thought that he would be obliged to do so. In fact he warned William that once the hereditary right of succession were given up an essential prerogative would have been lost and the very institution of kingship be put in peril. Other exclusions might follow; and the Duke of Monmouth might be preferred to Princess Mary. As his brother's daily warnings of republicanism were dinned into his ears, Charles II acted. He dissolved the second exclusionist Parliament on January 18, 1681, and ordered another one at once to be elected and to meet not in Westminster, always subject to the pressures of the London mob, but in royalist Oxford. He dismissed from his Council Essex, Temple and Sunderland, who were known to be Orangists and the friends of exclusion. He asked for immediate assistance from the French King, as James had been pressing him to do. And he gave his support, at least for the time being, to a compromise solution that while James should be allowed to take the title of King after his death, William and Mary as dyed-in-the-wool Protestants should be invited to become Protectors or Regents of the realm.

How did William react to all this? He thought that the dissolution of Parliament was a grave mistake; he feared that the next Parliament at Oxford would prove to be even more extreme, might indeed be republican in its sympathies. He still believed that exclusion was bound to come, although when Laurence Hyde later told Charles II that William's thoughts 'were still upon one expedient only', William expressed great indignation and was not mollified by hints of the regency solution.[12]

The first definite news of this scheme seems to have reached William towards the end of February 1681, just as the new Parliament was about to meet at Oxford. The King duly allowed the proposal to be put before the Commons, but they would not look at it. As usually happens in political life, a plausible compromise, which, if offered earlier, might have prevented a clash, when produced after tempers had become inflamed, proved ineffective and useless. Again the Commons prepared to pass the Exclusion Bill, but the two Houses of Parliament, meeting in Oxford, at once became involved in a complicated constitutional quarrel, and Charles, who meanwhile had been assured of the assistance he had sought from France, took the opportunity to get rid of his third exclusionist Parliament (March 28, 1681). No other Parliament was to meet in his reign.

33

To sum up: there was a strong feeling among leaders of English Protestant opinion that James must be stopped at all costs from mounting the throne as a Roman Catholic king. To prevent it, William was urged to come over to England while Parliament was sitting and exert his influence on behalf of the exclusionists. Charles II was sufficiently afraid of the dangers of revolution to be driven to suggest that William should actually be invited to act as a Regent after James succeeded. That was contemplated as a practical proposition. An alternative both to exclusion and regency was Halifax's proposal to reduce the powers of the monarchy and thereby strengthen the role of Parliament. Neither William nor James fancied that alternative: to them it savoured of republicanism. No one can say what might have happened if William had insisted on coming to England in the autumn of 1680 when the Exclusion Bill was for a second time passed by the House of Commons. But he hesitated to exert pressure or even to come out openly in favour of exclusion, and by the time he did come to England in the following year he had left it far too late.

Eight years afterwards Prince William had digested his lesson. By then the country had realized what it meant to have a Roman Catholic king of James's character. Once again some advocated exclusion, others regency, and there was widespread fear of a republican revival. But now when William came over to press his advice, again at the invitation of his Protestant friends in England, he took the precaution of bringing an army with him.

NOTES TO CHAPTER II

1. Dalrymple, ii, 224.
2. Sidney, ii, 46.
3. Prinsterer, v, 417.
4. *Ibid.*, 422.
5. *Ibid.*, 423–4.
6. *Ibid.*, 437.
7. Sidney, ii, 123; cf. Kenyon, 63.
8. Prinsterer, v, 437.
9. Dalrymple, ii, 305–6.
10. Prinsterer, v, 448.
11. Sidney, ii, 150.
12. Prinsterer, v, 484, 493.

CHAPTER III

The Last Years of Charles II: (ii) 1681–85

WHILE England was rent by internal political turmoil that brought her to the verge of civil war, King Louis XIV of France was already engaged upon fresh acts of aggression. The City of Paris had conferred upon him the title of 'Louis the Great' and the Marquis de la Fare claimed that he had become 'the arbiter of everything in this part of our hemisphere'. By intimidation, bribery and legal jiggery-pokery embraced under the name of 'acts of reunion', large slices of territory adjacent to land already under French sovereignty were annexed in Alsace, in Lorraine, and in neighbouring Franche-Comté without the need to declare war. William's uncle, the Great Elector of Brandenburg, disgruntled with the results of his Dutch alliance, moved over to the French side. The attention of the Emperor in Vienna was distracted by growing trouble in the east. Spain remained enfeebled. Only William of Orange himself persevered, in the face of every conceivable obstacle, in his hopes of forming a coalition, based upon an Anglo-Dutch agreement, to halt the French advance towards 'universal monarchy'.

At the beginning of March 1681, to the delight of his brother James, Charles II had concluded a secret verbal agreement whereby he became the pensioner of the French King for the remainder of his reign; he undertook to disengage himself by degrees from his recent public alliance with Spain, and Louis XIV promised in return not to attack the Netherlands. Ignorant of that agreement, William of Orange decided he must go over to England and try to impress on his uncle the importance of resisting the French domination of western Europe. That was what William's friends in Whitehall, the Orangists like Essex, Godolphin, Sunderland, Sidney and Temple, had long been pressing him to do. The French ambassador in London, egged on by messages from James in Scotland, had emphasised the need to counter any visit by William. 'It is time now or never to conclude this bargain,' he wrote in February,[1] 'for otherwise the

King of England will be obliged to put himself into the hands of parliament and of the Prince of Orange.' The Duke of York feared, he reported earlier,[2] that 'it was designed that the Prince of Orange should come over with a view that he might become the master of affairs and be established now in a manner which could not be changed hereafter'. Hence the hasty conclusion of the verbal agreement in March. But Charles II could hardly refuse to allow his nephew to visit him. Eventually William came over at the end of July, four months after the prorogation of the Oxford Parliament.

While William was making up his mind to visit England, his father-in-law was marooned in Scotland where he had been since the previous autumn; although he now held the post of King's Commissioner there, his attention was mainly concentrated on England. James had not approved of the calling of the Oxford Parliament and told William that he thought its dissolution had 'had a good effect'; for it had 'aimed at the destruction of the monarchy and if it had sat a little longer would have put all England in a flame'.[3] In spite of the part that the Earl of Halifax had played in defeating the Exclusion Bill in 1680 James was infuriated by Halifax's proposal that he should, when he succeeded, be reduced to the status of a monarch who reigned but did not rule. Halifax, he asserted, was 'an atheist without bowels' and thought if his 'timorous counsels' prevailed at Court all would be ruined.[4] Charles II at one time had contemplated an easy way out of his difficulties—namely, to induce James to rejoin the Church of England, and indeed James's brother-in-law, Laurence Hyde, was sent up to Scotland to see whether he could convert him. But James was adamant: it would be 'a base, mean thing', he told his friend, George Legge, 'besides the sin of it, to dissemble and deny my religion'.[5]

Naturally James did not relish the idea of William visiting England, while he himself was still confined in Scotland. And William's friends were a bit nervous: they thought that the Prince had been too obviously associated with the exclusionists and warned him that the King's closest advisers had complained that his letters were 'too high and too sharp'.[6] William's object was to remove such bad impressions and to induce King Charles to alter his foreign policy. As soon as he arrived at Windsor Castle he pressed on the King the need to protect the Low Countries against France. Charles retorted that he could only join an alliance with the United Netherlands and Spain to resist French aggression if he had a Parliament behind him. But he had been forced to dissolve his last two Parliaments because they had threatened the very existence of the monarchy; he had no cause to suppose that another Parliament would be any more reasonable: if he were to call one, he would be committing himself either to exclusion or limitations. The King then suggested that William might go up to London and have a talk with his friends there—the Whigs—and see if he could fix any arrangement with them. But the Whigs were still set on exclusion. And the King was afraid, in view of the radical feelings that prevailed in the City, if William were to be publicly entertained by the Lord Mayor and Aldermen, demonstrations against James would result. So the Prince was promptly called back to Windsor.

William was shocked by the state of affairs he saw there. (John Evelyn had noted in the previous year that it 'more resembled a luxurious and abandoned rout than a Christian Court'.) [7] Of all people, William selected the King's principal mistress, the French Duchess of Portsmouth, as the recipient of his criticisms. He told her that Charles II ought to pull himself together and re-establish his reputation at home and abroad. Otherwise, he thought, the King would sink into a state of nothingness from which he could not be rescued. So William returned to Holland, not having accomplished anything so far as the English Government was concerned. Some of his friends feared that he had actually done more harm than good. But the French ambassador, to whom the fullest account of the visit is owing, fancied that he had established useful contacts and that 'he believed that the worst that could happen to him was that he would have to wait until right of succession brought him the English Crown'. [8]

In Scotland James breathed a sigh of relief that his son-in-law's visit had passed off without trouble. He felt that the outlook for his brother, and for the future of the Stuart monarchy, was brighter than might have been expected, now that Parliaments had ceased to sit. 'Though not so absolute a master as I could wish,' he told William in his artless way, 'his [Charles II's] affairs will mend every day if he continue but steady to himself and his old friends and not let himself be deceived by those you say you were to go to speak with at London,' i.e. the Whigs: 'they have raised a devil they cannot lay and the less you have to do with such kind of people is no doubt the better.'⁹ A fortnight later he wrote to say that affairs were going well in England, and even better in Scotland where a Parliament over which he presided had disapproved of exclusionist measures. Indeed henceforward everything went swimmingly for James and the Tories for whom these were the years of triumph. Charles plucked up the courage to have the Earl of Shaftesbury imprisoned in the Tower, and, after his release, the Earl, who in the last days of his career was definitely backing the Duke of Monmouth as a Protestant claimant to the throne, fled to Holland to die in obscurity. In March 1682 James was allowed to return from Scotland; and that October a Tory was chosen Lord Mayor of Whiggish London.

The Whig extremists, that is to say those who were supporters of Monmouth or perhaps toyed with republican ideas, were now involved in the so-called Rye House Plot which was disclosed by informers in the summer of 1683. Although no convincing evidence was ever produced that any serious intention had existed to murder the King or his brother, incautious remarks and tales of half-baked conspiracies retailed by turncoats resulted in the suicide of the Earl of Essex and the execution of William Lord Russell and others. Some active Whig politicians and their hangers-on fled to Holland; the City of London was compelled to surrender its charter to the King; and during the last years of the reign Charles and James were able to govern without calling another Parliament and with French moral and material assistance.

Under these circumstances it was not surprising that Louis XIV was able to pursue his aggressive plans without effective interference from William of Orange. Indeed in August 1681 Louis ordered an attack on the city of Orange, William's patrimony in France; its walls were razed to the ground, an indemnity was imposed on its inhabitants, a decree was issued restraining its commerce, and no more Protestants were allowed to settle there. The English ambassador to France delivered verbal protests, for which William expressed his gratitude, but Charles II refused to exert any real pressure on his nephew's behalf.

If William of Orange could not rely upon the firm support of the English Court over so personal a matter as that, he could hardly expect help in resisting French aggression elsewhere. In September 1681 the French laid siege to Strasbourg, the only remaining independent territory in Alsace, which soon capitulated. In November an assault was launched upon Luxembourg, a fortress that commanded the communications between the Spanish Netherlands and Germany. William set about forming a defensive alliance with Sweden, Spain and the Emperor to halt the relentless French advance eastwards. For five months the Dutch ambassador in London vainly tried to persuade Charles II to take an active part in opposing France. The situation appeared critical. In the autumn it was said that 'the expectations of the world are either for a general peace or a general war'.[10] William tried to persuade his uncle that he was not a warmonger, that he wanted a general peace, and that he was genuinely concerned that the King did not trust him when he had 'so much zeal for his service'.[11] But the most that Charles would do was to offer his arbitration between France and Spain over Luxembourg; he refused to enter into any general scheme to bring pressure on France. William was informed that England was in no condition to make war, while the States of Holland, Friesland and Groningen were against the Dutch doing so. The commitment under treaty to send Dutch forces to the help of Spain was, however, honoured. Seeing the wasp's nest that he had aroused, Louis XIV then for the time being withdrew his troops from Luxembourg. By February 1683 William at last succeeded in holding a meeting of his allies, but the English Government refused to take part in it or even to send an observer.

These acute differences over foreign policy widened the breach between Charles and James on one side, and William on the other. Insisting that the French terms for appeasement ought not to be refused, Charles II stressed that the future of Orange itself depended on reaching a general treaty with Louis XIV. For the English King could not rid himself of the notion that his nephew was only concerned with his own personal interests. Vainly William sent over his friend William Bentinck as a special envoy to the English Court. He found Charles inviolably pro-French. When in the winter of 1683, provoked beyond endurance, the Spanish Government declared war on France, Charles and James merely expressed their regrets at such foolish behaviour. In July 1684 James told his son-in-law that there was nothing the States-General could do except to agree to the French proposal for a twenty-year truce on the basis of the *status quo* and added that the Spaniards had better agree too. In view of the opposition he was meeting at home and the distraction of Germany by a war then raging against the Turks in the east, William himself was obliged to give way.[12]

Questions of war and peace were not the only source of difficulty between William and his uncles. Another was the relations between William and the Duke of Monmouth. Monmouth, an attractive but rather shallow man, had allowed himself to be used as a tool by Shaftesbury when he, in the end, had preferred him to William as a candidate for the Protestant succession to the throne. In the last exclusionist Parliament it was said that Shaftesbury would have agreed to the regency proposal only if Monmouth had been named as regent. During 1680 and 1681 Monmouth had assiduously courted popularity: 'No pretender to the throne ever worked harder for a following than he did' (Ogg). But he over-reached himself and it is doubtful if he were ever seriously in the running. He avoided imprisonment for treason only because his father was so fond of him. When in 1683 Monmouth allowed himself to become involved in conspiratorial talk, his arrest was at last ordered, following the revelation of the Rye House Plot; he went into hiding and was believed to have fled abroad. But in November 1683 he gave himself up and made an oral confession of his guilt, though denying strongly that he had planned to assassinate his father or his uncle. However, he refused to put his confession in writing or accuse his friends. Again Charles II pardoned him. At the end of the year Monmouth went into exile in Holland, where his mistress joined him, and he was received in a friendly way by William and Mary.

Charles and James did not suspect William of being implicated in the Rye House Plot. The sympathy he expressed for the King's 'deliverance from bloody villains' was amicably accepted, and the Prince promised that the English envoy in Holland should obtain help in trying to arrest 'treasonable conspirators' who had escaped there.[13] But James was furious over William's warm treatment of Monmouth and suspected that he was not genuinely anxious to help round up the Whig exiles or other 'ill men out of England' who, as the English envoy admitted, 'confirm many people in this country in their unbelief of the plot'.[14] It was also alleged that William was giving commissions to Monmouth's friends in the English regiments that were still serving in the United Netherlands. James protested to both William and Mary, and induced the English envoy, Chudleigh, to make strong representations. William was furious at the impertinent tone used by Chudleigh and demanded his removal. He also maintained that he had done nothing wrong in treating Monmouth with friendliness, since he was the King's son 'whom he had pardoned for the faults he had committed'.[15] But James's suspicions were unassuaged. He was told that Monmouth was conferring with the Earl of Argyll, who had earlier escaped from Scotland after being condemned to death for treason when James himself had been the Commissioner there. In October 1684 the French ambassador reported home from London that 'the Duke of York remains of the opinion that the Prince of Orange and the Duke of Monmouth flatter themselves with the hope of being able to bring about a rising in one of the three kingdoms'.[16]

It is doubtful if Charles II himself was unduly worried about William and Monmouth. According to one account, he had let William know secretly that he wanted Monmouth to be well treated. It is hard to understand why William was so effusively friendly to Monmouth unless he hoped to please Charles II. In December 1684 Monmouth actually went over to England and paid his father a clandestine and, as it proved, farewell visit. Yet that same month when the Dutch ambassador defended William's attitude to Monmouth, the King 'laughed and said that the Prince of Orange was cleverer than anybody else if he knew how to manage a man whose aims were either to establish a republic in England or to support chimerical claims to which he could not succeed without the ruin of the Prince of Orange himself'.[17] A reasonable explanation may be that William wanted to keep a careful watch upon a man whose activities might conceivably jeopardize Princess Mary's chances of succeeding her father on the English throne and thus bringing England into the anti-French orbit. On a shorter-term basis it has been suggested that William might have hoped to use Monmouth to induce Charles II to change his mind on foreign affairs, though there is no firm evidence for this. Assuredly William neglected no opportunity, however remote, of pursuing the plans to which he had dedicated himself.

For during the last years of Charles II's reign William's own position in the United Netherlands and in world politics had been weakened and his own undimmed enthusiasm for resisting French designs in Europe had been damped. The Regents of Amsterdam

41

had successfully exerted their influence to prevent further Dutch military or naval assistance from being given to Spain. William had both been unable to raise fresh troops himself and had found his attempts to enlist active allies frustrated. Charles II had not only excused himself from involvement on the ground that he had too many troubles at home but had resented 'railleries' against 'a great king'—his friend Louis XIV. Charles and James in fact appeared to be pleased that William's influence was declining. When Sir Gabriel Sylvius, an unofficial intermediary, suggested in May 1684 that Charles II should use his good offices to prevent William's power from being destroyed, he received a very cold reception. On the contrary, Charles reiterated his loyalty to, and admiration for, the King of France and said that he pitied the Dutch people 'ruined by the fault and folly of those who govern them'.[18] James was openly delighted that his recalcitrant son-in-law was mortified and opposed in Holland. On October 3, 1684, he wrote to William telling him it was necessary for him to do his part to satisfy the King and that he had shown little consideration for what he had said to him which he thought 'of concern to our family'.[19] At the very end of 1684, according to French reports, Charles II was 'as dissatisfied as ever with the conduct of William of Orange'.[20]

So at the end of Charles II's reign James's position appeared to be as strong as William's was weak; James had been allowed, in effect if not in name, to resume his control of the English Navy; he attended the Privy Council and the Committee on Foreign Affairs; and he was constantly at his brother's side whispering poison in his ears about the plotting of the King's son and nephew in Holland. William, on the other hand, had reached the lowest point in his fortunes. He had met unyielding opposition to his plans both at home, abroad and in his wife's country. When the twenty-year truce with France was about to be forced on the United Netherlands in April 1684 William's confidant, Bentinck, had written to their friend Henry Sidney: 'Our affairs continue to follow their course, that is to say the road to our general destruction.'[21]

Some historians have suggested that in the very last months of Charles II's reign revolutionary changes were impending in England. The story largely derives from Gilbert Burnet's memoirs—Burnet was out of England at that time. 'The King,' he wrote, 'was observed to be colder and more reserved to the

Duke than ordinary' and he certainly did plan to send James back to Scotland for a few weeks. But that Charles really had a scheme on foot to call a Parliament in England (for which the ground had been prepared by a fairly wide remodelling of the borough charters, after the City of London's charter had been surrendered) or to change his foreign policy is doubtful. The evidence is meagre: the autocracy was working smoothly enough. An improvement in the Customs revenue had relieved the King's financial anxieties. Since his victory over the Whigs Charles had grown increasingly lethargic and had come to rely more and more on the society of his French Duchess whom he treated more like a wife than a mistress. At the same time he may well have felt the constant company of his dull and humourless brother rather irksome and have welcomed the idea of getting rid of him for a short spell. But James does not appear to have felt that he was unwanted; in fact he regarded himself as indispensable. It is true that he resented the fact that his brother-in-law Laurence Hyde, Earl of Rochester, had recently been deprived of the office of Lord Treasurer, and he disliked the fact that the witty and able Marquis of Halifax, whom he had never forgiven for promoting the policy of limitations on the monarchical power during the exclusionist crisis, still retained influence with Charles II, although his star was on the wane. In all probability all that Charles II wanted was a quiet end to his days; he can hardly have failed to perceive that his brother's fanatical devotion to his religion and his stubborn nature would spell trouble for the monarchy as soon as he himself departed from a world that had amused him a lot and bothered him not a little.

An eminent English historian once wrote that the shape of the Revolution of 1688 could have been detected from the letters that James wrote during the last years of his brother's reign.[22] Those letters certainly reveal the extreme naivety of James's temperament, his distrust of Parliaments, his fear of Monmouth, his jealousy of William of Orange, and his dislike of any measures that might detract from the autocratic power of the monarchy. During these years James wrote regularly and conscientiously to his son-in-law warning him, reproving him, advising him. Little did he recognize that he was dealing with a character far firmer and an outlook far wider than his own. Always in the background of his mind was the menace to the English monarchy of another civil war and the wistful belief that only a toughness

43

which neither his father nor his brother had ever shown could prevent the worst from happening. On the whole, he pictured the political landscape in black and white: those who were not with him were against him. But what he totally failed to realize was that his obsession with himself and his religion cut little ice with Prince William of Orange whose gaze was never far removed from the European scene as a whole. To that scene we shall now turn.

NOTES TO CHAPTER III

1. Dalrymple, ii, 299.
2. *Ibid.,* 295.
3. Prinsterer, v, 496.
4. *H.M.C. Dartmouth,* 11, V, 57, 60.
5. Cf. *Ibid.,* 67.
6. Sidney, ii, 214.
7. *Ibid.,* 108.
8. Baschet, Aug. 4/14, 1681.
9. Prinsterer, v, 512.
10. *The Dispatches of Thomas Plott and Thomas Chudleigh* (ed. F. A. Middlebush), 148.
11. Prinsterer, v, 550 *seq.*
12. Dalrymple, ii, 50.
13. Prinsterer, V, 582; *Correspondentie,* ii, 15.
14. *The Dispatches of Thomas Plott, etc.,* 233.
15. Dalrymple, ii, 63.
16. Baschet, Oct. 16/26, 1684.
17. Baschet, Aug. 21/31, 1684.
18. Baschet, Aug. 21 and 24 N.S., 1684.
19. Dalrymple, 11, 65.
20. Baschet, Dec. 19/29, 1684.
21. Grew, 78.
22. Ogg.

CHAPTER IV

Europe in 1685

EUROPE in the seventeenth century was divided among considerable states or great powers, or perhaps, more accurately, large political entities—like the Spanish empire and the Austrian Habsburg empire—and numbers of small kingdoms, petty princedoms, and dukedoms, which changed hands or were absorbed whenever a significant dynastic marriage took place.[1] The Spanish empire, though it still comprised the southern Netherlands, important parts of Italy and much of the New World across the Atlantic, was on the decline. At the beginning of the century it had lost the northern Netherlands which had achieved independence under William the Silent; in 1668 Portugal finally became a separate kingdom, while by the treaty of the Pyrenees (1659) Spain had been obliged to concede several frontier districts to France. The decadence of Spain had set in during the first half of the century. It suffered from economic uncertainties, from inflations and depressions, from a price revolution, from a lazy aristocracy and an incompetent or corrupt bureaucracy, from the frequent breakdown of public order, from a peasantry that often starved. Its vulnerability and large possessions aroused cupidity or concern throughout Europe.

Philip II, once the husband of Queen Mary I of England, had been a powerful king. But none of his grandiose schemes were realized. His grandson, Philip IV (1621–65), was an idle monarch dependent on ministers and favourites, including a nun to whom he confided his sexual excesses. He had to contend not merely with the loss of Portugal and the long war with France but also an exhausting civil war concentrated in Catalonia, the 'Ireland' of Spain. However, his territorial losses were not extensive; and when not long before his own death his daughter Maria Teresa was married to King Louis XIV of France it looked as if the régime of the Spanish Habsburgs might be fortified by the alliance. But, on the contrary, this very marriage whetted the appetite of the young Louis XIV. For Philip IV's successor,

Charles II, known as 'the Bewitched', was sickly and impotent. He lived a life of fantasy and disappointment. He was unable even to masticate his food. His half-sister's renunciation of her right to the Spanish succession on her marriage to Louis XIV had been made contingent on her dowry being paid by her father, but it was never paid. Thus through his marriage Louis might hope one day to lay claim to the whole of the Spanish empire for his family, the Bourbons. Meanwhile he did lay claim to possession of the Southern or Spanish Netherlands (roughly modern Belgium) on the ground that by local law these lands should descend through, or 'devolve upon', the female line, that is to say upon his Queen, Maria Teresa. On this excuse, during the regency of Charles II's mother, Spain was again attacked by France and compelled to yield fortresses in the Netherlands to her. And in 1668 Louis XIV concluded a secret treaty with the Holy Roman Emperor, also a Habsburg, whereby it was agreed that France and the Emperor should divide the possessions of Spain between them if Charles the Bewitched were indeed to die without an heir.

Some historians have asserted that this question of the Spanish succession dominated the history of Europe in the latter half of the seventeenth century. Certainly the whole world was aware of its explosive character. Supposing France did, for example, on one pretext or another overrun the whole of the Spanish Netherlands, then the strategic security of both the United Netherlands and of England, as well as of northern Germany— the heart, in fact, of Protestant Europe—would be menaced. Yet the pitiful Charles II,[2] the plaything of women and of priests, hung on to his life and his throne for more than thirty-five years and struggled, not unskilfully, for the preservation of Spanish imperial unity and integrity. If in the end the Spanish empire was to be partitioned between the Bourbons and the Habsburgs, it was not to come about until the second decade of the eighteenth century. Though its resources were small and its armies negligible, other powers propped up the declining kingdom of the Spanish Habsburgs, lit so recently by the genius of Velazquez and Cervantes. Meanwhile Louis XIV's ambitions were by no means confined to the acquisition of Spain for his heirs. In the sixteen-eighties he was aiming to extend the frontiers of France far beyond the Spanish Netherlands, towards the Rhine, and he even hoped one day to be elected Holy Roman

Emperor himself and to hold sway over the whole of middle Europe.

For Louis XIV[3] had all the instincts of a megalomaniac, the first of a succession of madmen who brought death and destruction to modern Europe. He had inherited a wealthy kingdom with vast natural resources and a large population, a victorious army and highly capable generals and diplomatists. Having intervened in Germany under the impulse of Cardinal Richelieu's foreign policy, France had emerged from the wars of the first half of the century with her prestige enhanced. After many vicissitudes the monarchy had recovered from the civil wars known as the wars of the Fronde, and Cardinal Mazarin, Richelieu's successor, had left the young king the heritage of a peaceful realm, directed by a centralized government, and valuable territorial acquisitions from the wars against the Spanish empire. But Louis XIV was determined to win personal glory at all costs. 'Love of glory,' he wrote, 'requires the same delicacy of touch and of approach as love of a woman.' He determined to exercise what was to him an endearing art. At home his minister Colbert stimulated industry and commerce and built up a French navy. Overseas his able diplomatic representatives worked to enhance French prestige: in its name even the Pope was insulted. Streams of money flowed through carefully sited channels to buy French supporters or to neutralize France's enemies. And war was threatened when diplomacy failed.

At first the French King advanced smoothly along his prepared paths of aggression. By the treaty of Aix-la-Chapelle of 1668 he obtained Lille and other frontier fortresses; by a group of treaties known as the Peace of Nymegen, concluded ten years later, he acquired Franche-Comté and more fortresses in the Spanish Netherlands. These gains and others exacted earlier by the treaties of Westphalia (1648) and of the Pyrenees (1659) were swollen by the lands brought under French control by the 'acts of reunion' in 1680–81. While William of Orange was hamstrung by the opposition of the States-General to any fresh military action, while the attention of the Holy Roman Emperor was diverted to the east, while England trembled on the verge of civil war and her King secretly took French pay, Louis was able to push his frontiers towards the Rhine. In his hands were concentrated Strasbourg and the whole of Alsace, Franche-Comté, much of Lorraine and many villages in Flanders as well as the key town of Luxembourg. He had drawn back from Luxembourg under pressure in 1682, but his soldiers had occupied it in 1684. By the truce of Ratisbon (August 1684) the important powers in Europe were compelled to recognize the French right to cling to all these territorial gains, however dubiously won, for a period of twenty years. William of Orange had worked not for such a one-sided truce but a general negotiated peace; if it had to be a truce, he had suggested, it should last for only eight years. But he could not induce his allies or even his own people to stand behind him. Thus in the years 1684-85 Louis XIV had climbed to the pinnacle of his power and glory in Europe.

Some French historians have placed the high-water-mark of Louis XIV's success earlier than that, around about the time of the treaty of Nymegen (1678-79). It is argued that the provocative conduct of the French in Alsace-Lorraine and in Flanders had excited such enmity that sooner or later they were certain to be forced to defend their conquests by war. The truce, it is contended, was generally recognized to be no more than a breathing space for consolidation, extorted by terror (the French had the largest army in western Europe) whereas by the treaties of 1678-79 France's expansion to the north-east had been recognized and sustained by public agreement.

Be that as it may, Louis XIV had no intention of standing still. If he paused for the moment, it was in order that he might later spring forward more effectively. Charles II of Spain might die at any time; he was married to a French princess, Louis XIV's niece: but it was known that he could have no children. One day the Spanish authorities might well welcome a French Bourbon prince as their king. Only the Austrian Habsburgs could stop a French prince from acquiring the throne of Madrid, and they might be prepared to acquiesce in it if they were offered a generous share of the Spanish empire, such as they had been offered, and had accepted, in the secret partition treaty of 1668. Otherwise there were only the Protestant powers, who might be neutralized or embroiled with one another. Thus the French King himself watched the international situation with the closest possible attention. Always a hard worker, he had now dropped the extravagant pleasures of his youth. After the death of his Spanish wife in January 1684 he was secretly married to the widowed Mme de Maintenon, a lady who had been the governess of his illegitimate children and was an exceptionally pious Roman

Catholic. While Louis awaited developments in Madrid and Vienna, he decided to unify his kingdom spiritually by expelling the French Protestants—the Huguenots—when he could not convert them. Their conversion or suppression had been his aim for several years: he wanted to demonstrate to the Roman Catholic world that he really was the Most Christian King. Finally in October 1685 he revoked the Edict of Nantes of 1598, which was the charter of Huguenot liberties, and tens of thousands of industrious Frenchmen, fleeing before an organized persecution, left their homeland to settle in England, Holland and Germany. The cruel means—the bullying and the torture—by which conversions had been attempted or achieved, as related by the exiles wherever they went, aroused anger against the French King throughout the Protestant nations. And this example of brutal bigotry contributed to political antagonism against France even in countries which, fearful of her might, had hitherto been prepared to cling to their neutrality at all costs.

How had it come about that the French were able to expand north-eastwards and acquire territory on the left bank of the Rhine by force or threats without meeting resistance from the Germans? France, it is true, had a population of eighteen or nineteen million people, but there were some twenty million Germans, some eight million Spaniards, five million English and Scots, and two or three million Dutchmen. The answer was that the Germans were divided among themselves. The Holy Roman Empire, though it still existed, was a ramshackle survival of earlier times. Already for many years French influence had been stronger in northern Germany than that of the Emperor. Some leading Germans, like the Electors of Brandenburg and Saxony, were French allies and in French pay. For ten years (1658-68) a League of the Rhine was established at Frankfort-on-Main consisting of German princes, but also of French and Swedish members which, though its declared aim was pacific, was a body patently hostile to the Habsburgs and subject to French pressure. The Imperial German diet met, but was rarely united or in agreement. Its troops were numerically smaller than those of France. At one stage in the latter half of the seventeenth century it was reckoned that Louis XIV could rely on the support of four of the seven princes who had the right to elect the Holy Roman Emperor. Louis thus hoped that, if anything should happen to the Emperor Leopold I, he might actually acquire this honourable

49

title for himself and so command or even attain wider allegiance among the rulers of Germany.

Whereas Louis XIV, who took over full authority in 1661, had inherited from Richelieu and Mazarin a highly successful foreign policy and well-organized military and economic resources as spring-boards from which to launch his policy of aggrandizement in Europe, the Emperor Leopold I, who succeeded his father Ferdinand III in April 1657 at the age of sixteen and was elected Holy Roman Emperor in July 1658, was left with a somewhat dubious heritage.[4] When the Emperor Charles V died he had divided his huge Habsburg empire into two parts. The Habsburgs of Vienna were junior and inferior to the Habsburgs of Madrid. They ruled over modern Austria and Silesia, Bohemia, Moravia and much of Hungary. During the Thirty Years War (1618-48) they had, on the whole, played a secondary part, but had been 'maimed, depopulated, and impoverished'. Plague and hunger then spread across the Habsburg lands; it is estimated that the population of Bohemia alone declined by nearly a half. Yet, as the late Professor Betts wrote: 'by the end of the century the Habsburg monarchy had become one of the great powers, hailed as the saviour of Christendom in the last and only permanently successful crusade, wooed as an ally by the maritime powers, feared as a rival by France.'[5]

How much did this remarkable achievement owe to the Emperor himself? Leopold I had perhaps been underestimated. A colourless figure, brought up by the Jesuits, of admirably cultured tastes and varied hobbies, something of an amateur musician, he was timorous in his decisions, very cautious and slow to make up his mind. Yet he had the advantage of having at his disposal really capable ministers and generals and quite an efficient diplomatic service. On the whole, he chose his servants wisely and was loyal to them. Although the overlapping between his rights as ruler of the Habsburg lands and his position as Holy Roman Emperor complicated matters, it enabled him to draw on a wide circle of helpers. In Raimundo Montecuccoli, Charles V of Lorraine, Max Emmanuel of Bavaria, Ernest Rüdiger von Starhemberg and later Eugen of Savoy he had soldiers fully comparable with the French marshals. Baron Lisola, the enemy of Louis XIV, was one of the ablest diplomatists of the century. It was he who constantly warned Leopold of the dangers from France.

But during the early part of his reign the Emperor had to contend with wars against Sweden, ruled by a line of ambitious kings seeking to extend their possessions southwards, and against the predatory Turks, whose Ottoman empire stretched from the eastern frontiers of the Habsburg empire to the Black Sea. In 1664 Montecuccoli defeated the Turks at the battle of St. Gotthard and a treaty was concluded at Vasvar; by this treaty Transylvania and parts of Hungary were temporarily abandoned to the suzerainty of the Sultan. Thus Leopold was able to turn his attention to the west, and in January 1668 concluded the partition treaty with Louis XIV which would have gained him a vast accession of territory on the extinction of the Spanish Habsburgs. But Lisola warned the Emperor, rightly as it proved, against French untrustworthiness. The attacks on the Spanish Netherlands in 1667 and on the Dutch Netherlands in 1672 were, he suggested, 'the beginning of the march of the enemy towards the gates of Vienna'.[6] The Emperor was gradually convinced: and during ten years when he was relatively freed from problems in the east (owing to Turkish absorptions in war elsewhere) seven years were spent in fighting France. Thus it was that William of Orange and the Dutch were able to count on considerable German help in their long-drawn-out struggle against Louis XIV. And so long as such allies could be collected on the mainland of Europe, the fact that William's uncle in England was the ally or client of Louis XIV was not of the first importance.

But in 1682 the Emperor Leopold's attention was once more distracted to the east. With his extremely vulnerable frontiers and relatively limited resources it was virtually impossible for him to fight simultaneously on two fronts. In 1678 Thokoly, a Magyar patriotic leader, started a revolt in Christian Hungary. This afforded an opportunity to the Turkish Grand Vizir, Kara Mustafa, to plan a major campaign against the Austrian Habsburg empire, with a base in Hungary. In the spring of 1683 a Turkish horde of some 100,000 men was concentrated under the flag of the Prophet in the neighbourhood of Belgrade. Its object was to overrun Hungary and then conquer Vienna.

The Emperor Leopold was most reluctant to turn away from his contest with France for the preservation of Germany in order to defend himself against the unprovoked aggression of the Turks. Vainly he strove to stave off the evil hour by diplomatic means. But the Sultan was persuaded that a magnificent chance had come his way. Leopold's own resources to deal with the Turkish armies were insufficient, and it needed a clarion call by Pope Innocent XI to save Europe from the infidels, to persuade the German princes and John Sobieski, King of Poland, to gather together for the rescue of Vienna. The siege by the Turks of the Austrian capital, which was hastily abandoned by the Emperor and his Court, began in July 1683. It was heroically defended by its garrison. And in September 1683 John Sobieski and Charles of Lorraine routed the Turks and drove them back into Hungary. The Emperor now had to decide whether he would pursue the war and expel the Turks from Hungary or turn his face back towards the west and use his victorious troops to check Louis XIV.

The French King had never actively assisted the Turks, though he had been on pretty good terms with them. But he had allied himself with the Hungarian rebels and was secretly delighted by the difficulties of the Emperor. He had refused his assistance in the Christian campaign to save Vienna. It was only the Austrian victory over the Turks that had induced him to make his offer of a twenty-year truce in the west. Under pressure from the Pope, the Emperor Leopold, who was a devout Roman Catholic, was induced to accept the truce of Ratisbon and instead of joining with William of Orange and the Spaniards in defence of the west, to sign a Holy League with Poland and the republic of Venice (at Linz, March 1684) aimed at the final destruction of the Ottoman empire. When the Most Christian King of France was invited to send his fleet to take part in the last of the Crusades, he refused.

Such broadly was the European situation in 1685. Spain in decline under an impotent and half-imbecile king; Germany divided; the Holy Roman Emperor absorbed in a crusade against the Turks; the French King aggressively feeding on his past successes. To the north, Sweden was still reckoned to be a considerable power. She had been the ally of France during the war against the Dutch, but had been humiliated by being beaten by one of the allies of the United Netherlands, Brandenburg, at the battle of Fehrbellin in 1675—a humiliation in the light of her magnificent military tradition in the first half of the century. The Brandenburgers had afterwards invaded Swedish Pomerania, while the Danes had attacked Scania. Only the intervention of French diplomacy prevented Sweden from suffering large territorial losses when the group of treaties was concluded that ended the war.

But the Swedes were not grateful to France; they resented not being consulted by their ally; and they refused for some time to ratify the treaties. Charles XI, an able but rather odd monarch, like most of the Vasas, was now determined to put his house in order and to make himself absolute in his kingdom. Thus for a time he tried to avoid becoming involved in European quarrels. He came to terms with the Danes in a secret treaty signed in 1679; he also concluded that the French alliance was of little use to him, especially as the French fleet was incapable of operating in the Baltic. He turned therefore to the Dutch. In September 1681 he at last ratified the peace treaty and signed a far-reaching treaty at The Hague whereby the two parties undertook to work for the maintenance of the *status quo* and to defend it, if necessary by force of arms. This treaty was the germ of the Grand Alliance which William of Orange was ultimately to construct against France. At the time it was neutralized because Louis XIV renewed his treaties with Brandenburg and concluded a treaty with Denmark which encouraged her to realize a long-felt ambition by attacking the independent duchy of Holstein-Gottorp. Thus Sweden and Denmark changed sides in the sixteen-eighties. And the confused situation in the Baltic, as we shall see, was to play its part in the events leading to the Revolution of 1688.

Though William of Orange[7] thus achieved some progress in his plans for containing the aggressions of Louis XIV when the Dutch–Swedish treaty was signed in 1681, he found that the opposition of the Regents of Holland and of Friesland to his forward policy was still firm. In 1682 as a result of William's diplomatic pressure on England and a Dutch undertaking to send troops to assist Spain in fulfilment of an existing treaty, Louis XIV had for a time to abandon his designs on Luxembourg. But when in the following year William had pressed for the raising of a larger Dutch army he had met with effective opposition, particularly from Amsterdam, which was determined not to be forced into another war with France. Van Beuningen, one of the Amsterdam Regents, who had gone over to England on a special embassy to enlist Charles II in the alliance against France, had come back in March 1683 feeling that the situation was hopeless and that it was as dangerous as it was useless to prepare for war.

This attitude in England, combined with the distraction of the Emperor by the Turks and the presence of Brandenburg and Denmark in the French camp, had effectively negatived all William's plans. The Stadholder never forgave Van Beuningen for his opposition to recruitment; he even asserted that he was a servant of France and that he deserved to lose his head. Feelings in Holland became inflamed. Shall we be compelled by the cowardly merchants of Amsterdam to submit to the might of the French King? William had demanded. In February 1684 he produced in the States of Holland an intercepted letter from the French ambassador to the United Netherlands as evidence of the intrigues between the French and the Regents of Amsterdam. When, in the end the States-General felt obliged to accept the twenty-year truce proposed by France, William was in despair. 'It is all the fault of those scoundrels in Amsterdam,' he asserted. He might have added that it was also the fault of his English uncle and father-in-law who seem—at any rate according to French reports—to have rejoiced at his set-backs in Holland. James assured William that the acceptance of the French terms in 1684 was the only means to peace. William did not believe it; he was convinced that the independence of his country had to be maintained by continuous and unflinching resistance to French aggression either in the Spanish Netherlands or in the Rhineland. A mere look at the map shows how these small but virile and prosperous Protestant nations—the United Netherlands, England and Sweden—supported, if possible by Denmark and Brandenburg—stood across the path of French mastery in Europe. If England, about to be ruled by a Roman Catholic king, were to range herself on the side of France, or if indeed she refused to enter an anti-French defensive alliance—that would be a fatal blow to William of Orange and to the security of the Dutch republic.

In fact the future was not so dark for William as it appeared to be at the end of 1684. In the first place, the Dutch Regents were as patriotic as he was, as patriotic as John de Witt had once been; they had no more intention of consenting to the French domination of Europe than they had once before of yielding to the tyranny of Spain. When the time was ripe, they would support their Captain-General. Secondly, James II, when he came to the throne of England, would prove himself, once he felt secure, to be proud, stubborn, and independent. He would not become the vassal of France; on the contrary, he would, much to the French King's wrath, renew existing treaties with the Dutch. Lastly, Louis XIV's policy of forcibly converting his own Protestant subjects to the Roman Catholic Church or, if they would not conform, driving them out of his kingdom, created a fierce reaction against France throughout the Protestant world. That gave William of Orange an opportunity he did not fail to grasp. His position at home and abroad was immensely strengthened. Once again he was able to direct the opposition to the French menace. But to do so successfully he required the active help of England. Hence the Revolution of 1688 has to be understood in its international setting.

Let us now turn to see what happened in England after King Charles II died.

NOTES TO CHAPTER IV

1. There is no entirely satisfactory general survey in English. David Ogg, *Europe in the Seventeenth Century* has often been reprinted. There is W. F. Reddaway, *A History of Europe 1610–1715* (1948). Two recent books which I have drawn upon are *The New Cambridge Modern History*, V (1961) and John B. Wolf, *The Emergence of the Great Powers 1685–1715* (1951). The volumes in E. Lavisse, *Histoire de France* are still useful.

2. J. Nada, *Carlos the Bewitched* (1963) is an amusing and valuable account of this monarch and period of Spanish history.

3. There are many books on Louis XIV and French history in the seventeenth century. One of the most reliable is A. de Saint Leger and Philippe Sagnac, *La Prépondérance Française sous Louis XIV, 1661–1715* (1949). Maurice Ashley, *Louis XIV and the Greatness of France* is a short introduction that has been reprinted several times.

4. See the late Professor Betts's chapter in the *New Cambridge Modern History*, V, 474.

5. See John Stoye, *The Siege of Vienna* (1964).

6. Cf. David Ogg, *Europe in the Seventeenth Century*, 235.

7. For a recent evaluation see P. Geyl's Trevelyan lectures in *History of the Low Countries* (1964), chap. VI; also P. Geyl, *The Netherlands in the Seventeenth Century, 1648–1715* (1964) and the works of Blok and Japikse.

CHAPTER V

The Conduct of King James II: 1685–87

ON the day that his brother Charles II died, King James, as the French ambassador in London reported, wrote to his son-in-law, Prince William of Orange, 'two lines with his hand merely informing him of the news, without adding any other testimony either of friendship or good will'. They read as follows:[1]

> I have only time to tell you that it has pleased God Almighty to take out of this world the King my brother. You will from others have an account of what distemper he died of, and that all the usual ceremonies were performed this day in proclaiming me King in the City and other parts. I must end, which I do, with assuring you, you shall find me as kind to you as you can expect.

That was the sour formula with which James usually concluded his letters to William when he was displeased with him. What he omitted to say was that on his death-bed Charles was received into the Roman Catholic Church. Also the late monarch left behind him two papers explaining why he became a Roman Catholic, which were a year later published on James's orders. John Evelyn noted, not entirely correctly, that Charles II was 'very obscurely buried . . . without any pomp and soon forgotten . . .'.[2] Still the fact remained that the King received a private burial in Westminster Abbey, thus saving his soul from the rites of the Church of England.

A quarter of an hour after his brother's death James entered the Privy Council chamber and made an impromptu and unscripted speech. In the course of the speech he said: 'I shall make it my endeavour to preserve this government in Church and State as it is now by law established. I know the principles of the Church of England are for monarchy and the members of it have shewed themselves good and loyal subjects, therefore I shall always take care to defend and support it.' The Privy Councillors, all of whom were at least nominally Anglicans, were delighted and pressed the King to publish his speech, which he did. But in retrospect James regretted what he had said. 'Though His Majesty intended to promise both security to their religion and protection to their persons,' explained his biographer,[3] 'he was afterwards convinced it had been better expressed by assuring them he never would endeavour to alter the established religion rather than that he should endeavour to protect it and that he would rather support it and defend the professions of it, rather than the religion itself.' In other words, James's policy was to tolerate the Church of England, not to maintain its exclusive place in the State.

James made his personal position clear enough when two days later he publicly went to Mass in St. James's Palace. Later, on April 23, he attended Mass in St. James's before going to Westminster Abbey for his coronation, from which some of the customary Anglican ceremonies were carefully omitted. But Anglican opinion was soothed by his promises to the Privy Council, promises which he appeared to repeat, though not in the same words, when he addressed his Parliament. For the time being he kept most of his brother's ministers including his brother-in-law Laurence Hyde, Earl of Rochester, who was promoted to be Lord Treasurer. Rochester was a leading Anglican. But the King's senior Secretary of State, Robert Spencer, second Earl of Sunderland, was a clever, highly unprincipled statesman who made himself indispensable both at home and abroad. James decided to call a Parliament at once; it was Sunderland who wrote to the Lords Lieutenant ordering them to exert their influence on the counties, while the previous manipulation of the corporation charters by the Crown in Charles II's reign gave the Government a persuasive power in determining the choice of members in the borough constituencies. Thus the House of Commons which met on May 19, 1685, was exuberantly royalist.

By the ruling classes James was welcomed as a sober, hardworking prince, quite unlike his frivolous brother. The Court, it was thought, had become solemn and moral without the profanity or buffoonery of its predecessor. That James should openly practise his own religion was deemed natural and even commendable. Yet to James it came as a surprise that his accession to the throne was passing off so peacefully, in view of the exclusionist crises and conspiracies that had occurred only three or four years back. '*C'est un coup décisif pour moi d'entrer en*

57

possession et en jouissance,' he told the French ambassador.[4] It is true that he was rather nervous at first, and if one may rely upon the French ambassador's other reports, felt that he might have to call upon King Louis XIV for support. His ministers even spoke of the Crown 'as yet tottering on their master's head'. But after his Parliament had been elected and proceeded to vote him generous revenues for life, his spirits rose, and with more confidence he began to consider bold policies for the future.

English historians have tended to depend largely on the voluminous dispatches of the French ambassadors in England for their descriptions of James's policies. There were two of these ambassadors, Paul Barrillon d'Amoncourt, the resident ambassador, and François d'Usson de Bonrepaus, the French Intendant-General of Marine, who came to England on three special missions in the course of James's short reign. Neither of these Frenchmen really understood English history or how the English political system worked. Barrillon was indolent and timorous and very much afraid of offending his master, Louis XIV, who was an assiduous reader of his dispatches: he preferred to tell the King what was likely to please him; for he was a born flatterer and, according to one French historian, he was cynical, unscrupulous, and an expert in the arts of corruption. Bonrepaus was an abler man and far less inspired by James II than his colleague was. We shall consider some of his opinions later. But the idea which has been derived from Barrillon's dispatches at the beginning of the reign, that James and his ministers were obsequious to the French King, in urgent need of his financial help, and ready to follow in his footsteps is not borne out by reading between the lines nor by the actual course of events.[5]

In one of his many letters in the first half of 1685 Barrillon told Louis XIV that James's aim was 'to establish the Catholic religion with the French King's assistance'. But what did he mean by 'establish'? During his brother's reign James had expressed his belief in liberty of conscience for all Christians, as indeed Charles II had done. According to one story, as early as 1669 James had told John Owen, a former chaplain of Oliver Cromwell, that he had no bitterness against the nonconformists; he was against 'all persecution for conscience sake', looking upon it as an unchristian thing and absolutely against his conscience.[6] Writing in 1683, Dr. Burnet observed that though James was very firm in his religion and very much devoted to his priests, 'yet when I knew him he seemed very positive in his opinion against all persecution for conscience sake'.[7] In one of his reports home Barrillon asserted soon after the King's accession that James did not intend to go so far as to favour nonconformists and Presbyterians since he regarded them as being really republicans, but at the same time he admitted that there was no question of his trying straightaway to make Roman Catholicism the State religion for 'it was a project so difficult to carry out—not to say impossible to carry out—that sensible people do not fear it'.[8]

In May the second Duke of Buckingham published a pamphlet entitled *Reason and Religion* in which he advocated liberty of conscience for all nonconformists. 'The King of England,' noted Barrillon,[9] 'could not prevent himself at first from praising this pamphlet,' although it alarmed the Anglicans. A little earlier Barrillon had written that James 'had thoroughly explained to him his intentions with regard to the Catholics, which are to grant them entire liberty of conscience and the free exercise of their religion; this is a work of time and it can be brought about only step by step'. What James in fact told him was that since he was aware of the aversion of the majority of the people of England to the Roman Catholic religion his aim was simply to 'establish it in such a manner as it could not be ruined or destroyed'.[10]

There was no question then of James immediately asking his Parliament for far-reaching measures in favour of his co-religionists. His primary objective was to get rid of the penal laws that prevented Roman Catholics from worshipping freely in their own way or required them to attend Church of England services. These penal laws were already virtually dead letters anyway. Later his plan was to obtain the abolition of the Test Acts which had deprived the Roman Catholics of equal civic opportunities with their fellow citizens. And he was also attracted by the idea of extending such opportunities to the Protestant nonconformists.

When Parliament met on May 19, 1685, James adopted, unwisely from his point of view, a rather bullying tone. For however carefully chosen they might be, the nobility and gentry of England were unlikely to allow themselves to be browbeaten for long. Did not a tradition of independence of the Crown stretch back at least to the early years of Queen Elizabeth's reign? Sir Edward Seymour remarked in the House of Commons that 'the people of England were strong in their aversion to the Catholic religion and were attached to their laws'. Following past precedents, the Grand Committee on Religion asked the King to publish a proclamation 'for putting the laws in execution against all dissenters whatsoever from the Church of England'. Extremely annoyed, James told the House its resolution was unacceptable to him. The Commons gave way. And in fact they proved cooperative over money matters if only because the royal Government at that very moment was threatened with a double rebellion.

Even before Parliament met, the Earl of Argyll, the Scottish Whig leader, who in 1681 had been condemned to death for treason and had fled to Holland, came over from that country to Scotland with the aim of raising his Campbell clan and others against King James II. Three weeks later the Duke of Monmouth—'the Protestant Duke'—his sluggish spirit stirred by bright memories of his popularity in exclusionist days—landed at Lyme in Dorset and afterwards proclaimed himself King at Taunton.

On July 2 Parliament adjourned, having voted the King additional supplies to deal with these rebels. James had by then collected such regular soldiers as he had at his disposal and dispatched them to fight Monmouth in the west of England. Argyll had already been captured in Scotland on June 18, but Monmouth was a bigger threat. James asked William to send over from Holland the three English and three Scottish regiments serving there in Dutch pay. The States-General complied with the request, but before these regiments could perform any useful part Monmouth had been defeated at the night battle of Sedgemoor, and on July 15 was executed.

These rebellions were inadequately prepared and concerted; their suppression was comparatively swift. But the anti-popery spirit which had flared up seven years earlier was by no means quiescent. For example, in the middle of May Dr. Titus Oates, the inventor of the Popish Plot, who had been tried, convicted, and punished for perjury, was put in a pillory in front of the Royal Exchange in the City of London. After he was released the mob rioted, upset the pillory, and pulled it to pieces; several persons had to be taken into custody before the uproar subsided.[11] When one of the Scottish regiments arrived from Holland nine of the soldiers defiantly drank the health of the Duke of Monmouth; one of them was shot and others flogged under the gallows.[12] The Somerset militia proved unwilling to fight against Monmouth and many of them went over to his side, and though he had only 150 men when he landed his army had swollen to over 3,000 before he was defeated at Sedgemoor. Very severe measures were carried out in punishment of the rebels and their numerous sympathizers in the west of England.

James had received a shock. He realized that his army was so small and some of his subjects were so disloyal that he was actually dependent upon assistance from abroad to maintain himself on his throne. It may have been for this reason that he now showed himself more friendly towards the Dutch, and in August 1685 renewed treaties with them. For in spite of all his promises Barrillon had not handed over any large sums of money from the French King, and James was not so stupid as to fail to understand that it would be fatal for him to rely exclusively on French aid—even if this were really forthcoming—to ensure the safety of his own position.

But gradually he recovered his nerve. Even before Monmouth's defeat Barrillon had reported: 'It seems to me that the King of England is very glad to have a pretext for raising troops, and he believes that the Duke of Monmouth's enterprise will serve only to make him still more the master of his country.'[13] George Jeffreys, the Chief Justice who had presided over the trials of the English rebels, was promoted Lord Chancellor; the Marquis of Halifax, long suspected by James of disloyalty to the monarchy, was dismissed from his post of Lord President of the Council and replaced shortly afterwards by the Earl of Sunderland, who had no other ambition than to please the King. When on November 9 James recalled Parliament to regale it with his account of Monmouth's overthrow he not only asked for a fresh supply of funds in order that he might strengthen his standing army, but insisted that, contrary to the Test Act of 1673, he intended to employ Roman Catholic officers in that army.

The House of Commons voted by a majority of one to postpone consideration of supply until the question of the Roman Catholic officers had been debated. Sir Thomas Clarges, brother-in-law of the famous General Monck, gave warning of the dangers of a popish king with a popish army. The House of Lords was even more outspoken. Viscount Mordaunt, who was to find fame as the conqueror of Barcelona in the reign of Queen Anne, said:

61

What we now see is not ambiguous. A standing army is on foot, filled with officers who cannot be allowed to serve without overthrowing the laws. To keep up a standing army when there is neither civil nor foreign war is to establish that arbitrary government which Englishmen hold in such abhorrence.

The Commons expressed its willingness to give the King more money, but tried to avoid a standing army either by granting it to the navy or by simultaneously passing a bill to remodel the citizens' army or militia. James was enraged by these evasions of his wishes and the criticisms of his policies and preferred to do without any more money at all. On November 20, 1685, he prorogued Parliament; in fact it was never to meet again. Barrillon was surprised. He thought the prorogation would have no other effect than to increase the discontent of the English people who were already upset with the conduct from the throne.

The King was outwardly little concerned. His peaceful accession, the generous revenues that had been voted him for life by Parliament when it first met and the complete defeat of Monmouth inspired him to press forward during the year 1686 with a plan to secure religious liberty for and give civic equality to his fellow Roman Catholics. He could not fail to applaud the success of his fellow monarch, Louis XIV, in purging his own kingdom of heresy. Since the French King's marriage to the pious Madame de Maintenon it had been his aim to have only the one religion throughout his kingdom. The Huguenots he regarded not merely as heretics but also as potential rebels. Every means was therefore used to enforce their conversion, culminating in the revocation of the Edict of Nantes. Protestant churches were henceforth closed; military pressure (*'dragonnades'*) and even torture were employed to prevent backsliding; those who were caught trying to escape from the country were sent to the gallows. Yet an exodus of tens of thousands took place, of whom a large number arrived in England.

The English King at first admired all he heard of Louis XIV's labours for his Church. But soon doubts assailed him. His subjects were worried whether their own sovereign, being such an enthusiastic convert, might not try to imitate his brother in the faith. Protestants feared he would go to extremes; Roman Catholics, or at least the wiser among them, were anxious, lest the French persecution might have adverse reactions on their own chances of freedom of worship. In fact it seems that it was more the strength of his own position at home that persuaded James to go forward with his policy of toleration; the more he heard about the events in France the less he liked them. Before Christmas he was giving instructions that the English ambassador in France should make sure that the English Protestants there who were not naturalized Frenchmen were entirely free from molestation, and he was also instructed to do everything in his power to help those who were naturalized and 'to appear on their behalf'.[14]

When the French special envoy, Bonrepaus, paid his first visit to England in January 1686, he was not impressed by King James. The King, he reported, 'is not so much master of himself nor so great a man as I had been led to expect'.[15] He was stubborn, fussy over small things, and dominated by his Queen. Bonrepaus reported that although both the Whigs and Tories feared the King would be encouraged by the repeal of the Edict of Nantes, James was perturbed by what he had heard about the brutality of French methods of conversion. The refugees arrived in England bringing tales of the *dragonnades*, of torture and rape. Bonrepaus in fact thought it wise to repudiate all these stories either as exaggerated or as the work of subordinates who had exceeded their instructions. James had agreed to a fund to help the refugees and had contributed £500 out of his privy purse towards it. It is true that such refugees were expected to join the Church of England, but it was then of course the only official Protestant Church. In that same month there were rumours that Roman Catholic regulars (those who belonged to a religious order) were going to be prosecuted in the United Netherlands merely on account of their faith. James was assured by his son-in-law that this was not the case. In expressing his gladness at the news, James wrote that he was of the opinion that 'it was the very hard usage the Huguenots had and still have in France which made that affair of the regulars talked of where you are'.[16]

It is clear not only from the dispatches of Bonrepaus but also of Barrillon that James did not at all approve of the French Government's treatment of the Huguenots. A good deal was made of the fact that James ordered the burning of a book by a French Protestant minister named Claude, condemning the persecution, which had been distributed in London both in a French and an English version: the Lord Chancellor had advised against the burning of the French version. But James had explained that 'dogs defend each other when attacked; so do kings'. What it did not mean—so Barrillon told his master—was, 'as ill-intentioned people suggested', that James approved the revocation of the Edict of Nantes. James also told the Dutch ambassador when explaining his own religious policy to him later in the year and commenting on that of the King of France that he 'detested' Louis XIV's conduct 'as not being politic, much less Christian'; he himself, he said, aimed at 'nothing else but liberty of conscience' and 'that so many honest people should not remain slaves to laws introduced in a singular manner'.[17]

James's problem and its proposed solution were therefore different from those of the King of France. In fact James moved at first rather slowly and seems to have envisaged helping his fellow-religionists in a broad context of a wider religious toleration. After Parliament was prorogued Presbyterians and other nonconformists began to hope that they might obtain liberty of conscience forthwith 'since the Anglicans failed the King in the last session of parliament'. At the very beginning of 1686 the Dutch ambassador reported that it was being publicly said that the King as Head of the Church would grant a general freedom of conscience to all dissenters. As Easter approached, the King became conspicuously religious. 'The busy time of devotion is now here,' observed a newsletter on April 6, 'His Majesty, God bless him! one of the zealousest. Ten hours a day sometimes.'[18] Father Edward Petre who was now generally known to be his Jesuit adviser, urged him to make some forward move. The King gave permission for the printing of Roman Catholic writings, and propaganda pamphlets were published. Henry Hills, the royal printer, was himself a Roman Catholic. In the summer a military camp of some 14,000 was established at Hounslow with a chapel where Roman Catholic officers might attend Mass every morning.

In the spring too a general pardon (with certain exceptions) had been issued and 1,200 Quakers were released from prison in England and Scotland. Anabaptists as well as Quakers made public their gratitude to the King. By July it was reported that 'politics were on the gallop' and that 'the King seems determined to push on in religious matters as far as he possibly can'.[19] In June a collusive case was tried in the Court of King's Bench—Godden *v*. Hales—which decided by a majority of eleven judges

64

to one that the King had the right to dispense with the Test Act of 1673 in individual cases, in this instance in order to allow a Roman Catholic to hold a commission in the army; on July 15 an Ecclesiastical Commission was set up (to which the King's powers as Supreme Governor were delegated), which could suspend clergy or deprive them of their functions. One of the first things the Commission did in September was to suspend Henry Compton, the Bishop of London, because he in his turn had refused to suspend a London clergyman who had preached against Roman Catholicism. Earlier a special envoy had been sent to the Pope and a papal envoy was received in Whitehall. The Marquis of Queensberry was dismissed from his office as Royal Commissioner in Scotland when the Scottish Parliament failed to sanction the suspension of the Test Acts, and was himself replaced by an administration largely controlled by Roman Catholics. Although James thus carried out a twofold policy of relieving individual Roman Catholics of their disabilities and giving offices and commissions to Roman Catholics by suspending recent statutes (several Roman Catholic peers were now appointed to the Privy Council), he told the Spanish ambassador in August that 'he would force no man's conscience but only aimed at the Roman Catholics being no worse treated than the rest, instead of being deprived of their liberties like traitors'.[20]

In the light of these measures it was natural that during the second half of 1686 the conviction should grow among the subjects of King James that their monarch was plotting to impose his own religious views upon all of them. In Ireland Lord Tyrconnel, since May the Lieutenant-General of the Irish Army, a Roman Catholic himself, was engaged in undermining the authority of the Earl of Clarendon, the Protestant Lord Lieutenant; in Scotland Queensberry was demoted; in England the recall of Parliament was postponed from time to time by a series of prorogations. That autumn the policy of trying to persuade Members of Parliament to do the King's will by repealing the Penal and Test Acts—a policy known as 'closeting' was started. At the Court itself a struggle took place between Rochester, the King's brother-in-law, who had resisted the setting up of the Ecclesiastical Commission, and Sunderland who was determined on the overthrow both of Rochester in England and of his brother, Henry Hyde, Earl of Clarendon in Ireland.

This struggle was drawn out. Rochester was pro-Dutch and

Sunderland was pro-French; Sunderland in fact was the paid agent of the French King, from whom he received a pension of £7,000 a year. The rumour was rife that soon the Hydes would be dismissed. In fact they clung on to office until the end of the year. That autumn Sunderland made it pretty clear to his master that he was sympathetic towards his religion and available for conversion at any suitable moment. But Rochester and Clarendon, though ambitious men, refused to be tempted. 'As poor as I am,' Clarendon wrote when he heard of his brother's dismissal,[21] 'I hope God will give both you and me the grace to beg rather than that we should falter in the religion wherein we have been bred. . . .' Vainly James had begged Rochester to study again the papers that King Charles II had left for the edification of posterity. Though, according to Rochester, the King 'wept almost all the time he spoke to me', he told him, as he had told Halifax a year earlier, that 'no man must be at the head of his affairs that was not of his own opinion [on religion]'.[22]

The Hydes lost their offices at the end of 1686, though some Protestant ministers were still retained in ministerial positions. Policy, however, was settled by Sunderland and the Roman Catholic group over which he regularly presided. Loyal Protestants became increasingly unhappy about the King's favouritism. The Earl of Chesterfield, a staunch royalist, wrote that December:[23] 'Though we have now a prince, whose study is his country's glory, whose courage would give him lustre without a throne, whose assiduity in business makes him his own chief minister, yet heaven, it seems, hath found a way to make all this more terrible than lovely. . . . Men are generally discontented, and dread being shown some other way to heaven.' The Marquis of Halifax wrote to William of Orange on January 18, 1687, that the nation remained firm and averse to change: 'so that conversions are so thin and those which are so little fit to be examples that the prevailing party is not a little discountenanced by making no quicker progress.'[24] Ten days later John Evelyn, who over twenty-five years earlier had rejoiced after the restoration of Charles II in seeing the Cromwellians' corpses being hanged at Tyburn, wrote, 'the Lord Jesus defend his little flock and preserve this threatened Church and nation'. In the course of 1686 the Dutch ambassador reported anti-popish riots in Oxford, Worcestershire, Warwickshire, Bristol and Scotland; only the prompt action of the Lord Mayor had prevented demonstrations against the Mass in the City of London, though even he had been unable to suppress an outburst on Guy Fawkes Day. Even Barrillon admitted that the decision in the Godden *v.* Hales case (for which the way had been prepared by the dismissal of four judges) was much disliked, though there were no open protests.

Yet the resident French ambassador did not fancy that King James was moving fast enough. He thought that he was wasting time, was getting older, and that what he did might be reversed by his successor. The King's efforts to induce Members of Parliament to commit themselves to legislating for religious equality were meeting with resistance; and it was felt that even if the House of Commons agreed to 'liberty of conscience' opposition would certainly be encountered in the House of Lords. James's own aims were clear enough and common knowledge. For instance, he wrote to the Duke of Beaufort on February 12, 1687, saying that what he intended to have done when Parliament did meet next was to 'have the two Tests and penal laws repealed that my Catholic subjects may be in the same condition as the rest of my subjects are'.

It was at the beginning of 1687 that King James finally made up his mind to issue a royal proclamation suspending the laws against Roman Catholics and nonconformists by the exercise of his royal prerogative. He had been contemplating this step for at least a year. On February 12 a proclamation was published in Scotland under powers granted to him by an Act of 1669; the declaration extended liberty of worship to all Christians except only the extreme Presbyterians who met in field conventicles and had proved themselves to be unruly and rebellious. On April 5 a declaration of liberty of conscience was published in England; James had previously explained to his son-in-law that in order that 'all my subjects may be at ease and quiet and mind their trades and private concerns' he had 'resolved to give liberty of conscience to all dissenters whatsoever, having ever been against persecution for conscience sake'. That was also to be stressed in his published life: 'it was always his settled opinion,' wrote his biographer, 'that men's consciences ought not to be forced.'[25] Here too the argument that liberty of conscience was helpful to trade was repeated. 'Trade he had much at heart,' wrote the Earl of Ailesbury, 'and his topic was, liberty of conscience and many hands at work.'[26]

The declaration suspended all the penal laws and excluded

office-holders from obeying the Test Acts. The King's aim was also stated to be to obtain Parliament's approval later, thus admitting by implication that his extensive use of the prerogative was exceptional. But he made it clear that he would prefer his subjects to be of his own religion. 'We cannot but heartily wish,' stated the declaration, 'as it will easily be believed, that all the people of our Dominions were members of the Catholic Church, yet we humbly thank Almighty God that it is, and hath of long time been our constant sense and opinion (which upon divers occasions we have declared) that conscience ought not to be constrained nor people forced in matters of mere religion.' A fair field, one might say, but plenty of favours.

Favours were also shown to nonconformists, many of whom presented addresses of thanks to the King. But at the same time efforts were exerted to soothe the Church of England. It was, however, less the two declarations than James's attempts to persuade his ministers and leading officers in the army and navy to become Roman Catholics or to force Roman Catholics into posts from which they had been excluded by statute that frightened the Church. Every post, wrote Sir John Reresby in February 1687,[27] 'brought news of gentlemen laying down their appointments and papists for the most part being put in their places'. Only a week after the declaration was published in England the King tried to compel the Fellows of Magdalen College, Oxford, to accept a worthless Roman Catholic as their president. There was precedent enough for the King making a nomination. And though James, with his belief in civic equality for all Christians, might understandably feel that the Anglican monopoly in Oxford and Cambridge ought to be broken, that indeed was to assault the Church of England where its heart beat most strongly.

Such was the point that had been reached when Prince William of Orange sent over a special envoy, Everard van Weede, Lord of Dijkvelt, to see King James on his behalf and to explore the feelings of the English ruling class. Dijkvelt's mission is generally considered to have been the first obvious step that led along the road to the Revolution of 1688. But before we examine it, we shall first sketch the attitude of mind and conduct of William of Orange before he arranged the mission.

NOTES TO CHAPTER V

1. Dalrymple, ii, 114.
2. Evelyn, iv, 415.
3. Clarke, ii, 4.
4. Dalrymple, ii, 104.
5. Cf. my article in *Historical Essays 1600–1750* (1963).
6. Turner quoting Macpherson, I, 51.
7. H. C. Foxcroft, *A Supplement, etc.* (1902), 51–2.
8. C. J. Fox, *op cit.*, xliii.
9. *Ibid.*, lxxv.
10. Dalrymple, ii, 147.
11. Add. Mss. 34508, f. 19 v.
12. *Ibid.*, f. 66 v.
13. Dalrymple, ii, 169.
14. *H.M.C. Downshire*, I, i, 77.
15. Letter of Feb. 7 N.S., 1686, cit. Durand.
16. Dalrymple, ii, 177.
17. Baschet, May 3/13, 1686; Add. Mss. 34512, f. 48.
18. *Ellis Letters* (2nd series), iv, 90.
19. Cavelli, ii, 113.
20. Mackintosh, 678.
21. Clarendon, ii, 126–7.
22. *Ibid.*, 117.
23. Chesterfield, ii, 327.
24. Dalrymple, ii, 187.
25. Clarke, ii, 106.
26. Ailesbury, 103.
27. Reresby, 444.

CHAPTER VI

The Conduct of Prince William of Orange: 1685–87

WHEN King James came to the throne the relations between him and his son-in-law were frigid. Prince William had resented the removal of his old friend Henry Sidney from the post of English ambassador to the United Netherlands and disliked Thomas Chudleigh who had a long spell as his successor. He thought Chudleigh was impertinent to him and on one occasion the Prince poked him on the nose with his cane. Chudleigh's replacement by Sir Bevil Skelton at the beginning of the new reign only improved matters slightly. Skelton was described by one of his colleagues at The Hague as a lightweight and very unreliable.[1] When William had asked permission to appoint Sidney as commander-in-chief of the English and Scottish regiments serving in the United Netherlands, the request was rejected nominally on the ground of Sidney's lack of experience. James wanted the Earl of Carlingford, a Roman Catholic, to be given the post; but William would not hear of that, and eventually the command was offered to the Earl of Pembroke, who had about as little military experience as Sidney. In England the Dutch were represented by a conscientious ambassador, Arnold Van Citters. But Van Citters was not treated very seriously at the English Court, and when William wished to be sure of getting into close touch with his father-in-law, he had to send over a special envoy whom he personally trusted; this was all the more necessary as it was made clear to him from the start that he would certainly not be welcome in England himself.

The first special Dutch envoy to arrive in London at the outset of the reign was Hendrick van Nassau-Ouwerkerk who was sent over to congratulate James upon his accession. Ouwerkerk had instructions to try to establish more friendly relations. William, it seems, told him to explain to James that he repented his faults towards the late King of England and would do all he could to repair them. At first James was wary. According to Barrillon (whose reports must be suspect since he was under orders to sow as many dissensions between James and William as he possibly could) the King told him that he was obliged to preserve appearances with the Prince of Orange 'in order to prevent the popular party finding a head', but that 'he knew the Prince too well to be deceived by him'.[2] James warned Ouwerkerk that William would have to change his attitude on foreign as well as on home affairs, that is to say he must be less hostile towards France; more specifically, William was asked to order the Duke of Monmouth to leave the United Netherlands, to remove politically unreliable officers who were serving in the English or Scottish regiments there and to replace them by others recommended by James, and to keep him informed about such measures as he proposed to take abroad diplomatically. William promised to do all that he was asked; Monmouth was told to leave the country (though later he secretly returned); and when Skelton arrived at The Hague he was able to state that William and James were now much more friendly.

But the unimpeded departure by sea both of the Earl of Argyll and the Duke of Monmouth, three weeks later, from the United Netherlands to launch their rebellions against King James's Government soon cooled this tepid harmony. On each occasion Skelton had warned the Dutch and asked that the rebel sailings should be stopped. He told the States that Monmouth was hidden in Holland and actually provided a list of eighty Whigs and republicans known to be on Dutch territory and in which towns they were to be found. Not one of them was put under arrest. The various Dutch authorities blamed each other for Monmouth's safe departure in Dutch ships navigated by Dutch sailors. But William himself was not only Captain-General but also the Admiral-General of the United Netherlands, and few doubted that he could have prevented both Argyll and Monmouth from collecting arms and hiring ships if he had genuinely given his mind to doing so. The people of Amsterdam were openly sympathetic towards the rebels, and it was said that Monmouth's flag was flaunted in Dutch streets. William was a ruthless politician; the evidence is only circumstantial, but he must surely have closed his eyes to Monmouth's preparations and departure for England, even though he certainly hoped that his invasion would fail.[3] Indeed he may well have imagined that James would be obliged to invite over Dutch troops under his own command to help repel such an invasion, and thus give him at one stroke the opportunity to destroy his Protestant rival for the English succession and place his father-in-law under a debt of gratitude.

As soon as the news of Monmouth's landing in Dorset was known in Holland William sent over a more eminent ambassador than Ouwerkerk, his personal friend, William Bentinck. Bentinck was instructed to apologize for the escape of the rebels and to lay the blame on French assistance. Bentinck said that Monmouth had been seen at the French ambassador's house, and Skelton was told that only the French possessed the large financial resources necessary to enable Monmouth to buy arms. It is noticeable, however, that when Bentinck wrote to William from London on June 30 to say that James did indeed think that the French might have been responsible for helping the invaders—though he did not wish to show his resentment until the rebellion was suppressed—William ignored the report.

In his instructions Bentinck was told to offer every assistance to James in overcoming the rebels. William was most anxious to come over himself and to provide any generals or other officers needed. James understandably rejected these offers, but asked that the six regiments in Dutch service should be dispatched to England. They arrived too late to be of any material help; but James was not sorry that he did not have to make use of them since he was suspicious of their loyalty.

For his part William followed the course of events with the closest attention. According to Skelton, he was 'passionately disappointed' that he was not allowed himself to go over to England.[4] He seems to have been taken by surprise that Monmouth had been able to recruit so big an army in western England and to hold out there for as long as he did against the King's forces. 'God grant that we shall soon hear of new measures being taken against the English rebels,' he wrote to Bentinck on June 26;[5] four days later he expressed his concern that Monmouth was moving freely about the west; a fortnight later he praised God that the rebellion had been crushed and Monmouth captured. In his last letter to Bentinck in England he added realistically that he hoped that the six regiments would be promptly returned to Holland and said that he did not want Roman Catholic officers appointed in the place of any who might in the future resign.

In writing to express his pleasure at Monmouth's defeat and to stress the inseparability of the interests of the two nations, William now observed that 'everybody knew where the help for the rebels came from'.[6] At the time James accepted the Dutch assurances that the whole thing was a most unfortunate accident, caused by the complications and restrictions of the Dutch federal constitution. But in his posthumous memoirs he certainly laid the blame squarely upon William. The Earl of Ailesbury, also writing long after the event, recorded that he had heard at the time that Monmouth had disclosed his designs to the Prince of Orange who had sent over Bentinck to inform James and with the offer to come over himself so as 'to have the Duke sacrificed who was his rival'.[7] Fletcher of Saltoun, who had accompanied Monmouth on his expedition, told the first Earl of Dartmouth later that 'he had good grounds to suspect that the Prince under-hand encouraged the expedition with a design to ruin Monmouth'.[8] Monmouth himself denied that he had told William of his plans, but it is unquestionable that the Prince had received pretty good intelligence of what was on foot ten days before Monmouth sailed down the Texel on his fatal expedition, and yet failed to stop him.

But whatever James may have thought at the time—and it is possible that he suspected the French as well as the Dutch of aiding Monmouth—he was impressed by the promptitude with which the six regiments were sent over from the United Nether-lands and of the need for him to remain on friendly terms with the States-General. He had the sense to see that close dependence on France would do his cause no good with many of his subjects. In any case it was far from certain that help would be provided by Louis XIV. The French King was annoyed when in August James renewed the existing treaties with the Dutch and blamed Barrillon for not warning him that this might happen. He also demanded that Barrillon should send back the substantial sum of money with which he had been provided to tide the English King over any awkward corner. In view of the defeat of Monmouth and the voting by Parliament of generous supplies for life to James, the French reserve fund was no longer thought likely to be needed.

The temporary thaw in the relations between William and his father-in-law, deriving from the promptitude with which the English and Scottish regiments were sent over to England after Monmouth's invasion and from the signature of the Anglo-Dutch treaty, did not last very long. The French ambassadors in London and The Hague did everything they mischievously could to stir up trouble by whispering campaigns. In the autumn of 1685 William had to ask for the dismissal of his wife's almoner, Dr. Covell, and two of her bedchamber-women on the ground that they were engaged in a conspiracy to sell information to the English ambassador, Skelton. William was also dismayed by James's prorogation of his Parliament in November since he had regarded it as a safeguard against any pro-French moves by the English monarch.

James, for his part, was unable to shake off his old suspicions of his son-in-law, dating back to the exclusionist days, or forget William's former friendliness towards Monmouth. Nor was he pleased to learn from Skelton that he was receiving 'many words but no deeds' about the expulsion of such Whigs, Monmouthians and republicans as remained on Dutch territory.[9] When Bonrepaus arrived in England in January 1686 he immediately reported that 'the King of England regards the Prince of Orange as his enemy'[10] and after he had been in England for three months he was able to go even further and say, 'the King of England can scarcely hide his hatred for, and jealousy of, the Prince of Orange'. The French ambassadors improved the shining hour by pointing out that the obstruction in Parliament to the King's policies had been due to the Orangists and they played with the idea of trying to convert the King's younger daughter, Princess Anne, and her husband, Prince George of Denmark, to the Roman Catholic religion so that there should be Catholic candidates available for the succession instead of William and Mary, should James die.

In the course of 1686 a curious English document fell into the hands of Van Citters, the Dutch ambassador in London. This document, entitled 'A Remonstrance made to the King of England by his Council', advocated the exclusion of Princess Mary from the succession, a close alliance with France and a war against the Dutch. King James stated at once that the document was a forgery and was extremely angry at the suggestion that he was a vassal of France or that he had plans to alter the hereditary succession. Indeed these two proposals were quite out of character, though it is not impossible that they might have been seriously put forward by some of the King's extreme Roman Catholic advisers, such as Father Petre. They may even have been stimulated by Bonrepaus who, as has been noted, had plans to convert Princess Anne. They certainly contributed to the

French objective of causing dissension between the English and Dutch Governments. Indeed a fairly wide distribution of copies of the document may have meant that it was disseminated for propaganda purposes.

In any case James's actual policies during 1686, the favouritism that he showed towards Roman Catholics, and the building up both of a standing army and of his naval forces aroused anxiety not only among his Protestant subjects but among Protestant rulers abroad. The impartial reports of the Tuscan envoy in London at the time make it clear that there was a strong undercurrent of discontent not only against the renascent English Roman Catholics, as witnessed by the sporadic riots, but also against the King himself. An attempt by some of the Protestant ministers of the King to provide him with a Protestant maîtresse-en-titre (she was an old flame, Catherine Sedley, who got as far as a title, Countess of Dorchester, and a house in St. James's Square) failed owing to the vigilance of the Queen and the Court priests. The dismissed Marquis of Halifax, one of the most influential figures in the kingdom outside the Government, firmly refused to change his mind about supporting the repeal of the Test Acts—he asked sarcastically why if the judges had given the King the power to dispense with the laws such a repeal was necessary—and he re-established a cautious correspondence with the Prince of Orange.

Prince William had several visitors from England in the course of 1686. His friend Henry Sidney joined him at Cleves (where William was visiting his uncle, the Elector of Brandenburg) and then departed on a mysterious visit to Italy. Dr. Gilbert Burnet, the active divine who had been on friendly terms with many of the Whig leaders in King Charles II's reign, was welcomed at The Hague both by William and Mary and taken to some extent into the Prince's confidence. The Earl of Danby, once Charles II's chief minister, who was finally released from prison at the beginning of James II's reign, also opened a correspondence with Prince William and made several attempts to get over to Holland to see him; Barrillon, however, evidently speaking of the feeling at Court, observed that Danby was 'recognized to be a partisan of the Prince of Orange and does all he can to strengthen his party',[11] and the Earl was refused permission to travel abroad. Later in the same year Viscount Mordaunt, a rising and eccentric young genius, who had been so openly critical of James in the last session of Parliament, arrived at The Hague in October and, according to Burnet, pressed William to undertake 'the business of England', that is to say he advocated his active intervention. 'This,' wrote Burnet, 'appeared too romantical to the Prince to build upon it. He only promised in general that he should have an eye on the affairs of England; and should endeavour to put the affairs of Holland in so good a posture as to be ready to act when it should be necessary.' William also added that should the King attempt to alter the established religion or deprive his wife of her rights or 'raise forged plots to destroy his friends', then he would 'try what he could possibly do'. Though there is a story that the Elector of Brandenburg had earlier suggested to William that he should go over to England with 10,000 men, Burnet's is the first solid piece of evidence that exists that the idea of William intervening in England was discussed during the reign of James II. On the whole, Burnet's memoirs have stood up pretty well to historical examination; but parts of them have proved to be untrustworthy; and Halifax, who knew Burnet well, once observed that he 'has a swiftness of imagination no other man comes up to'.

The principal source of dissension between William and James during 1686 was the presence of numerous English and Scottish political exiles on Dutch soil. Some had been there ever since the time of the Rye House Plot; others had managed to escape back there after having been, directly or indirectly, involved in the rebellions of Argyll and Monmouth. They hid themselves among the mercantile classes of Amsterdam and Rotterdam or pretended to be studying at the university of Utrecht. The most notorious among them were Robert Ferguson, an indefatigable Scottish plotter, Sir Robert Peyton, said to be a republican formerly prominent in the City of London, and Dr. Gilbert Burnet, who was used by William as a collector of intelligence from England and afterwards as a propagandist. Most Amsterdammers were sympathetic towards the Whigs and republicans who were living among them; it was with the connivance of the Amsterdam naval authorities that the rebels of 1685 had originally set out. To protect them from extradition Peyton and Burnet were both naturalized as Dutch citizens.[12]

Sir Bevil Skelton was under constant pressure from his Government to secure the arrest and extradition of all those rebels who had been excepted from James's general pardon. In the

76

spring of 1686 James himself wrote to William protesting about the number of former rebels known to be living in Amsterdam. The Anglo-Dutch treaties were invoked, and eventually the States-General were induced to publish a resolution ordering that a *plakkaat* or proclamation should be published in all the Dutch Provinces demanding the departure of the English rebels from the country. But though in May James recorded his pleasure at this decision, two months later he was complaining that the proclamation had been published only at The Hague. By August the Dutch ambassador in London was assuring the King that the *plakkaats* had now reached all the States of the Union, but he soon had to admit that they had not yet appeared either in Friesland or in Groningen. Later the English King grumbled because the Dutch had failed to arrest Ferguson, Peyton or Burnet. Perhaps fearing that Skelton's heart was not in the business, he decided in September to replace him by a Roman Catholic named Ignatius White who boasted the title of Marquis d'Albeville bestowed on him by the Holy Roman Empire. But Skelton had certainly done his best. He had delivered a stream of protests both in writing and in words. On one occasion he had suddenly appeared at a service in the English church at Utrecht and frightened the English exiles there. He had made personal representations to William and Mary, who replied that it was a matter for the States. At home he had suggested that he might come to terms with some of the exiles, providing them with a royal pardon in return for their betraying the whereabouts of their friends. Before he finally left the United Netherlands he actually tried to organize the kidnapping of Peyton from Rotterdam. But the citizens protested; the authorities of Amsterdam asserted that they had made Peyton a burgher; and when an official protest was delivered by the Dutch ambassador in London, James was forced to eat humble pie and state that Skelton had acted without his permission and would be reprimanded. But he seems to have told Skelton in confidence that he was pleased with his effort and that he would see that no one who had been concerned in it should suffer.

If William was still anxious to keep up friendly appearances, and placate his uncle and father-in-law, he was by no means merely absorbed by the question of Anglo-Dutch relations. When Burnet arrived at The Hague in 1686 he noted how 'the depression of France was the governing passion of his whole

77

life' and how his chief fear then was that James would so upset his own subjects by his policies as to 'throw him into a French management'. Early in 1685 a new treaty had been concluded with his other uncle, the Elector of Brandenburg, who later became more positively antagonistic to the French because he disapproved of the revocation of the Edict of Nantes. Fear was felt in many parts of Germany about coming French acts of aggression; earlier ones were not forgotten and remained to be revenged; Louis XIV was expected to try to seize the Palatinate, to which his sister-in-law had a hereditary claim, when the Elector died. Then Prince William also looked anxiously towards the Holy Roman Emperor, the nominal leader of Germany. Most of his forces were still fully occupied in the war in Hungary. But the campaign was going well and the fall of Buda in September was a decisive event. The formation of the League of Augsburg, with the object of maintaining the existing international treaties —clearly intended as a defensive move against France—to which the Emperor and other German rulers adhered that August, showed that at least they were conscious of the dangers that lay ahead. The French King, for his part, was eager to thrust forward as far as he could into Germany before the Emperor Leopold, finally relieved of the war against the Turks and the rebel Hungarians, should turn back towards western Europe and, in spite of the truce of Ratisbon, attack him.

Because the French diplomatic and military hold upon northern Germany had been weakened by the defection of the Brandenburgers and the Swedes from their former French alliance and because of the menace that the French might see in the League of Augsburg, William might well have had reason to fear that the French King would try to redress the balance in Europe by concluding an offensive alliance with England. After all, James's principal minister who dealt with foreign affairs was in French pay; so was the English ambassador in Holland. Throughout 1686 constant reports were received in the United Netherlands of the strengthening of the English armed forces. Could the object be a fresh war against their old trade rivals? In August Van Citters started transmitting alarmist reports to The Hague of military activities foreshadowing an Anglo-French offensive alliance. King James II was pressed to deny these stories, but refused to do so. Consequently the rumours grew louder. In November 1686 the French ambassador at The Hague reported

78

that the people of Amsterdam (formerly rather friendly towards France) were nervous over the English naval preparations and were afraid that an Anglo-French attack on the Netherlands was coming in the following spring. The same story (which was reported back from Holland by Skelton) arrived in the English Court. However, in the middle of November the Dutch ambassador in London reported:

> The general conversation at Court is now that His Majesty's affairs are not in a fit condition, nor has he the inclination to go to war with anyone, and that the great naval armaments are made for no other purpose than to place himself in a situation for defending himself and thereby to cause himself to be considered the more both at home and abroad.[13]

A few days later Van Citters added that the rumour that a war with the Dutch was contemplated in the spring had been officially denied at the Court, and that it had also been explained (truly enough) that the state of preparedness of the English Navy was exaggerated. The fact was that James II had by now decided to publish his two declarations of liberty of conscience,* and the stirrings of discontent in his kingdom during the year made him aware that he might be required to employ force to sustain his policies at home.

In some history books the events of 1686 have been wrongly pictured. It has been suggested that James was the slave of France and that already William was deeply worried over the threat of an Anglo-French offensive against him. The old *Cambridge Modern History*, for example, discussing the events of 1686-87, observed that Louis XIV, in pursuit of his grandiose aims in Europe, 'received the full support of James II, under whose rule England had become "the corner-stone of the fabric" of French aggression'. There is no evidence for this whatsoever. Equally William—even though he was in no sense the architect of the League of Augsburg, though that myth is still sometimes repeated—was as much, if not more, concerned over Germany, notably over the behaviour of his uncle in Brandenburg and of the Emperor in Vienna, as he was over James II's cavortings at Whitehall.

The King of England, in fact, was wrapped up in his own domestic plans and what he desired at this time, as we shall see

* Appendix A.

79

in the next chapter, was to persuade his son-in-law to give them his support and approval so that James's fellow Roman Catholics might be assured of equal treatment not only during his own life-time but in the future. What William wanted was to be certain that James was not driven by his own stupidities or excesses into an enforced dependence on the King of France. The Prince hoped that he could persuade James II to realize his European responsibilities, just as he had vainly tried to induce Charles II to accept them six years earlier. Viscount Mordaunt may have suggested to William that he would ultimately be obliged to intervene in England; the Elector of Brandenburg may, quite likely, have discussed the same idea with his nephew during 1686. Nevertheless as yet no new factor had entered into the general situation that could urgently impel William to undertake an expedition so fraught with political and military dangers. But when Dijkvelt set out for England as Dutch ambassador extraordinary in February 1687 he was under instructions to make a very thorough reconnaissance of the ground. For anything might happen.

NOTES TO CHAPTER VI

1. D'Avaux, iv, 210.
2. Dalrymple, ii, 114.
3. The late Sir Winston Churchill's remarks on this in the first volume of his book on Marlborough are realistic.
4. S.P. 84/220, f. 7.
5. *Correspondentie*, ii, 21–2, 28.
6. Cf. S.P. 84/220, f. 5 v.
7. Ailesbury, 114.
8. Burnet, iii, 25 note.
9. Skelton to Sunderland, June 12/22, 1686, in S.P. 84/220.
10. Baschet, Jan. 10, 1686.
11. Baschet, May 17/27, 1686.
12. Cf. Maurice Ashley, *John Wildman*, chap. XIX.
13. Letter of Van Citters, Nov. 9/19, 1686, in Add. Mss. 34508.

CHAPTER VII

Towards the Revolution: 1687

THE mission of Everard van Weede, Lord of Dijkvelt, to England in 1687 is generally held to have been a turning-point on the road that led to the English Revolution. Not as much is known about the mission as might be wished. Dr. Burnet, the Scottish clergyman in exile at The Hague, for example, states in his memoirs that he was commissioned 'to draw his [Dijkvelt's] instructions, which he followed very closely'.[1] It is highly unlikely that William of Orange, who was a statesman, would have left this task to an exile whom he always regarded as a busybody. The truth is that the relations between the United Netherlands and England—and between William and James—had deteriorated, and an exchange of ambassadors was arranged in an attempt to resolve differences. At the same time as Dijkvelt was sent as a special envoy to London, Skelton was replaced by D'Albeville as English ambassador at The Hague, and each mission had, in the late Dr. Japikse's words, 'a parallel aim, open as well as secret'.[2]

Dijkvelt's mission arose out of the many rumours that had been crossing the North Sea during the previous autumn and winter about the scope of James's naval and military preparations. Might, for example, disputes over the Indies be used as a pretext for an act of aggression similar to the Anglo-French assault in 1672? Dijkvelt was therefore ordered to negotiate over the situation in the Indies, to examine the extent of the English armaments, and to inquire into King James's policies at home and abroad. Before he left he was also informed about Prince William's views on religious toleration. William Penn, a leading Quaker and a personal confidant of James II, had come to see the Prince in the previous November in order to sound him informally about whether he would give his public support to the repeal of the penal laws and Test Acts, which the English King had so much at heart. Dijkvelt was instructed to state in broad terms that while William and Mary favoured toleration as such, they regarded the

81

Test Acts as essential to the maintenance of the Stuart monarchy and the Protestant religion; for without them the confidence of the King's subjects in his impartial administration would be undermined. Just after Dijkvelt was being received for the first time by King James, William was sent an extraordinary letter by the Countess of Sunderland warning him in dramatic terms how unwise it would be if he were to fall in line with the King's religious proposals. She advised him that there were 'no offers, no dangers that will not be very artificially showed to Monsieur Dickfield', as she called him in Anglo-Saxon style.[3] Since the Earl of Sunderland was King James's principal minister, such a warning was calculated to make a profound impression on William, even if, in fact, Sunderland himself had no hand in his wife's letter. The Prince realized that his father-in-law required the most delicate handling on a matter so close to his heart and told Bentinck that he thought Dijkvelt could better explain to the English King about '*la grande affaire de la religion*' by word of mouth than he could himself by writing.[4]

James refused to see Dijkvelt until D'Albeville had been officially received in Holland. D'Albeville, who was himself a Roman Catholic, did his utmost to persuade William to agree with his master's views about toleration. Later on he seems to have intrigued against William (his reputation as an intriguer had preceded him); he was certainly in French pay and had promised to work in collaboration with the French ambassador at The Hague; but neither the French nor the Dutch ever trusted him, and, without being incompetent, he proved an even less successful representative in Holland of his Government than his predecessors, Skelton and Chudleigh.

When James first saw Dijkvelt he was anxious to be conciliatory. The King expressed the opinion that the dispute over the Indies, which related to the island of Bantam, west of Java, could be settled; he made light of the fears of the States-General that he was getting ready to make war upon them; his army and navy, he explained, had simply been neglected and needed to be brought up to a higher state of efficiency. He asked that the proceedings against the English officers who had been involved in the attempt to kidnap Sir Robert Peyton should be dropped and that they should be allowed to return home. The question of Orange was discussed and no doubt the King assured Dijkvelt that the English ambassador in Paris (Sir William Trumbull who was about to be replaced by Skelton) was making representations on his behalf. So far, so good. But the day after Dijkvelt arrived James's declaration of liberty of conscience was published in Scotland and that was soon to be followed by a similar declaration in England. Both these declarations showed clearly that James not only intended to abrogate the penal laws, but to dispense with the Test Acts.

If the King felt that by thus using his royal authority, which had been upheld by the Courts as lawful, he was entitled to ignore the statutory restrictions upon his Roman Catholic and nonconformist subjects, why was it that he was so anxious to have the Test Acts abolished by Parliament when it was obvious that it was going to be extremely difficult to persuade members to do this, since they were for the most part enthusiastic supporters of the Anglican establishment? The answer was, first, that he could not have Roman Catholics in either House unless the Act of 1678 was first repealed, since it had been decided that Parliament had the right to determine the nature of its own membership. As to the Act of 1673, which he had been allowed to nullify after the Godden *v.* Hales test case, he was afraid that his policy of conferring offices of State on Roman Catholics and dissenters would be reversed by his successors unless either the Act were repealed or he could induce his likely heirs, that is to say his two daughters, to promise their personal approval for its repeal.

Hence the pressure that King James now attempted to bring to bear on William and Mary through Dijkvelt and D'Albeville. (Princess Anne was also under royal pressure in England.) On his master's behalf Sunderland held out large but vague promises to Dijkvelt if he would announce that William and Mary agreed in principle to the repeal of the Tests. Dijkvelt handled the question as tactfully as he could. He did not openly express disapproval either on his own or on the Prince of Orange's part of the two declarations of liberty of conscience, but he appears to have hinted to the King that in William's view the constant and continuing pressure on influential persons to repeal the Test Acts and the extension of his use of the royal prerogative to suspend them might create such grave fears among his Protestant subjects as to bring about a revolution. If Dijkvelt went as far as this—and our sources for these conversations are not entirely satisfactory—it made little impression on the English King. On the contrary, while Dijkvelt was still in England, James wrote to his son-in-law telling him how satisfied people were with his declarations and how all was 'at ease and quiet'.[5]

According to the contemporary chronicler Nicholas Luttrell, James received during 1687 and 1688 altogether 200 addresses from dissenters and others approving of his declarations, including some from the London livery companies. Such a reception inspired him with the hope that a new Parliament might be fashioned by the reliable Sunderland to repeal the Tests and even made him wonder whether his son-in-law and two daughters might not in the end be persuaded to rally behind him in giving their approbation to 'liberty of conscience for all'. Was that not, after all, a policy already prevailing in the Dutch Provinces?

William and Mary were polite but inflexible. They insisted that if the Roman Catholics in England were given equality of opportunity in political life, they would not be satisfied, but would press on 'till they were masters'. The fear was also expressed by Dijkvelt—and here he was surely speaking for Prince William— that if by some means or other the repeal of the Tests were forced through Parliament and in consequence the Church of England were alienated, the monarchy might be overthrown and be converted into a republic as it had been forty years earlier. Then the Stuarts would count for nothing.

In addition to his official mission Dijkvelt had been told to give assurances on William's behalf to the leaders of the English ruling classes outside the official group at Court; to make it clear to the bishops, for example, that if William and Mary came to the throne they would not permit the destruction of the Church establishment, even though the Prince himself was a keen Calvinist and a Presbyterian. The Protestant nonconformists were told that while the Prince and Princess did not favour the repeal of the Tests, they none the less thoroughly approved of liberty of conscience, and indeed, if it were practicable, would support the comprehension of nonconformists within the Church of England, as had been proposed in 1660. Dijkvelt was in fact instructed to give as agreeable an impression of William as he could: to show that he was neither arbitrary nor imperious, as might reasonably have been deduced from recent happenings in Holland, and that he held liberal, but not too liberal, views on the subject of religion.

Dijkvelt was more successful with the secret than with the official side of his mission; he carried back with him to Holland in the early summer of 1687 a batch of amiable letters privately written to the Prince. Perhaps the most significant of these came from Lord Churchill, a former brigadier-general in the royal army who, though he was an intimate servant and former pageboy of King James, was now through his wife, who was her Lady of the Bedchamber, on the closest terms with James's younger daughter, Princess Anne. Anne had also been badgered by her father to change her religion or at least to give her public support to the repeal of the Tests. In a letter dated May 17 Lord Churchill explained that the Princess had ordered him to speak to Dijkvelt on her behalf;[6] she had received the Dutch envoy publicly but had only muttered the politenesses proper to princesses; Churchill assured Prince William that she 'was resolved by the assistance of God, to suffer all extremities, even to death itself, rather than be brought to change her religion'. Princess Mary had sent her sister a letter by Dijkvelt which Anne had answered earlier, telling Mary how the King their father had refused to allow her to visit her sister in Holland. But she begged Mary to inform no one except William that she had even thought of coming over and that her father had forbidden her: 'for tis all treason that I have spoke'. In his own letter Churchill assured William that he was resolved 'although I cannot live the life of a saint, if there be ever occasion for it, to show the resolution of a martyr'.

Apart from the letters of Princess Anne and Lord Churchill, one of the most revealing that the Prince received came from the Bishop of London who explained in a tortuous way how the Protestants in England looked to William as a leader and how 'if the King should have any trouble come upon him, which God forbid, we do not know any sure friend he has to rely upon abroad, besides yourself. . .'. Dijkvelt also carried over letters from the Earls of Danby, Nottingham, Halifax, Devonshire and Russell, from Arthur Herbert, the two Hydes, Lord Lumley and others. Most of them were written in very cautious phrases, but, after all, there was no real need for them to write at all. For Dijkvelt, who 'kept a great table', had seen and spoken to them and was able to take verbal messages to his master. By the very act of writing they indicated that they depended upon the Prince's protection if the King's religious mania got out of hand. Dijkvelt had sensed the atmosphere of doubt and fear in London, the pressures that were being brought to bear on all and sundry to accept the King's religious policies or religious opinions.

While Dijkvelt was still in London, Admiral Herbert, a capable if bucolic naval commander, had resigned his official posts rather than agree to the repeal of the Tests. Soon he was to go over to Holland. The Earl of Shrewsbury, one of the younger peers, who had not yet met Prince William, was to arrive at The Hague that autumn with a letter of introduction from the Marquis of Halifax who described him as 'without any competition the most considerable man of quality that is growing up amongst us'.[7] Halifax himself told the Prince that he was sure there was unlikely to be a new Parliament in the near future and that James's 'great design' was still held up for lack of sufficient influential converts. When Bonrepaus reached England in July, soon after Dijkvelt left, on his second visit, he reported that only one of James's ministers was serving him with single-minded fidelity. He thought that Sunderland, Godolphin and Churchill were already working in secret to merit the favour of the Prince of Orange. Jeffreys was described as 'very extravagant' and the Roman Catholic camarilla were alone thought to be completely loyal to the King.[8]

What were the results of the Anglo-Dutch exchange of ambassadors? That James was disappointed is evident. At first he hoped that when Dijkvelt on his return from England conveyed to his son-in-law his personal messages and arguments in favour of William and Mary giving their support to the policy of repeal, they would change their minds and endorse 'liberty of conscience to all dissenters whatsoever'. But William's reply to a letter from James, defending his declaration, which was brought over to Holland by Dijkvelt, was to tell his father-in-law pretty bluntly that he could not do anything contrary to his religion and would not agree with what James asked of him. When James realized the hopelessness of his task, he felt dismayed and at last complained about the meetings that had taken place between Dijkvelt and the powerful persons who were no longer members of his Government, such as Halifax and the two Hydes. And he ended his letter of protest with the old sour formula: 'I shall always be as kind to you as you can expect.'[9]

What were William's reactions to Dijkvelt's reports? Here posterity is in the dark. For what is important is what Dijkvelt actually said to William and that we do not know. He could tell his master that there was no immediate likelihood of the King of England making war on the Dutch or concluding a close alliance with France. But what was his view about the domestic situation in England? In the letters that he brought back with him from influential men the message for William was invariably to the effect that Dijkvelt would tell him all that had taken place. He will 'give you a full account', wrote Clarendon; Dijkvelt 'knows everything', said his brother Rochester. Danby repeated that he was eager for a personal conference with the Prince, if only it could be arranged. Halifax again informed him that a new Parliament was unlikely.[10]

Unquestionably it was on the holding of a new Parliament that William fastened his attention. James had now at last in July, soon after Dijkvelt's departure, dissolved his Parliament of 1685 and was starting a campaign to pack a new Parliament that would favour the repeal of the Tests. But here lay the unknown territory. Dijkvelt may well have told the Prince that it was most unlikely that James and Sunderland would be able to organize such a Parliament in the near future. If an election were held, it was quite on the cards that a House of Commons, still composed of Anglicans, would show itself extremely hostile to the monarchy, as it had done in 1640. William may have felt that if and when a Parliament were called it might be his duty to intervene in England, not in order to protect the liberties of its people, but to save the Stuart monarchy from destruction. After all, he was a Stuart and his wife was the heiress-presumptive to the throne. For him it was essential that the Government of England should be a friendly one: he knew that on the mainland of Europe a lull prevailed that might precede a storm. For would not Louis XIV be tempted to strike again in Germany before the Emperor Leopold turned his attention back from the Hungarians and the Turks? So William decided that he needed still more information about the state of affairs in England, and in August he sent over another trusted ambassador extraordinary in Count Zuylestein, his own cousin, 'a person the more dangerous because under the appearance of a man of pleasure and a soldier he had great talent for business' and was 'entitled to a degree of confidence from the English malcontents'.[11] The nominal reason for his visit was to commiserate with the English Queen on her mother's death. His real object was to confirm the contacts established by Dijkvelt, and to collect the latest intelligence about the state of affairs in England.

'From July to October, 1687,' observes Professor Kenyon in

87

his biography of the Earl of Sunderland, 'the English government was moving in a void, without confidence, expectation or hope for the future'. But a distinction needed to be drawn between the King, who was never more set on having his own way, and his ministers, who were becoming highly nervous both about the domestic and the foreign situation. James was pleased by the peaceful manner in which his declarations of liberty of conscience had been accepted in England and Scotland. In July he had received D'Adda officially as Papal Nuncio to his Court, and proceeded to try to mediate between his cousin Louis XIV and Pope Innocent XI over a prolonged dispute which had cast a blight upon the unity of Roman Catholic Christendom. It is true that the sixth Duke of Somerset, one of the greatest noblemen in England, had refused as Lord of the Bedchamber to conduct the Nuncio to his first audience at Windsor on the ground that to do so would have been against the law (according to Burnet, he told the King 'you may be above the law, but I am not'); one of Charles II's illegitimate sons, the Duke of Grafton, had to take over from him in a hurry. It was from about this time, the beginning of July 1687, that James II determined to abandon all hope of obtaining support from his existing Parliament and to try to fashion another one to do his will.

'Closetings' of Members of Parliament—that is to say personal interviews conducted by the King—had gone on ever since the previous year. James now decided to ask the Lords Lieutenant of the counties to carry out closetings on his behalf throughout the whole kingdom. They were instructed to call together their deputy lieutenants, sheriffs, justices of the peace, officials of the boroughs, and other prominent local people and ask them individually whether, if they were chosen Members of Parliament, they would be in favour of taking off the Tests and the penal laws; alternatively, whether they would assist the election of members who were so committed; and finally if they would support the King's declaration of liberty of conscience by living on friendly terms with Christians of all persuasions. Most of the existing Lords Lieutenant, however, preferred to resign or be dismissed rather than to put these three questions, nominally on the ground that to exert such pressure would be constitutionally improper, though of course Members of Parliament were normally selected largely by agreement among the influential men in the counties. So, as a first step, the King had to appoint new Lords Lieutenant.

Nine Lords Lieutenant were dismissed in August; a further four in December. Some of the new appointees were Roman Catholic. They were asked when they went on their rounds to collect the names of suitable Roman Catholics and nonconformists to add to the justices of the peace. In September the King himself went on a 'progress' through the west of England, going as far north as Chester. According to what Dr. Burnet heard, he was very gracious to the dissenters he met, even to former adherents of the dead Monmouth. 'He ran out,' wrote Burnet, 'on the point of liberty of conscience: he said this was the true secret of the greatness and wealth of Holland . . . He everywhere recommended to them the choosing of such Parliament men as would concur with him in settling this liberty as firmly as the Magna Charta had been: and to this he never forgot to add the taking away the Tests.'[12] When he came to Oxford he addressed the Fellows of Magdalen College, reprimanding them extremely angrily for their disloyal conduct in refusing to accept his original Roman Catholic nominee as their President and then being reluctant to repudiate their own choice and replace him by the crypto-Catholic Bishop of Oxford. (Later a special royal commission achieved the King's wishes only by pressure and afterwards most of the Fellows were expelled.) But, on the whole, the King was satisfied with the results of his progress.

However, he had less reason to be pleased with the answers to the three questions put by his new Lords Lieutenant. Throughout the kingdom the local gentry evaded, almost to a man, the pressure to commit themselves in advance of an election. In most places the stock answer was that those elected to the House of Commons would have to decide what to do when Parliament met; in answer to the third question it was generally said in a pious way that they were willing to live in peace with their neighbours, according to the precepts of the Gospels. Even appointments of officials likely to be loyal and friendly to James did not help his cause very much. The Dutch ambassador in London estimated that in December 1687 one third of the sheriffs were Roman Catholics, one third dissenters and one third moderate Anglicans. But even such sheriffs, who were in a position to play a vital part in elections, were cautious. It was noted, for example, that 'many of the popish sheriffs have estates, and declare that whoever expects false returns from them will be deceived'.[13]

The answers given to the Three Questions in most counties

have survived and show an almost unanimous opposition among the influential persons consulted to the repeal of the Test Acts. That became clear even before the returns were completed. The Dutch ambassador reported home at the end of the year that only six out of seventy gentlemen in Norfolk answered the questions as the King wished, and about the same proportion in Wales. Bonrepaus, who was in England at the time, noted that the Lords Lieutenant did not find things as the Court would have liked: 'even in the most friendly counties only six people favour repeal of the Tests, in others none'. Earlier Van Citters had written to the States-General that the news from all quarters was that the nobility and the leaders of the nation were not to be persuaded to remove the Tests; the only possible exception was in Lancashire 'where they are for the most part Catholics and fanatics'.[14] As to the boroughs, as distinct from the counties, even here manipulation was far from easy. The King told his Council that he intended to purge the parliamentary corporations of hostile elements, but in fact events proved in 1688 that however often they were purged the ultimate result was not to ensure compliance when it came to religion. And if a House of Commons could not be packed to do the King's will, it was even more certain that in a House of Lords where the Catholics could not take their seats, men like the proud Duke of Somerset and the astute Marquis of Halifax were not going to be browbeaten into a reversal of all the anti-Catholic laws.

The King's ministers and advisers, apart presumably from fanatical Catholics like Father Petre, realized the position. Whichever way Sunderland analysed the situation, he could not feel in the least optimistic. Nor could the Lord Chancellor, Jeffreys. But the King himself was adamant. 'If His Majesty get not a parliament to take off the Tests within six months,' said Lord Dover in late November, 'he will go out of England.' '*Le Roi d'Angleterre*,' reported Barrillon on December 1, '*est resolu de poursuivre ses dessins, quelque opposition qu'il trouve.*'[15] A fortnight later Van Citters reported that the King had told his Council that he was anxious that his declaration of liberty of conscience should be passed as a law and that anyone who failed to concur with him would be dismissed from office. Thus throughout the winter of 1687–88 and the early spring of 1688 the policy of trying to pack a Parliament continued. In March there was a rumour that such a Parliament would actually be called in May. But by then other important things were happening. For from early November 1687 the Roman Catholic Queen Mary of Modena was known to be pregnant, thus holding out the prospect of a Roman Catholic dynasty so long as the hereditary succession was upheld; and from that time on the English Government was busy taking steps to strengthen its military resources against all eventualities.

What can William of Orange have been thinking to himself as news of these events and of James's political frustrations kept arriving by every post from England? Van Witsen, a Dutch Regent, said afterwards that the roots of the Revolution of 1688 were to be found in Dijkvelt's visit to England. D'Avaux, the French ambassador at The Hague, an extremely well-informed diplomatist, dated the beginnings of the Revolution from about August 1687 when Count Zuylestein returned to Holland carrying more confidential letters for William from his well-wishers in England. Though others were to describe the decision as not having been taken until June 1688 when a son was born to James II and Mary of Modena, the Earl of Shrewsbury, who was an important actor in the revolutionary conspiracy, was to tell Halifax that William would have invaded England had the Prince of Wales never been born.

We have seen that even earlier than 1687, in the first half of 1686, suggestions had been made to William by Viscount Mordaunt and the Elector of Brandenburg that he should lead a force over to England. Political schemes and military plans of such magnitude were not to be carried through in days or even in a few weeks. No large-scale military expedition against even a relatively stable government in England had been achieved successfully since 1066. Even mighty Caesar had experienced his difficulties in overcoming British barbarians. Only chaos and disorder had smoothed the path of King Henry VII. The Spaniards had sailed through the Channel a hundred years earlier, but had never looked like landing an army. Clearly the idea of possible active intervention had existed in William's mind for a long time, conceivably ever since 1681. The missions of Dijkvelt and Zuylestein were reconnaissances of the whole political and military situation in his father-in-law's kingdom. If there was the slightest thought in the minds of the Prince and of his closest advisers of undertaking an expedition so fraught with dangers before the end of September 1688, that is to say before conditions of wind and weather favourable to sailing ships were likely to vanish, then active preparations would have to begin before the winter of 1687–88 was over. Thus it can hardly be doubted that strategic appreciations and concrete plans were already being taken into consideration after the reports of Dijkvelt and Zuylestein had been seen and digested.

The main political question in William's mind was clearly whether James really intended to call a Parliament and if so, what kind of Parliament it would be. Once James had in session a Parliament ready to back him over his religious policies, the chances of intervention were poor. William had witnessed and no doubt studied the fate of the Duke of Monmouth, whose backers in London had failed him. The Prince had to feel sure that he himself would receive the fullest moral and political assistance if he came to England. That, it seems, is what he wanted most: he never counted on military or material aid arranged by his English sympathizers. The fight, if it came to a fight, would be between professionals, not amateurs. But was not Napoleon I to claim that the moral to the material was in war as three to one? Politically William could look back to the precedents of 1680–81. Then it had been proposed in Parliament that William and Mary should come over to act as Regents, as tutors to a Roman Catholic king who reigned but did not rule. That proposal had been put forward by quite moderate men (like Halifax) in order to thwart the exclusionists whose policy threatened to bring hereditary monarchy to an end. Now might there not be a threat of exclusion in reverse? Quite apart from Mary of Modena's pregnancy, which was not known for certain until November 1687, might there not be some truth in the rumours that, under pressure from his Jesuit advisers, James would try to prevent the coming of a Protestant successor? That very winter James had written long letters to Princess Mary, trying hard to persuade her to become a Roman Catholic. Princess Anne too had been proselytized. Either a Roman Catholic successor or a Parliament orientated towards popery might carry England over into the French camp. Alternatively—and that one believes was William's biggest fear—James's increasingly unpopular actions might give birth to a new republican movement and destroy the monarchy altogether.

Every week the Dutch ambassador in London sent fresh reports of anti-Protestant pin-pricks.[16] A popish master was appointed to a school in Bath; when James was in Oxford he attended Vespers with the Roman Catholic Master of University College;

the Protestant President of Magdalen College was finally deposed; Father Petre became a member of the Privy Council and was promised a cardinal's hat; the Duke of Berwick, James's illegitimate Roman Catholic son, was appointed Lord Lieutenant of Hampshire and became responsible for the defence of Portsmouth; a Roman Catholic, Sir Roger Strickland, was to command the Channel fleet. In November William took a positive and significant decision: he determined to make known not merely to James but to the world at large precisely where he and his wife stood on the question of the repeal of the Test Acts. He got his friend, Caspar Fagel, the Grand Pensionary of Holland, to write a letter (which Dr. Burnet translated into English) in answer to an inquiry from a Scottish Presbyterian, James Stewart, explaining that they were ready to concur in the repeal of the penal laws, provided that Roman Catholics continued to be excluded from both Houses of Parliament and from public employment. Roman Catholics, they thought, should be allowed the same degree of liberty of worship as they possessed in Holland; but the Test Acts must be retained. James was most annoyed over this open letter. At first it was pretended in Whitehall that it was not genuine. But a continuing flood of pamphlets printed in Holland made it clear that Fagel had indeed spoken for his master. In vain a reply was produced entitled *Parliamentum Pacificum* or *The Happy Union of King and People in a Healing Parliament*. Already the Fagel–Stewart correspondence had created a sensation.

That same autumn the Marquis of Halifax, a brilliant pamphleteer, anonymously published his *Letter to a Dissenter* in which he argued that it was not really to the interests of the nonconformists to support the repeal of the Tests. He urged that popery was by its very nature an exclusive religion, and once the Test Acts were repealed the English people might be forced into the Church of Rome. More important than this war of words was the request that was soon put forward officially by King James II that the English and Scottish regiments in Dutch pay should be permanently returned to England. The inspirer of this request was the Earl of Sunderland, now himself teetering on the edge of conversion, who, it has been suggested, thus hoped to strengthen the position of the Roman Catholic party in England if James should suddenly die. It seems a rather complicated motive, but Sunderland had an over-subtle mind. At any rate it was not a particularly feasible proposal. In the first place, James did not possess the funds to pay for the upkeep of six additional regiments, and Sunderland had to try to induce Barrillon to persuade his King to pay for them: that indeed was to put James under the patronage of France. No wonder that Sunderland asked, if the scheme went through, that he should be awarded an additional 'gratification' by the French King and a promise of his protection in case of trouble.[17] Frankly he admitted that he needed enough money to put him in a state to face with less concern the revolutions that happened so frequently in English history. In the second place, it was highly unlikely that the States-General would agree to the release of the regiments without putting up a great deal of resistance. It was generally recognized that the mere request was certain to poison the relations between the two nations and to arouse the suspicion that an Anglo-French attack on the Dutch was in contemplation. Thus the Dutch would be alienated without the French being necessarily committed. Finally, after their long sojourn in the Netherlands would these regiments prove loyal to a popish sovereign?

Too late Sunderland realized that this proposal was a blunder of the first order. In February 1688 Van Citters reported to the States-General from London that the English King was expected to put thirty-eight men-of-war to sea in the spring; that a Parliament was to be called in the hope that it would prove anti-Dutch; and that the demand for the recall of the regiments from Holland was accompanied by growing rumours of a coming war. Thus, if in the winter of 1687–88 William was in fact considering the possibilities of intervention in England, an operation which would require the fullest support from the States-General and from leaders of opinion throughout the United Netherlands, by lending substance to alarmist reports James and Sunderland had played right into his hands.

William's final decision would have to be reached on practical grounds in the cause of *Realpolitik*. His aim was to prevent and not to start a civil war in England; to assert his wife's right of succession to the throne; to stop James from concluding a military alliance with France. These were the great simplicities. William had no intention of allowing himself to be pushed into a sudden or desperate enterprise by a few discontented English politicians. He listened, above all, to the Marquis of Halifax who advised him to play a waiting game. He knew that many people in England regarded him as a ruthless Prince who had once adopted a fierce attitude towards the Dutch Republican party and had quarrelled frequently with the rulers of Amsterdam. The Whig interpretation of history, stemming from Sir Edward Coke and realized in history books written soon after William died, made the Prince of Orange into the saviour of immemorial English liberties, the spiritual heir of Simon de Montfort and John Pym. So, in effect, he came to be. But that was not the main motive for the actions that precipitated the Revolution of 1688. Before they are detailed, we shall, however, turn back and consider the political theories and constitutional ideas that lay behind the Revolution and may have contributed in some measure to its bloodless success.

NOTES TO CHAPTER VII

1. Burnet, iii, 164.
2. Japikse, ii, 219.
3. Sidney, ii, 257; cf. Pinkham, 40–1, and J. P. Kenyon in *Cambridge Historical Journal*, No. XI.
4. *Correspondentie*, i, 31.
5. Dalrymple, ii, 181.
6. W. S. Churchill, *Marlborough*, i, chap. XIII.
7. Foxcroft, *A Character of the Trimmer*, 236.
8. Mackintosh, 387.
9. Dalrymple, ii, 185.
10. *Ibid.*, 197.
11. *Ibid.*, 200.
12. Burnet, iii, 179.
13. Johnstone, Dec. 8, 1687, cit. Mackintosh, 218 v.
14. Add. Mss. 34510, f. 63 v.
15. Add. Mss. 34515, ff. 33–5, cit. Kenyon, 169; Baschet, Dec. 1/11, 1687.
16. Add. Mss. 34510, *passim*.
17. Baschet, Jan. 5 N.S., 1688 (P.R.O. 31/3/175, f. 357).

CHAPTER VIII

Political Theory and the Revolution

THE Stuart kings of England all had far-reaching ideas about the extent of their political authority, and William of Orange, himself a Stuart on his mother's side, had frequently behaved extremely autocratically in his dealings with the Regents of Holland and of other States of the Dutch Union. But in any case the seventeenth century was becoming an age of absolutism, though less enlightened than in the following century: for examples, the Kings of France and of Sweden alike aimed to restrict the political power and influence of their more important subjects: and the divine right of kings to rule was almost a commonplace. Yet at the same time a social rumbling was to be heard, which burst into a fearful storm in the middle of the century. In greater or lower degrees the whole of Europe was faced with revolution, though it took different forms. In England it resulted in the victory of Parliament over King Charles I; in the United Netherlands it inflicted a setback on the House of Orange. However, the hereditary executives largely recovered their lost ground: in 1660 Charles II was restored to the throne of his fathers; in 1672 William became Stadholder as well as Captain-General of the United Netherlands. Both Charles II and William of Orange had learned a lesson from revolution and restoration. James II, coming to the throne in 1685, had not learned the same lesson or had forgotten it; or perhaps, as some historians argue, he had learned an altogether different lesson: that a tough line of conduct was the best assurance against revolutionaries and to yield to pressure was foolish if a king wished to rule as well as to reign.

The Stuarts, who in three centuries of kingship in Scotland had never been effectively absolute and indeed had frequently been tossed about and humiliated by a turbulent aristocracy, had looked with admiration on the authority and influence of the Tudors in England. Realizing that his position was likely to be much stronger in England, James I when he came south incautiously put forward grandiose claims for the rights of mon-

archy. Yet before the time of the Tudors the kings of England—
and indeed of other countries in Europe—were never thought of
as absolute monarchs. 'The subordination of government to a
moral standard and to spiritual authority,' it has recently been
observed,[1] 'was probably the outstanding feature of much political
thinking: the use of political power was considered to be limited
both by the reason implicit in customary law and by God's will
and purpose as embodied in the law of nature.' It is true that
when King Henry VIII repudiated his allegiance to the papacy
greater political power came to be concentrated in the hands of
the English monarchy, and once the Tudors became Supreme
Heads or Supreme Governors of the English Church it was more
difficult to insist on spiritual or moral limitations upon the
authority of the Crown. But the idea that the sovereign was completely supreme was never admitted without question by the
majority of those who thought about politics in seventeenth-
century England. Against King James I's far-reaching claims
(which he had the sense not to press too far) Sir Edward Coke, the
famous jurist, and his friends, comprising leading members of the
House of Commons, lawyers and antiquarians, advocated the
doctrine that the King was subject, if not to the moral and natural
laws, then certainly to the immemorial laws of the English people,
dating back at least to Anglo-Saxon times, and enshrined in such
documents as Magna Carta, coronation oaths and other cherished
constitutional acts of the middle ages. Coke would never have
agreed that the Tudors had destroyed 'feudalism' and erected an
absolute monarchy responsible solely to the Almighty in its place;
for he insisted that the King was subject to laws tested by experience and that he needed regularly to consult his subjects assembled
in Parliament.[2]

Up to the outbreak of the civil war in 1642 what most English
political thinkers believed in was not royal absolutism but what
they called 'mixed monarchy'. Men as politically opposed as
Coke and Francis Bacon would have agreed that, in theory at
least, there could be and should be no disharmony between the
executive, the legislature and the rule of law. Where the difference
was to arise was over the reserve or emergency powers of the
monarchy, generally called the King's prerogative powers, but in
fact signifying simply the basic authority which any effective
executive expects to exercise. It was only after the civil war broke
out that different political ideas were expressed. Yet at first the

97

royalists argued that a constitution consisting of a 'mixed monarchy' could not function if the powers of the monarchy were reduced as much as the parliamentarians now claimed they should be, while the parliamentarians argued that Charles I in many of his actions, especially his arrests of Members of Parliament and his imposition of taxes by prerogative means, had violated the whole spirit of the English constitution and ignored the rule of law handed down from generation to generation. Convinced that the King was incorrigible, political writers who sought to justify the civil war then began to suggest that Parliament itself ought to be the sovereign power in the community while the King carried out purely ceremonial or administrative duties under Parliament's supervision. Philip Hunton, Henry Robinson and William Prynne were among those who argued in such a way.[3] It was not until King Charles I started the second civil war, having been defeated in the first, that even more extreme views were expressed. In his *Tenure of Kings and Magistrates* written in 1649, John Milton observed that 'the power of kings and magistrates is nothing else but what is only derivative, transferred and committed to them in trust for the people to do the common good of them all'. The people therefore, he argued, had the right to depose a king at any time, even though he were no tyrant, and to decide, 'merely by the liberty and right of freeborn men', to be governed as they thought best.

During the ten or eleven years before the Stuarts were restored to their throne many constitutions or schemes of government were tried or came under public discussion. Never in the history of England were republican writings more prolific or varied than they were in 1659. And the greatest political thinkers who wrote during this period, Thomas Hobbes and James Harrington, produced theories which were no comfort to the Stuarts or the advocates of hereditary monarchy and could indeed have been made equally applicable to a republican form of government.

It is usually said by historians that political theories or philosophies when absorbed and disseminated bring about constitutional changes. But the fascinating thing about the history of political thought in seventeenth-century England is that the theorists, for the most part, wrote not to urge changes but in justification of the existing political facts. King James I's books justified the divine right of the Tudors to govern without restraint; the political pamphleteers who wrote in the sixteen-forties invented a case for the sovereignty of Parliament instead of the system of 'mixed monarchy'; Milton, Harrington and Henry Vane in their different ways approved a sort of republican oligarchy; men as different as Oliver Cromwell and John Lilburne, the Leveller leader, favoured a widening of the bases of electoral power, though neither of them was in the least a democrat in a modern sense. And republicans who wrote during the reign of King Charles II thought in terms of the rule of an aristocracy of virtuous men—or a 'chosen people'—which they had seen to exist during the Interregnum.

During the first eighteen years after Charles II was restored to the throne there was comparatively little political writing, though the works of Hobbes were read and refuted. A 'mixed monarchy', or what has been called by the greatest authority on this reign a 'semi-constitutional' monarchy, was established. Parliament sat, if discontinuously, throughout the whole of the period. Charles II accepted the restrictions on the power of the monarchy to which his father had agreed in 1640 and 1641. No attempt was made to levy taxes without the consent of Parliament or to interfere with parliamentary privileges or deliberately to pervert the law (that was hardly necessary in view of the flexibility of the judges). It was not until the exclusionist crisis blew up in 1679–81 and King Charles II's first 'long' Parliament had been dissolved that men began to apply their minds again seriously to questions of political theory and to examine the constitutional foundations of the existing Government.

When the crisis came the royalists were rather stuck for an apologist. No question arose of their making use of the works of Thomas Hobbes who, though he had a brilliant mind and friends in Court circles, was considered by most of his contemporaries to be a cynic and an atheist; moreover his arguments did not necessarily lead to belief in the value of the kind of monarchy that actually existed. So they turned to the writings of a Kentish country gentleman, Sir Robert Filmer, who had been dead for thirty years, but whose books had been written to support the Stuart cause at the time of the civil war. His *Patriarcha, a Defence of the Natural Power of Kings Against the Unnatural Liberty of the People*, originally circulated in manuscript before the civil war, was printed in 1680 and it excited lively interest.[4] It was ironical that he should have begun his book by stating that the doctrine

99

that mankind was born with freedom from all subjection and at liberty to choose what form of government it pleased was one fostered by 'Papists and Jesuits', since the monarchy that he was now being called upon posthumously to sustain was itself becoming unpopular mainly because of its close relationship to the Roman Catholic Church. In 1670 Charles II had promised the French King that he would aim to convert his subjects back to Roman Catholicism; in 1673 James had laid down his public offices rather than admit to the validity of a Test Act requiring public servants to vouch for their Protestantism. If the hereditary monarchy of England was again in danger, as indeed it was in the sixteen-eighties, it was because it was tarred with this papist brush, made manifest to the English public in general by the discovery of the so-called Popish Plot.

Anyhow, Filmer was used to show that the monarchy had been created by God, that the subordination of Adam's children to their father was 'the fountain of all regal authority' and that this authority was handed down through Noah to the Stuarts. Filmer was no defender of 'mixed monarchy' as some royalist writers had been. To him 'mixed monarchy' was an 'impossibility' or 'contradiction', for the State then, he said, becomes a democracy, and there is no such thing as a democracy. But while Filmer agreed with Hobbes that mixed monarchy was another name for anarchy, he disagreed with his view that men are naturally equal or with Milton's view that they are born free. A political State, he argued, is simply an enlarged human family: subjects must obey their king, as children obey their father. That was prescribed by Holy Scripture. Thus Filmer had a clear-cut opinion about the basis of political obligation and he employed historical precedents and commonsense reasoning to expose political arguments deriving from such shadowy concepts as 'the state of nature' and 'the rule of law'.

At the same time that *Patriarcha* appeared, another book of Filmer's, *The Freeholder's Grand-Inquest Touching Our Sovereign Lord the King and His Parliament* (1648), was reprinted: in this Filmer argued from a study of medieval statutes that Parliament's privileges were derived from and governed by the King. Parliament was no court but was subject to the monarchy. Filmer's arguments were taken seriously in spite of their dependence on Old Testament stories and dubious constitutional history. Though a modern historian has written that the immediate and enduring success of *Patriarcha* was 'a pathetic reflection of the absence of any truly critical element in the conservative thinking of the time', yet there was more substance to Filmer's arguments than vague assertions of indisputable right and the theories of conquest which had previously been employed to promote royal absolutism.

At this time, largely by accident, the power of the Government to impose a censorship on books temporarily came to an end, and thus it was legal for pamphlets to be published in support of views that could be condemned as subversive, though the authors might be had up for seditious libel. Three writers sat down to tackle the doctrine of the inviolability of hereditary monarchy put forward by Filmer: the authors were Sir James Tyrrell, a man of Filmer's own class, Algernon Sidney, the brother of Prince William's friend Henry Sidney, who was prominent among the exclusionists, and John Locke, an Oxford don who was the personal friend and servant of the Earl of Shaftesbury, the exclusionist leader in Parliament. As it happened, Sidney's book was not published until after he was dead—he was executed for the part he was alleged to have taken in the imaginary Rye House assassination plot—and the manuscript of his book was used in evidence against him at his trial, while John Locke's work did not appear until after the Revolution of 1688 succeeded. But all three books illustrate the kind of arguments that were being put forward at that time to refute such notions as the divine right of kings and the obligation of subjects not even to resist a tyrant.

Tyrrell's book, *Patriarcha Non Monarcha* (1681), was attributed to 'a Lover of Truth and of his Country', bearing the name of Philolethes. Tyrrell argued that he was only defending the existing state of affairs against an advocate of tyranny. The Government of England, as it was established, he asserted, was the best of its kind. Tyrrell was not prepared to go all the way with Philip Hunton, whom Filmer had attacked. 'I have nowhere maintained with Mr. H. in his treatise which our author writes against [he wrote] that ours is a mixed monarchy, though limited by law, and therefore shall not maintain, as he does, the King to be one of the Three Estates.' But Tyrrell pointed out that mixed monarchies did exist elsewhere in the world (thus refuting Filmer's view that they were impossibilities) and he quoted the writings of Puffendorf, the German jurist, in support of them. Tyrrell insisted that supreme power must be limited by some law; all sovereignty was ultimately dependent upon consent; and the past history of England showed that the King had always consulted Parliaments and acknowledged the rule of law. When King John conceded Magna Carta to his subjects, the assertion of their ancient rights by the nobility and people of England was never condemned or declared to be a rebellion, except of course by the Pope.

Sidney's arguments were more far-reaching than those of Tyrrell, though they have never been considered to be particularly subtle. In fact he reverted to old doctrines of 'natural law'. Government, he said, with Milton, is derived from the consent of the people: 'the liberty of the people is the gift of God and Nature'. Government is carried out by magistrates appointed by the people and the magistrates are not necessarily a hereditary dynasty. As with Milton, Sidney believed that what the people had once granted they might take away again at any time. The general revolt of a nation against a tyrant could therefore never be called a rebellion. Sidney expounded his views not only in the manuscript that shocked the judge at his trial but also in a speech delivered on the scaffold, which was afterwards published. These views were summarized in a pamphlet entitled *Sidney Redivivus*, which appeared in 1689. Sidney believed, this pamphlet explained, that 'the power of kings is founded on the consent of the people who have a right to call them to account for maladministration and to restore themselves to their native liberty'. This original power of the people was delegated to Parliament; the rights and powers of magistrates in every country was that which the laws made them to be. The King is as much accountable to the people as he is to God. The trouble with Filmer was that he failed to understand that magistrates were made for and by the people.

It was no wonder that such ideas were deemed horrid at Sidney's trial. The notion that the King was responsible to his people as well as to God, that he was a mere magistrate, and that his powers could legitimately be taken away from him if he were considered at any time to have misused them, was anathema to all good royalists and indeed to all good Anglicans. Yet these ideas were not expressed merely by Sidney but by other exclusionists in the sixteen-eighties and they represented a fundamental criticism of the traditional authority of hereditary monarchy. The right of rebellion in fact could not have been more clearly formulated than it was by Sidney. 'When nations,' he wrote in his posthumous *Discourses*, 'fall under such princes as are either incapable of making a right use of their power or do maliciously abuse that authority with which they are entrusted, those nations stand obliged by the duty they owe themselves and their posterity to use the best of their endeavours to remove the evil, whatever danger or difficulties they may meet in their performance.'

John Locke, a far profounder political writer than either Tyrrell or Sidney, does not seem to have gone as far as they did in advocating the right of rebellion.[5] It is not clear precisely how far he did go because his famous book, *Two Treatises of Government*, was not published until after the Revolution of 1688, although it is known that much of it was written at the same time as the other two critics of Filmer were writing. Moreover, modern commentators on Locke's work are by no means in agreement over exactly what he did mean: for example, the very last chapter of his book entitled 'Of the Dissolution of Government' is held to be 'not at all explicit about what actually happens when people find themselves at liberty to entrust new hands with the government'. Nevertheless it can hardly be doubted that Locke's doctrines permitted a rebellion, at any rate if it were approved by Parliament. Mr. Peter Laslett, the recent editor of the *Two Treatises*, says that 'the trend of Locke's statements about the ultimate right of the people to revolt is quite unmistakable'. Mr. Maurice Cranston, his latest biographer, observes that 'the right to rebellion . . . is central to the argument of the book'.

From what does this right derive? Locke invented a 'state of nature' and 'a law of nature' which really represented his view of what mankind was or ought to be. In the 'state of nature' men were free and equal and according to 'the law of nature' no one ought 'to harm another in his life, health, liberty or possessions'. But the power of punishment that every man has in 'the state of nature' to enforce 'the law of nature' may lead to disorder. Hence men make a 'compact' to set up a magistrate and thereby secure an ordered society. In agreeing to do so, they do not surrender their natural rights; on the contrary, the principal aim of government is to protect the individual's liberty and property. Thus, in Mr. Cranston's words, Locke was 'an early champion of the minimal state'.

The government which men set up, according to Locke, was therefore a fiduciary trust. The consent that men gave to government was a tacit consent. The object of government was not to reduce men's liberties (at any rate in theory) but to extend them by conferring protection upon their 'natural rights' as laid down by the 'law of nature', rights approved by God. A government may be dissolved if either the legislature or the executive commits a breach of its trust, and another government be put in its place.

Can the people then at any time take up arms to overthrow the Government? Is it right for them to do what they did in 1642, to 'set upon their king'? In his last chapter Locke quoted approvingly from William Barclay, 'the great champion of absolute monarchy', where he argued that if a king himself endeavours to overturn his Government or make himself dependent upon another king, then indeed the King may be resisted. In the very last paragraph of his book Locke explains that if those in authority 'commit miscarriages' they forfeit the supreme power, which reverts to society, 'and the people have the right to act as supreme, and to continue the legislative in themselves, or erect a new form, or under the old form place it in new hands, as they think good'.

Locke, Mr. Cranston points out, regarded absolute monarchy as a real and present menace, and asserts that he made the right of rebellion explicit. Who were the rebels to be? Professor C. B. Macpherson, whose essay in refined Marxism, entitled *The Political Theory of Possessive Individualism*, has been much praised, has argued that 'the people' who were given by Locke the right to decide whether or not 'constituted civil authority' had broken its trust were not the people as a whole: 'he [Locke] was consistent throughout in wanting a civil authority which could secure the basic institutions of a class society.' But few historians have ever imagined that Locke was a democrat in the modern sense of the word. The consent to government on which his political philosophy was founded belonged (both in theory and in fact) to the property-owning or possessing classes or whatever one likes to call them. The main point, so far as these theorists were concerned, was that authority was not conferred on the Stuart kings exclusively by the Almighty through the monarchy's descent from Adam and Eve or in any other way but by the politically active and influential among the King's own subjects. Though in a way such thinkers looked back to the older theories of 'mixed monarchy' subject to the moral law, they increasingly emphasised a view of political obligation which derived not from God but from man. Theirs was an empirical, utilitarian view of society.

There is one other consideration which is being examined by present-day historians. It has been suggested that perhaps too much stress has been laid in the past upon the importance of religion in the latter half of the seventeenth century. This was a formative period in the development of modern science. It was the age of Isaac Newton and the Royal Society. Men, it is suggested, were no longer so worried about theology as they used to be or even about the relations between Church and State; they were moving towards a much more secular outlook on society. God had retreated from being the spirit of the universe to being a mere clockmaker. Neither Hobbes nor Milton nor Locke was an orthodox Christian. Much of the political reasoning of the time was cast in a traditional mould for tradition's sake. All this is true up to a point. But one must not overlook the historical facts. How was it that a Parliament, so enthusiastic about the restored monarchy and the Church of England as the first Parliament of Charles II had been originally, had been moved towards the idea of excluding the legitimate heir to the throne from his right of succession? It was simply because he was a Roman Catholic. Why was it that James II provoked many of his leading subjects to conspire against him? Because he had employed his prerogative powers to try to achieve equality for all Christians. It may be that what both King and Parliament were concerned about was material things, about possession of offices and of property. Lord Willoughby was to say in 1688: 'it was the first time any Bertie was ever engaged against the crown . . . but there was a necessity either to part with our religion and properties, or do it.'[6] Yet few men doubted that a Supreme Power governed the world and many believed that the Almighty guided it, as Cromwell had believed, as William of Orange believed. Newton, the greatest scientist of his time, was a keen theologian. What men quarrelled about was not whether God existed but whether the Almighty had designed it so that kings should rule absolutely—as enlightened despots—or whether governments were made for the governed, who could remove rulers if they menaced their God-given rights.

In the second half of his *Two Treatises of Government* Locke laid emphasis on the importance of Parliament or 'the legislative'. In his chapter 'Of the Subordination of the Powers of the Commonwealth' he says that 'in a Constituted Commonwealth' there can be but one supreme power which is the legislative. Even where the executive is vested in a single person and the legislative is not always in being, the legislative still has the power to resume the execution of the laws when it finds cause and to punish any maladministration. Nor does the right of the executive to assemble or dismiss the legislative give the executive a superiority over it, for this is a 'fiduciary trust' placed in him for the security of the people. It is true that in all 'moderate monarchies' and 'well-framed governments' several things must be left to the discretion of the executive where the laws are silent, but since the end of government is the public good, the prerogative has to be exercised in conformity with the laws laid down in Parliament. In any case, the right of the executive to make laws is a right delegated to it by Parliament, which retains its superiority.

Two other authors writing in the sixteen-eighties stressed the role of Parliament as forming an essential and historic part of the English constitution. In his *Ancient Rights of the Commons of England Asserted* William Petyt, a barrister, aimed to undermine the suggestions in Filmer's books that monarchy (which, he said, stretched back to Adam) was far older than Parliament and that such powers as Parliament possessed were privileges granted by kings. Parliament and the law, he asserted, were immemorial. King William of Normandy was no real conqueror of England since he and his successors had confirmed the Anglo-Saxon laws. The Norman and Angevin Kings had met freeholders or representatives of the freeholders in a common council of the realm which was in fact a true Parliament. Petyt was supported and supplemented in his reasoning by his pupil and friend, William Atwood, who in two books, served, in Dr. Pocock's words, as 'a combatant on the historical wing of the Filmerian controversy'. They revived a line of reasoning, once used by Sir Edward Coke, that the English monarchy was subject to a rule of law stretching back to time out of mind; Magna Carta and the Petition of Right of 1628 had confirmed the recognition by the monarchy of the existence of fundamental, unchangeable and inalienable laws, while the historic position and importance of Parliaments were a proof that England had always been governed by a 'mixed monarchy', not by the absolute monarchy defended by Filmer.

Two other notable contributions to political and constitutional theory were in circulation in the sixteen-eighties: one was *Plato Redivivus*, written by Henry Nevile, a friend of James Harrington, and published at about the same time as Filmer's *Patriarcha*. While Filmer admitted no real restrictions on the monarchy, Nevile, who had been an active republican before the restoration of Charles II, went to the other extreme and advocated a reduction of the King's authority. The sovereign power, he said, resided in the 'three estates' of King, Lords and Commons, and he thought that in terms of property the King's share of political authority had become excessive; for, like Harrington, Nevile believed that in a stable society the holding of political power must be related to the distribution of landed property. He urged therefore that the making of war and peace, the control of the army and navy, the nomination of officers of State and the control of the public revenues should all be taken away from the King and put into the hands of four councils, while Parliament should be elected to meet every year and ensure rotation in the membership of the governing councils.

A more realistic political argument came from the Marquis of Halifax in his *Character of a Trimmer* which circulated in anonymous manuscript from about the year 1684. Halifax wished to persuade his readers of the virtues of a mixed monarchy and a middle-of-the-road policy. The pamphlet, it seems, was provoked by a royalist article written by Roger L'Estrange, who defended the existing monarchy and mocked moderation. Halifax praised the laws as jewels, attacked Louis XIV and the policy of close alliance with France, upheld the principles of the Test Acts and the exclusion of Roman Catholics from public life, and argued that the penal laws against them should not be abrogated except by statute, though he favoured mildness in their administration. 'The Trimmer' was a man who avoided all extremes in politics, of monarchy, 'a thing that leaveth man no liberty', on one side, of a commonwealth (or republic) which was 'too hard for the bulk of men to come up to', on the other. King and kingdom, he thought, were 'one creature, not to be separated in their political capacity'.

Thus during this period when the censorship of books was temporarily in abeyance, when the exclusionist controversy was still raging, and when the names of 'Whigs' and 'Tories' first entered the English language as describing those who favoured and those who abhorred the calling of Parliament in the last years of Charles II, there was a good deal of theoretical political writing, anonymous and at times fantastic, but implicitly critical of the

Stuart monarchy. Undoubtedly it was sparked off by the exclusionist movement; if exclusion of the Roman Catholic James could not be achieved, then the power of the monarchy must be clearly limited and defined, as Nevile and Halifax urged. Most of these writers argued a case for the supreme role of Parliament; some of them invented plausible historical arguments for the subjection of the monarchy; a few of them walked a thin line between political theory and treason.

Should the view be accepted that John Locke's book was written 'to promote a revolution'? It seems more likely, in the light of recent researches, that its primary aim was to justify the exclusion of James from the throne when he was still Duke of York and to allow the Duke of Monmouth to take his place, as Locke's patron the Earl of Shaftesbury wished. In any case the *Two Treatises of Government* was not circulated until after the Revolution and its argument in favour of the right to rebel—often obscurely worded—can hardly have made much difference to the plans of William of Orange who, as we shall see, came to England not to promote a rebellion but to enforce the calling of a Parliament.

There is, however, one indirect way in which such writings may have contributed towards the Revolution of 1688; that was by conjuring up the fear in William's mind that a genuine alternative to the rule of James II was the restoration of republicanism in England. James himself, as we have observed, was deeply afraid of a republican movement in the sixteen-eighties: a few former republicans, notably John Wildman,[7] were mixed up both in the Whig plottings that followed the failure of the exclusionist movement and the invasion of Monmouth in 1685. The kind of doctrines aired, in however vague and wrapped-up phrases, by Algernon Sidney and Henry Nevile suggested that republican ideas were still floating around, ideas that had proliferated twenty years earlier, in 1659. When William of Orange worried about the growing unpopularity of his father-in-law and concerned himself over James's failure to call Parliament in 1686 and 1687, he may well have been anxious, above all, about a possible reaction in the form of a revolt against the monarchy as such; for if a revived republican movement were a success, not only would it deprive his wife of her chance to come to the throne, but it would ruin his own opportunity of being able in the future to influence the course of English foreign policy.

Even after William established himself in England and his

father-in-law fled abroad, the Prince still feared above all the re-establishment of a republic or Commonwealth, emerging from the Revolution that he himself had unleashed; for that might have proved a very different form of government from the 'mixed monarchy' advocated by so many political thinkers, who were not absolutists, as the ideal constitution (even if in practice under Charles I and Oliver Cromwell it had proved almost unworkable).[8]

To sum up: some of the ablest political theorists of the later half of the seventeenth century had by their arguments justified a right of rebellion against a misguided king, and to that extent aided William of Orange, when he invaded England, thundering against popery and arbitrary power; but, at the same time the arguments that they used tended to undermine the fabric of monarchy itself. And William's aim of course was to save the monarchy, not to destroy it.

NOTES TO CHAPTER VIII

1. W. H. Greenleaf in *English Historical Review* (1964), LXXIX, p. 747.

2. For Coke see J. G. A. Pocock, *The Ancient Constitution and the Feudal Law* (1957) and Christopher Hill, *Intellectual Origins of the English Revolution*, chap. V. I have discussed this point in a booklet entitled *Magna Carta in the Seventeenth Century* (University of Virginia Press, 1965).

3. See J. W. Allen, *English Political Thought 1603–1660* (1938); W. K. Jordan, *Men of Substance* (1948); William Lamont, *Marginal Prynne* (1963), *etc.*

4. See R. Filmer, *Patriarcha*, ed. P. Laslett (1949); J. W. Allen, *op. cit.*

5. See Peter Laslett's edition of the *Two Treatises* (1960) and Maurice Cranston, *John Locke* (1957) and authorities there cited.

6. Cit. Christopher Hill, *The Century of Revolution*, 238.

7. For John Wildman see Maurice Ashley, *John Wildman*.

8. See B. Behrens, 'The Whig Theory of the Constitution in the Reign of Charles II', *Cambridge Historical Journal* (1941), vii. For a broad view of seventeenth-century political thought see W. H. Greenleaf, *Order Empiricism and Politics* (1965).

CHAPTER IX

The Invitation

GRANTED that at the turn of the year 1687-88 William of Orange
had decided that on certain conditions he would be ready to
intervene in England, what kind of conditions did he have in
mind? After all, it was possible at least to plan a large-scale
military operation and then, if it were not needed, to call it off;
what was virtually impossible was to come to a decision at the
very last moment and then scrape the barrel to find the necessary
resources when the way had been insufficiently prepared either
strategically or politically.

One condition that might make intervention necessary was
the birth of a son to King James II and Queen Mary of Modena.
Mary was now nearly thirty and most of her previous children
had been girls; none had survived beyond the age of five. (The
taint in the children of the later Stuart crowned heads had come
from their wives. For the fathers proved themselves capable of
doing their parts. Charles II had two sons who showed some
military capacity in the Duke of Monmouth and the Duke of
Grafton; James's son by his mistress, Arabella Churchill, the
Duke of Berwick, was to become an outstanding soldier.) Ever
since it was known in November 1687 that the Queen was
pregnant the birth of a son was considered a serious possibility.
The King would regard such an event as happy for his cause; and
until then it was thought he would not come to any extreme
resolutions. 'If the Great Belly should in any way fail,' it was
reported to William Bentinck by an intelligencer in England,
'the Court will take much warmer measures.'[1] On the other
hand, how would the discontented Protestants—those leaders
of opinion who had sent letters offering their services to Prince
William by the hands of Dijkvelt and Zuylestein—behave if a
Roman Catholic Prince of Wales were to be produced? The
Imperial envoy in London reported home towards the end of
March 1688: 'Judicious people think if a prince is born an effort
will be made to prevent the Catholic succession.'[2]

The question for William, then, was whether the birth of a prince would provoke a civil war which might destroy the monarchy or at any rate paralyse England as a factor in European affairs. The kingdom had, after all, accepted the idea of having a Roman Catholic king in 1685 without demur, although at the time of the exclusionist agitation that had seemed most unlikely. Had James now in fact so upset his Protestant subjects that they would resist the coming of a Roman Catholic successor? After all, even if a prince were born, he might not long survive. We have already noted the testimony of the Earl of Shrewsbury that William would have invaded England if a prince had never been born. The tone of the letters written to the States-General by the Dutch ambassador, to William Bentinck by his intelligencers and to the Prince of Orange by his political friends suggests that the Prince and his Dutch colleagues were far more concerned over the immediate possibility of King James packing a pro-Roman Catholic and pro-French Parliament ready to do his will than they were over the ultimate likelihood of a Roman Catholic heir succeeding to the English throne.

Over the shaping of a Parliament there was indeed a struggle between the King and his son-in-law. By informing the public through Fagel's letter that he was opposed to the repeal of the Test Acts William had nailed his flag to the mast for all to see. Many papers were printed in Holland and dispatched to England giving warnings about the dangers of removing the Tests. Henry Sidney had written asking for thousands of copies of this propaganda to be sent over; and thousands of copies of Fagel's letter were in fact printed. A Dutch intelligence service established in London by Sidney helped to diffuse this propaganda. Under its impact James II gave up all hope that William would alter his views; according to one account, when it was suggested to the King that William might still be induced to change his mind, he answered that he knew the Prince better than they did; that he was 'a man inflexible'.[3] And so would James himself have liked to be. William Penn, his principal nonconformist adviser, had attempted to persuade the King to press for a Parliament ready to repeal the numerous penal laws, but to abandon for the time being the hope of ending the Tests. That was thought by independent observers to be a practical proposition and was supported by the Earl of Sunderland. But James then stuck to his full plan. He still hoped for a complacent Parliament.

In November 1687 it had been rumoured that a Parliament would be called in March; but when March arrived, it became known that the King had no intention of summoning a Parliament until after the Queen had given birth to their child, an event expected about the end of June.

In any case the various methods employed to secure a suitable Parliament had not yet held out much hope for the King. Some of the Lords Lieutenant commanded to put the Three Questions in the counties had been dismissed or resigned; some had been replaced by Roman Catholics; James's loyal Protestant Lords Lieutenant like Sunderland, Jeffreys and Rochester (Rochester had been well treated by the King financially after he had ceased to be a minister and was not the stuff of a martyr) had been unable to make any impression on the counties they visited; Sunderland in April postponed a visit to Warwickshire in view of the general failure elsewhere. The leading gentlemen in Cornwall and Devon, once the heart of royalist enthusiasm, had proved recalcitrant. The Earl of Bath insisted that however often he changed the deputies and justices of the peace, they would never agree to placing their religion in danger. Even in Lancashire, a county strong in Roman Catholic deputy lieutenants and J.P.s, more than two to one, according to Lord Molyneux, the Lord Lieutenant, openly declared themselves to be against the King's proposals.

Some Lords Lieutenant put the questions formally, but made it clear that they were not at all concerned over the answers they received. As to the boroughs, orders requiring them on one pretext or another to surrender their charters to the Crown had been given ever since 1681 and many new charters issued—often referred to at the time as 'obnoxious'. James's purpose had been so to remodel the charters as to be sure that his policy of religious toleration would be fulfilled. Consequently he had actually in some cases called in charters issued by his brother. Yarmouth's charter had been 'regulated' more than once; so had that of other towns. In the course of 1688 thirty-five new charters were issued after the old charters had been surrendered in response to a writ of *quo warranto*. Lawyers were kept busy all over the kingdom. In Cornwall alone no fewer than sixteen new charters were granted in the first year of James II's reign. Yet the Earl of Bath's reports suggested that it was unlikely that M.P.s elected in the Cornish boroughs would favour the repeal of the Tests.[4] Elsewhere all the indications were that however much the Government fiddled with the charters, by nominating members of corporations, by exempting them from oaths and tests and even by restricting the franchise, it was as difficult to be sure of obtaining from the boroughs representatives in the House of Commons who would favour the King's religious policies as it was from the counties. That was the reason why the Marquis of Halifax, who closely followed the manoeuvres over electing a fresh Parliament, insisted in his messages to William of Orange that he had no need· to worry about the likelihood of a Parliament being called in the near future or of its approving the royal programme. Still that was not precisely how William himself was looking at the matter; for his position was a paradoxical one. It was true that a Parliament that was subservient to the King might be dangerous to his own interests; on the other hand, a Parliament exasperated against the King—like the former exclusionist Parliaments or the Long Parliament in 1642—could provoke a situation as dangerous to the stability of the monarchy as the former civil wars had been.

More important to William than either the birth of a Roman Catholic prince or the summoning of an extremist Parliament was the question of a possible military alliance between James II and Louis XIV directed against the Dutch. Such a possibility appeared to be real when the demand was put forward by King James's Government that the six British regiments in Dutch pay should be sent back to England. The Earl of Sunderland, who had at first regarded this demand as a wonderful coup, afterwards came to recognize it as a first-class blunder. For nothing was better calculated to provoke the Dutch and to induce them to support William's campaign for rearmament. Not only did the Dutch Government positively refuse to send back the regiments intact, but the French King, who had been invited to subsidize the payment of the recalled regiments, became more and more tepid about the whole idea. Indeed it suited him for the Dutch and English to be at loggerheads. Eventually on March 14 King James published a proclamation ordering the return of all his subjects serving in the United Netherlands. Though a large number of officers did return and become available as the nucleus of new regiments, most of the non-commissioned officers and men stayed with the Dutch. And it was not until May that the French were persuaded to offer a small contribution towards the cost of raising these new regiments.

As to the navy—and it was the naval situation that was really crucial in Anglo-Dutch relations—the behaviour of James and Sunderland over the recall of the regiments actually stimulated the recruitment of Dutch sailors to man a fleet of some twenty warships for a summer guard. Louis XIV showed himself far more concerned over the state of James's navy than with his army. The French Navy was pretty fully committed to the Mediterranean theatre and Louis XIV was afraid that the Dutch might employ theirs when the spring came to assist the Swedes against the Danes, who were the allies of France. If James were to make available a large fleet and if he could be persuaded to lend his support to the Danes, that would neutralize Dutch activities in the Baltic and the North Sea and help prepare the way for renewed French aggression in northern Europe. Thus even the obscure contest between the Scandinavian kingdoms over Holstein played its part in the history of the English Revolution.

James was certainly worried over the Dutch naval preparations at that time, just as the Dutch authorities closely watched the activity in English shipyards; and a state of mutual suspicion and fear was engendered. On the whole, the reports received by William were soothing. The Dutch ambassador in London thought that the English King just did not possess the means to put a big fleet to sea, even if he wanted to do so. (That incidentally was what Sunderland was then telling the French.)[5] According to Dutch intelligence from England, when Sir John Berry, a naval commander, was ordered to stand by in February he told the King that if it were a question of getting ready for action, he had better 'put no popish officers in', for 'he was sure that the seamen would knock them on the head'.[6] And the French ambassador in Holland was of the opinion that even if James were capable of raising a big fleet that would only serve as an excuse for the Dutch further to increase their own. By the middle of May Sir John Evelyn noted in his diary that 'the Hollanders did now alarm his Majesty with their fleet so well prepared and out before we were in readiness'.[7] Thus each side grew more nervous of the other. Lord Dartmouth was sent to look at the defences of Yarmouth. In the United Netherlands the ports and other towns were being fortified and plans laid to double the size of the fleet. Louis XIV for a time continued to press James II to fit out twenty-five men-of-war instead of the mere twelve chosen for the summer guard on which preparations were begun in February. But all that James could be persuaded to do in the French interest was to publish a general declaration against disturbers of the European peace, and in time the King of France lost interest. James, though he himself had been a sailor, attached more importance to his army than to his navy. He rightly recognized the military difficulties involved in an invasion from the sea. But realizing his relative naval weaknesses, he did not wish to incite the Dutch. Barrillon was persuaded that one of the reasons why James kept on putting off the calling of a Parliament was that he feared that if he did call a Parliament to meet during the summer 'Dutch warships would come to the English coasts and the Prince of Orange would omit nothing to stir up trouble and prevent Parliament doing what was asked of it by revoking the penal laws and the Tests'.[8]

But the real reason why James postponed the calling of Parliament was that he was by no means sure that such an assembly would in fact favour his ends. Change though he might his Lords Lieutenant, the answers to the Three Questions were always discouraging; change though he did, by regulation or by the issue of *quo warranto* writs, the membership of the parliamentary boroughs, there somehow did not seem to be enough loyalists, dissenters and Roman Catholics to go round. 'The persons placed in the new corporations,' wrote the Dutch ambassador on May 1, 'mostly all are of the same maxims and ideas as those that are removed from them, through which they often alter one and the same corporation two or three times in one month.'[9] Danby assured William of Orange at the end of March: 'Our zeal for the Protestant religion does increase apparently every day in all parts of the nation and the examination of the minds of the nobility and gentry had made such a union for the defence of it throughout the kingdom' that it could not be supplanted except by violence.[10] The Marquis of Halifax wrote a fortnight later that there was 'rapid motion without advancing a step'.[11] The men 'at the helm', he asserted, were divided; the great thing for William to do, he thought, was to do nothing, but wait for the good consequences of the Court's divisions and mistakes.

By now King James had decided to abandon for the time being, the idea of calling Parliament; though Sunderland collected somewhat more promising reports from the agents that he had sent out to the constituencies than he had obtained from the traditional hierarchy, he could see that he had no hope of getting together a Parliament that was likely to do the King's will before the autumn; and finally he succeeded in overcoming the various groups of advisers who clustered around Whitehall and in persuading the King at least to postpone holding Parliament until after the Queen's delivery. According to the Papal Nuncio, from whom an account of the decisive meeting about this question comes, Sunderland observed bluntly that 'the Anglicans were now utterly estranged from the Government'.[12]

In the light of this view it was strange, but typical of the fatalistic policy of James II, that he now proceeded to provoke the leaders of the Church of England beyond endurance. They had already been angered by the King's treatment of the Fellows of Magdalen College, Oxford. Oxford, after all, had long been the heart both of the Church and of the royalist faith. It had been Charles I's headquarters throughout the first civil war. When Parliament met at Oxford in 1681 its discomfiture had been evidence of the turning of the tide against the exclusionists. Vainly had the Commission for Ecclesiastical Causes given instructions that the expelled and deprived Fellows of Magdalen should be offered no livings. The monarch ignored all the danger signals. Even when the Bishop of Oxford, who had been forced on the College as its President, died, the King would hold out no olive branch to the Anglicans. The new President, Bonaventura Gifford, was yet another Roman Catholic, one of four papal vicars in England, and the College, now 'filling apace with Popish priests, and others of the Roman communion, they seized wholly upon the College chapel for the uses of their religion'.[13] Magdalen was a *cause célèbre* in the higher echelons of the Church. But James spread resentment throughout the rank-and-file of the Church of England by ordering the clergy to read his declaration of liberty of conscience, which he reissued on April 27, from every pulpit in the country.

The Order in Council, published on May 4, stated that the declaration was to be read in London churches on the Sundays May 20 and May 27, and on June 3 and June 10 elsewhere. Precedents enough existed for such an order: the pulpit was the best means of broadcasting royal wishes. But the bolder and more Protestant-minded of the church leaders determined at last to make a united stand. Among those prominent in the movement were Henry Hyde, Earl of Clarendon, the King's

116

brother-in-law by his first marriage (less time-serving than his brother, the Earl of Rochester), William Lloyd, Bishop of St. Asaph, and the suspended Bishop of London. On May 12 Clarendon dined at Lambeth with the ageing Archbishop of Canterbury, William Sancroft. He must have screwed up the Primate to action. For on May 18 Sancroft wrote out in his own hand a petition to the King requesting him to withdraw the Order in Council on the ground that the foundation of his declaration of liberty of conscience was illegal, being based on his dispensing power which had often been condemned by Parliament.* When the petition was presented to James he was thunder-struck. This, he exclaimed, 'is the standard of rebellion', or 'of Sheba', according to another account.[14] That same evening the bishops' petition was printed and distributed throughout London. In consequence the following Sunday the great majority of the clergy of London refrained from reading the King's declaration from their pulpits.

The King's first reaction was that the seven bishops must be punished for their temerity. But how? His advisers were divided. It was rumoured that even the papists were for temporizing and that 'the only new advice given the King was to hasten out the fleet and new-model the army'.[15] A general indecisiveness prevailed at and around the Court. Sunderland and the Lord Chancellor Jeffreys were for damping down the affair; they suggested that the King should admonish the bishops rather than try them or punish them. Again might not the bishops be suspended by the Ecclesiastical Commission which had dealt with Bishop Compton and the Fellows of Magdalen? Or could they be tried at common law for treason? Ultimately it was resolved, on the counsel of Jeffreys, that the bishops should be prosecuted for seditious libel before the Court of King's Bench. When they refused to enter into recognisances for their appearance at the Court they were arrested and sent down the river to imprisonment in the Tower of London.

The day after the bishops were taken to the Tower the Queen was carried in a sedan chair from Whitehall to St. James's Palace where she planned that her lying-in should take place. During her pregnancy she had been subjected to terrible psychological strains. Long before the child was born gossip had it that the whole thing was a Roman Catholic plot. On January 15 the

* Appendix B.

Earl of Clarendon had noted in his diary that 'the Queen's great belly is everywhere ridiculed . . .'. On March 27 the Earl of Danby wrote to William of Orange: 'many of our ladies say that the Queen's great belly seems to grow faster than they have observed their own to do' and expressed the hope that Princess Anne should be on the spot to watch the performance of the midwife.[16] In fact Princess Anne departed for Bath at the end of May. Those malicious gossips who did not voice the suspicion that the Queen was really suffering from 'dropsy' asserted that the father of the child could not be the King, but might be the handsome Nuncio, Count d'Adda, or even Father Petre, the King's Confessor.

However, at ten o'clock in the morning of June 10 a son was born in St. James's, three or four weeks before the expected time. Few royal births have been more fully documented.[17] Only the Archbishop of Canterbury (who was in disgrace at Court) and Princess Anne were missing from the crowded State bedchamber in which the birth took place. Immediately after the delivery the child was carried into the next room where, it was claimed afterwards, a substitution took place. In no time at all every sort of rumour was floating around London. Princess Anne, who had not been at the lying-in or delivery, hastened to inform her sister Mary that though it was possible that the birth might have been genuine, she did not believe it herself nor did thousands of others.

The unhappy parents were not yet aware of all this tittle-tattle. The Mass was celebrated in Whitehall, the 'Te Deum' was sung, fireworks were let off and cannon fired. Within twenty-four hours of his birth the Prince of Wales was privately baptized according to the Roman Catholic rite and the Pope was named as his godfather. It was no wonder that his two stalwart Anglican step-sisters, Anne and Mary, insisted on questioning the authenticity of the birth and gave vent to the opinion that he probably would not live very long. The wish was father to the thought. But William of Orange himself had no immediate doubts. Prayers for the Prince were said in Holland; and William promptly sent over his trusted relative, Count Zuylestein, to convey his congratulations and sound out the reactions of the Protestant nobility to this unwelcome and inconvenient event.

Meanwhile the Earl of Sunderland and others of the King's advisers had soon realized that the arrest of the seven bishops, like the recall of the regiments from Holland, was a political blunder of the first magnitude. 'The whole Church,' the Papal Nuncio informed the Pope, 'espouses the cause of the bishops. There is no reasonable expectation of a division among the Anglicans, and our hopes from the nonconformists have vanished.'[18] Indeed, much to the disgust of the King, leading nonconformists visited the bishops when they were in the Tower to convey sympathy. Sunderland and Jeffreys tried to persuade the King that the birth of his son offered an admirable opportunity for him to grant a general pardon and thereby save his face. But the King was not to be moved. The bishops themselves took a high line. When they were in the Tower they refused to pay the customary fees to the Lieutenant, Sir Edward Hales. When they were brought from the Tower 'thousands of people stood on each side of the river making great shouts, the bells rang, and people hardly knew what to do for joy'.[19] James II reviewed three battalions in Hyde Park and the Dutch ambassador thought it was 'surprising that in view of so great a concourse of people so very much affected for the bishops a general insurrection did not take place'.[20] Appearing before the King's Bench with their counsel the bishops pleaded not guilty, refused to make any admissions, but eventually agreed to stand their trial on June 29 after small personal recognizances from them had been accepted.

Although the bishops' counsel raised a number of rather ridiculous objections to the Crown's case (such as that there was no proof that the bishops had signed the petition) in essence the argument was a simple one. The Crown maintained that the petition was a seditious libel because it impugned the King's honour. It was libellous to say that a justice of the peace was dishonest in carrying out his duties; how much more libellous it was to claim that His Majesty did not know how to carry out his. To publish such a statement was to stir up mischief among the people and therefore the libel was seditious. The bishops' counsel, insisted, however, that all this was irrelevant; no libel had in fact been published by the bishops; they had merely exercised their rights as loyal subjects to submit a humble petition to the Crown. The fact that they had asked the King to withdraw an order because his dispensing power had been declared illegal by Parliament had nothing to do with the case. The King's rights were not being decided by the trial, only the rights of his subjects.

Four judges tried the bishops before a jury, to which the

verdict whether the petition was a libel or not was left. The Lord Chancellor Jeffreys, who had himself formerly been the Chief Justice of the King's Bench, told the Earl of Clarendon that the public trial was extremely unfortunate and that 'as for the judges, they are most of them rogues'. He also said on June 14 that James II had changed his mind under the pressure of some 'who would hurry the King to his destruction'.[21] Be that as it might, two of the judges, Chief Justice Wright and Sir Richard Allibone, a Roman Catholic, summed up against the bishops and two in their favour. The jury had to sit all night without heat, food or light to consider their verdict. First thing on the morning of Saturday, June 30, it found the bishops not guilty. Huge crowds awaited the verdict and broke into loud cheers when they heard it. 'The giddy rabble continued their disorderly joys till Sunday morning,' reported a newsletter, 'making bonfires all Saturday night.'[22] The fires were lit even in front of St. James's Palace and an effigy of the Pope was burnt. The people, according to the Imperial envoy in London, were 'bold and insolent' not in the least afraid of the soldiers, and the King's dispensing power was now being generally called into question.[23] And it was not only the mob who rejoiced. The nobility threw money to the crowds as they indulged in their pope-burning. The King was staggered at the news of acquittal. Before and during the trial he had visited the army camp at Hounslow which was supposed to be there in order to overawe the capital. Instead of that, even the soldiers cheered when they learned of the verdict. Typically, James dismissed the two judges who summed up for the defendants. He also planned to summon the bishops before the Ecclesiastical Commission and even to punish all the clergy who had refused to read his declaration in their churches. But that would have been to make war on the entire Church of England, and the matter was postponed indefinitely.

Well before the birth of the Prince of Wales and the trial of the seven bishops William of Orange had been completing his plans for intervention in England. War, he felt sure, was coming in Germany and he had no wish to have either a hostile or neutral England, with a powerful fleet and a growing professional army lying on his flank. About the middle of April Edward Russell, an admiral and a cousin of the dead Whig martyr, William Russell, and another admiral, Arthur Herbert, whom James II had forced to resign, visited William of Orange in Holland.

Russell told the Prince that 'he was desired by many of great power and interest to speak very freely to him'. He and his friends, he said, were under heavy pressure from the Court. At the moment they were united. But if the army proved both loyal to the King and obnoxious to the nation, they might be compelled to yield to the King's wishes. That at least is Burnet's account of what Russell said. What is not open to doubt is the nature of William's reply which was to the effect that:

if he was invited by some men of the best interest and the most value in the nation, who should both in their own name and in the name of others who trusted them invite him to come and rescue the nation, and the religion, he believed he could be ready by the end of September to come over.[24]

The Dutch Pensionary, Caspar Fagel, appears to have earlier suggested the same condition on behalf of the Prince. In May the French ambassador at The Hague had been reporting with increasing urgency that he was sure that the Prince of Orange would 'hazard all' if a son and heir were born to King James.[25]

Russell and Herbert returned to England, but on May 24 Herbert wrote to William to say that he understood from Russell that it was the Prince's wish that he should join him in Holland and that he intended to do so shortly. Arthur Herbert was a remarkable character. He had served in the Dutch wars and ten years earlier when he was already a vice-admiral he lost an eye in an accident. In 1683 he was reported to have kept a harem in Tangier. He had lost £4,000 a year when he had resigned from his posts rather than become a Roman Catholic; he was said to be the darling of British seamen. William welcomed him with open arms. In a letter of June 17 he told Herbert how pleased he was that he was satisfied with what Russell had said to him on his behalf and promised him that he would be well looked after if he came to Holland.[26] On May 31 Lord Lumley wrote to the Prince offering his personal services, and earlier the young Earl of Shrewsbury had expressed his anxiety to go over to Holland: so had Lord Latimer, a son of the Earl of Danby. On June 9, the day after the arrest of the bishops, Shrewsbury had again written to the Prince, and nine days later while the bishops were awaiting their trial William was assured that the letter of invitation for which he and Fagel had asked would soon be forthcoming. It was then hinted that besides Henry Sidney (who was William's principal agent in England and had organized an intelligence service on his behalf), Shrewsbury, Danby, Bishop Compton, and the Earl of Nottingham were ready to commit themselves to rebellion. In fact Nottingham backed out, though he did not reveal his knowledge of these treasonable transactions to the King. And on June 30, 1688, the required letter of invitation was signed by the 'Immortal Seven': Shrewsbury, Devonshire, Danby, Lumley, the Bishop of London, Edward Russell and Henry Sidney.* The Marquis of Halifax and Lord Mordaunt, who had at one time been enthusiastic for William to intervene, like Nottingham refrained from signing the letter of invitation, but kept the secret. The letter was carried over by Herbert disguised as a common sailor.

The letter pointed out that 'people generally' were dissatisfied with the Government's behaviour in regard to religion, liberties and properties, 'all of which have been greatly invaded'. It was asserted that nineteen out of every twenty people in the kingdom were desirous of a change and would be ready to take part in a rising against the Government, if they received the promise of protection against the royal forces. 'It is no less certain,' the letter observed, that 'the greatest part of the nobility and gentry are as much dissatisfied, although it is not safe to speak to many of them beforehand.' The common soldiers, it was thought, were 'averse to the Popish religion'. But there was a real danger of a packed Parliament. Therefore the Prince should come over soon, presumably to prevent this, and the signatories would 'attend' his 'landing'. On the same day Sidney wrote a letter of his own to the Prince advising him to seek the services of Marshal Schomberg, a famous French general now in the service of the Elector of Brandenburg, to command an invading army and to leave Zuylestein in England until the conspirators had received their answer.

Undoubtedly it was the birth of the Prince of Wales—or his alleged birth, for according to the letter of the Immortal Seven, 'not one in a thousand believed the baby to be the Queen's' —and the trial of the bishops which screwed up these men to commit themselves in black and white to 'a rising' against the throne. Modern historians are divided over the quality of the men who thus committed themselves. In the opinion of the late David Ogg, a close student of the reign, 'only one name, that of

* Appendix C.

122

Lumley, could be considered obscure'. Lord Lumley, the owner of a modest estate, was a former royalist and a convert from Rome who had been alienated from the King. Professor Kenyon, on the other hand, maintains that 'their importance has been greatly inflated' and 'William received remarkably little support from the English nobility'.[27] It is perfectly true that neither Nottingham nor Halifax nor Rochester, three of the most influential figures outside the King's Government, had the courage to go so far. Halifax, by nature a trimmer, a man of wealth,was always a coward and remained so after the Revolution. But Halifax had lent his help with his effective, if anonymous, pamphlets. As events proved, men like Nottingham, Clarendon, and the Duke of Ormonde were entirely sympathetic, but did not have the courage to risk all until after William had landed. But there is little solid ground for doubting the statements of men like Danby or the Dutch ambassador, Van Citters, that during the first half of 1688 the King's policies and methods had thoroughly upset the bulk of the English nobility and that even Roman Catholic peers had been trying to moderate the King's insistence on pressing, by hook or by crook, for the repeal of the Test Acts by a packed Parliament.

Of course William himself did not look at the questions in the same light as these English Protestant conspirators. Their fears were for their religion, their property, their position in the establishment. When he sent over Zuylestein to congratulate the King and Queen on the birth of their son, he had already made up his mind to intervene in England later, if the military and political situation allowed, to enforce an Anglo-Dutch alliance. What worried him were, first, James's naval and military preparations, presaging an alliance with France, and, secondly, the dangers that might arise from calling a packed Parliament or even the King's extremism provoking a civil war from which he himself might be excluded. The arrest of the bishops and the birth of the Prince of Wales had created a sense of an immediate crisis. James had been busy inspecting his army and had sent a fleet of twenty men-of-war and four fireships to the Downs under command of the Roman Catholic Rear-Admiral Sir Roger Strickland. At the same time the French King was at last offering to help James not with small sums of money to pay for his new regiments or to expand his fleet but by actually stationing a squadron of sixteen French warships brought from the Mediterranean to

Brest, ready to unite with the English Royal Navy if need be. That offer was put forward and fully discussed between the French and English Courts during June. But the only result of the negotiation, which quickly became common knowledge, was to heighten Anglo-Dutch tension and to convince William of Orange that he must hurry forward his preparations for his operation in England.

NOTES TO CHAPTER IX

1. Letter of Dec. 8, 1687, Nottingham University Library, P.A. 2110a.
2. Cavelli, ii, 181.
3. Letter of Nov. 18, 1687, Nottingham, P.A. 2101b.
4. 'Note on Borough Charters in the Later Seventeenth Century', by R. B. Pugh (unpublished); Add. Mss. 34510, f. 112 v.
5. Baschet, March 1/11, 1688, etc.
6. Letter of Feb. 6, 1688, Nottingham, P.A. 2141a.
7. Evelyn, iv, 582.
8. Baschet, April 30/May 10, 1688.
9. Add. Mss. 34512, f. 77 v.
10. Dalrymple, ii, 216.
11. Foxcroft, *A Character of the Trimmer*, 244.
12. Mackintosh, 649–60, cit. Kenyon, 191.
13. J. R. Bloxham, *Magdalen College and James II* (1886), xxvii.
14. A. Tindal Hart, *William Lloyd* (1952), 100.
15. Add. Mss. 34515, f. 68.
16. A. Browning, *Thomas, Earl of Danby*, ii, 120.
17. Cf. J. P. Kenyon, 'The Birth of the Old Pretender', *History Today*, June 1963.
18. Mackintosh, 253.
19. Add. Mss. 34510, f. 125–39 v.
20. *Ibid.*
21. Clarendon, ii, 49.
22. *Ellis Letters*, 2, iv, 110.
23. Cavelli, ii, 236.
24. Burnet, iii, 229–30; a letter from William to Bentinck of April 19/29, 1688, makes it clear that this interview took place in April.
25. D'Avaux, vi, 129.
26. Egerton Mss. 2621, f. 6.
27. Ogg, 202; J. P. Kenyon, *The Nobility in the Revolution of 1688*.

CHAPTER X

Final Preparations

As soon as William of Orange received his letter of invitation from the Immortal Seven preparations for the invasion of England were intensified. Earlier, as Captain-General, William had obtained from the States of Holland a vote of 4,000,000 gulden for his military needs; it was assigned to fortifications, but in fact it was used for other purposes. During the late summer a recruiting campaign was launched to enlist 9,000 sailors for service with the Dutch Navy. There was now closer cooperation between the Prince and the States than there had been for years: even Amsterdam was friendly. This was partly because the revocation of the Edict of Nantes and the influx of Protestant refugees had aroused resentment against the King of France. The merchants of Amsterdam were also offended by a tariff war started by the French Government; an attempt to create an entrepôt for their commerce at Dunkirk had proved abortive. Thus the Dutch burghers were touched both in their religion and in their pockets by French policies and were readier than before to listen to William's pleas for rearmament.

William himself felt sure that war was coming again to northern Europe. On May 24 the Archbishop of Cologne, a Bavarian prince who was one of the Imperial Electors, had died. His Coadjutor or understudy was Cardinal Wilhelm von Fürstenberg, who was notoriously a French tool, as he had proved himself to be before when he was Bishop of Strasbourg. If Fürstenberg were chosen by the chapter to succeed at Cologne, then this key town would be confirmed as a French dependency. On May 28/June 7 William wrote to Bentinck, who was in Hanover, that the death of the Elector would cause a great change in affairs and wondered whether the Emperor and the German princes would unite to prevent this attack on their interests. French intentions were not long concealed, for soon after the Archbishop died troops were dispatched to the Electorate of Cologne to uphold Fürstenberg, whose succession was opposed by the Emperor. Just before this, the Elector Palatine also died (on May 16) and Louis XIV put forward claims in the name of his sister-in-law, who was the sister of the dead Prince. It was generally believed that Louis XIV was planning to undertake operations in Germany before the Emperor turned back his attentions from the east. Here were excuses and opportunities for aggression. Louis feared that sooner or later the Emperor would repudiate the truce of Ratisbon and invoke the defensive treaty of Augsburg against him. Therefore he would strike first. William expected the French King to attack in Germany as soon as the harvest was in.

The problem that faced William now was whether he dared to carry out his planned invasion of England, lest during his absence the coming European war should surge over the Dutch frontiers. It was necessary for him to raise two armies: one to take with him to England, the other to leave behind him to guard the United Netherlands in case of unprovoked French aggression while he was away. In the third week of July he sent his trusted friend William Bentinck to hire troops from Cassel, Hanover and Celle. Prince Frederick III, who had succeeded the Great Elector in Brandenburg and was a cousin of William of Orange, was more friendly to the Dutch than his father had been and more consistently anti-French. Bentinck had been in Berlin in May and William himself was to pay the Elector an important visit at the end of August. The Elector was taken into William's confidence about the operation against England and undertook to keep watch on the Rhine. In July and August troops were sought from Saxony and Brandenburg and the Prince of Waldeck, a veteran general greatly trusted by William, received reinforcements from Würtemberg with which to help guard the Dutch frontiers. By September Brandenburg troops had occupied the city of Cologne. In the last week of August a military camp was in the process of being formed by the Dutch between Grave and Nymegen, warships were being made ready, and flat boats collected. Meanwhile it was essential for political developments in England to be closely watched and for James II to be deluded as long as possible about the plan for invasion.

The two principal directors of the Dutch intelligence service in England were William Bentinck, who had an English wife and considerable knowledge of England, at The Hague, and Henry Sidney in London, both men being intimates of the Prince. The previous November a certain James Johnstone, a Scotsman with useful contacts at Court (he was, for example, on friendly terms with one of the Queen's Bedchamber women), set up an intelligence service under Sidney's supervision.[1] Gilbert Burnet, another Scot, had valuable sources of information in Scotland and England. Edward Russell, a spearhead of the conspirators, had a sister in Holland and was therefore able to cross the Channel frequently without arousing suspicion. Letters were sent from England in cipher, but were usually carried over by a safe messenger. The printing presses in Holland published propaganda, such as a pamphlet entitled *Le Royaume Usurpé et L'Enfant Supposé*.[2] In general, it seems that William's arrangements were as complete and effective in 1688 as they had been when organized on his behalf by Peter du Moulin in the sixteen-seventies.[3] Information received could be checked against that obtained in the normal way through the Dutch ambassador in London. But it is likely that Johnstone's information, gained through Sidney and his fellow-conspirators, was as good, if not better than that of Van Citters. Early in July Van Citters was recalled home for consultation and he did not return to London until the middle of September when William's military preparations had been almost completed.

The task of hoodwinking James was not too easy. Many things could not be concealed. For example, after Admiral Herbert arrived in Holland, he was appointed to a command in the Dutch fleet. Herbert was a proud and sullen man and said to have been jealous of Lord Dartmouth who was to be put in charge of James's navy. Dartmouth in England later challenged Herbert to meet him in a duel at Ostend; William, however, persuaded Herbert that it was better that he met Dartmouth on the high seas.[4] Herbert was created Admiral of the North and Vice-Admiral of Zealand with a pension for life; also he was given the colonelcy of a Dutch regiment. He soon made his presence felt. He proposed to William to send Dutch fishing boats to the English coasts to collect intelligence; he suggested that after the return of Zuylestein, Dijkvelt should be sent over to London on some excuse to spy out the land; he urged that topographical information should be gathered from friendly Englishmen who knew the north and west coasts; and in general that the system of spies and agents in England should be strengthened. William was doubtful about some of this advice. For example, he could not think of any reasonable excuse for dispatching Dijkvelt to England again. He believed that Van Citters should be able to collect the necessary military and naval intelligence, and he left it to Herbert himself to acquire the geographical information he needed.[5]

All that was below the surface, but the intensive recruiting of sailors, the fitting out of ships, and Bentinck's missions to Germany were public knowledge. The cover plan was to make out that these preparations were directed against France and not against England. James II was fully aware that the death of the Elector of Cologne and French support for Fürstenberg would, as he put it, 'cause a noise'.[6] It could therefore be hinted to James that only a naval or military alliance concluded by him with the French King would oblige the Dutch to point their arms in his direction. Before Van Citters left London in July he assured the English King of the peaceful intentions of the Dutch Government. Its navy, he explained, was too small to attack England. After his return in the middle of September Van Citters again saw James and this time informed him the Dutch naval rearmament was for use against the Algerians, to support the Swedes, or to impress the French in Germany; there was no thought of a descent upon England.[7] Ambassadors in those days were reckoned to be 'great spies' and were expected to lie for their country. But perhaps Van Citters was not let into the secret.

It should not be imagined that the deception of James II and his ministers was entirely successful. The air of Whitehall and of London was thick with rumours during the summer. Everyone at the centre of affairs recognized that June and July were critical months at home and abroad. The deaths of the Elector Palatine and the Elector of Cologne; the birth of the Prince of Wales; the arrest and trial of the seven bishops; the open French offer of naval assistance to James II—all these justified the Imperial envoy in London in forecasting that 'affairs move daily towards a catastrophe'.[8] Both doubt and fear were engendered. The bishops had hesitated to defy their King, the Supreme Governor of their Church. One bishop was reported to have said that he had fourteen arguments for obeying the King—a wife and thirteen children—and only one against, his conscience. One of the jurymen at the trial of the bishops was the King's brewer; he was supposed to have said that if he voted for the bishops, he would never brew for the King again and if he voted against them, he would brew for no one else. The rumour that the Prince of Wales was suppositious was widely believed, in spite of all the witnesses carefully summoned by the King and all the official rejoicing. 'Be it a true child or not,' it was reported to William Bentinck, 'the people will never believe it.'[9] When D'Albeville, the English ambassador in Holland, gave a banquet followed by fireworks to celebrate the happy event it was boycotted by the Dutch and by other Protestant diplomatists at The Hague. Princess Mary had made searching inquiries of her sister Anne about the genuineness of the birth, and afterwards prayers for the Prince ceased in the royal Dutch chapel. It was felt by many that the English Court had concocted a wicked plot to deprive William and Mary of their right to succeed and that they might well take action to enforce their right. On June 18, 1688, a week after the birth, James Johnstone wrote: 'the people have got a foolish maggot in their heads that the Prince is coming over with an army (and at Court they say if ever he comes, he must come now).'[10] Furthermore, 'the rabble in the country' were saying that they hoped Prince William would bring over the Duke of Monmouth with him; for 'they neither believed in his death nor in the Prince of Wales's life'.[11]

Such rumours were confined neither to 'the people' nor 'the rabble'. On August 7 Dr. Tenison, then the vicar of St. Martin's-in-the-Fields, London, and afterwards an archbishop of Canterbury, told one of his friends that the Prince of Orange 'intended to come over with an army to our relief'; three days later he repeated the same story to John Evelyn, who noted it in his diary.[12] Others besides the Immortal Seven knew about the invitation to William; for not only Nottingham and Halifax but the Duke of Ormonde and other peers were certainly sounded. In the middle of August when Louis XIV sent Bonrepaus as his special envoy on his third mission to England he told King James II that the Prince of Orange had 'fifty-one warships ready for a descent on England'. His information was reasonably exact; for by the third week of August William had finally made up his mind to go forward with the operation and was completing his plans.

In England, then, these summer months were filled with doubts, fears and confusion. The Earl of Sunderland, a politician of cynicism and acumen, tried at one and the same time to strengthen his personal position and to modify and guide James's policies. Sunderland attained his first objective by at last declaring himself to be a Roman Catholic. Nobody seemed to be much impressed by his conversion, but it did the trick with the King and Queen. Sunderland then again tried hard to persuade James to reduce his demands for the repeal of the Tests, pointing out how deeply Anglicans had been upset by the trial of the bishops and how much the Roman Catholic dynasty had been fortified by his having a son. But James was not to be shifted from his goal. He still hoped to use the dissenters as a counter-balance to the Anglicans: three nonconformists were introduced into his Privy Council and parliamentary agents were sent around the constituencies to report upon the attitude of the dissenters. But, according to Evelyn, it was feared that the nonconformists might have been unduly affected by the trial of the bishops and the subsequent threats to punish the clergy and have been induced to believe that the King's aim was 'to extirpate the Church of England' first and themselves afterwards. Halifax told William of Orange on July 25: 'I look upon it [the prosecution of the bishops] as that which hath brought all the Protestants together and bound them into a knot that cannot easily be untied.'[13] In his own *Letter to a Dissenter*, a scintillating anonymous pamphlet, Halifax himself had helped to tie the knot.

Over foreign affairs James and Sunderland were faced with an awkward dilemma. If the rumours were true and the Dutch were contemplating an immediate attack on England, then they urgently needed the help of France. On the other hand, if they openly sought and accepted French assistance, would not that provoke the Dutch and upset their own people? They therefore decided to refuse Louis XIV's offer of naval support and let it be known to the Dutch ambassador. They did what they could to increase their own resources; they pushed on with the formation of the new regiments; they sent out officers to inspect fortifications; the King himself visited the Buoy of the Nore to review his fleet; and Sir Roger Strickland undertook cruises in the North Sea.

At first the royal Government was lulled into a renewed sense of security by Dutch assurances, but by August it felt scared for a number of reasons. The English ambassador in Holland came over to London and expressed his considered view that a Dutch invasion of England was imminent. The blatant way in which William and Mary had thrown doubts on the genuineness of the Prince of Wales provided good grounds for suspecting their intentions. Then towards the end of the month Bonrepaus arrived in London with instructions to say that it was certain that the Dutch armaments were meant for use against England and to try to arouse James from his 'surprising lethargy'.[14] But before he saw the King, James had acted. All naval leave was stopped and army officers sent to join their garrisons. Arrangements were made to fit out fresh warships and call up more men; Lord Dartmouth as an experienced naval officer was sent to inspect the fortifications at Chatham; and more readiness was expressed to consider French help.

When Bonrepaus saw the King of England on August 28 he told him bluntly that if he did not believe that the Prince of Orange was preparing to attack him, he was the only person in Europe who was of this opinion.[15] Three days later James confided to the French special envoy that he planned to divide a navy of thirty-two warships and ten fireships between the Downs and Portsmouth and was ready to contemplate a treaty embodying the former offer of cooperation from sixteen French ships, based on Brest. Bonrepaus in fact offered eleven men-of-war and three fireships, and a treaty was actually drawn up, though both the numbers of ships and the date of their joining were left blank.

But ten days later the whole scare was over. James and Sunderland had decided to make it known that a Parliament would definitely be called in November and thought that the announcement would soothe public opinion. They did not believe that there was any likelihood of rebellion at home—with the memories of the Duke of Monmouth's failure still fresh in people's minds—and without help from home they did not see how the Dutch could effect a landing. Finally the news that Louis XIV was beginning to mobilize troops on the Lower Rhine was thought to be quite enough to keep William of Orange in Holland.

Contradictory rumours continued to float around, notably among the ladies. On August 25 the Countess of Rutland was informed by a newsletter sent to her at Belvoir that[16] 'the Prince of Orange hath written a very obliging letter to his Majesty to assure him that the States-General hath not the least thought of being the aggressors at this juncture' and would act only defensively. Yet a week later the Countess of Sunderland was writing to Sidney from Windsor to say that 'there was talk more than ever of the Dutch invading'.[17] At the same time the French changed their minds about the Dutch intentions. On August 29 the French Minister of Marine, Seignelay, wrote to Bonrepaus that 'intelligence from Holland suggests that the Prince of Orange would not attempt anything against England this year', since he had insufficient resources and sailors.[18] Seignelay had already refused to make any precise commitment about the strength of the naval help he could provide and had inquired why James II had not sent for his Irish troops. In any case the French King had little intention of giving James much by way of assistance because he was already too involved in Germany. On August 19 Bonrepaus had been instructed by Louis XIV to ask what arrangements the King of England had made for his safety in case he was unfortunately (*par malheur*) abandoned by his subjects![19] So on September 3 the meaningless draft naval treaty was signed, and Bonrepaus left England, after reporting home: '*On est persuadé içi sur les derniers avis d'Hollande que le Prince d'Orange n'entreprendra rien cette année.*'[20]

But meanwhile the French had put their foot into it, so far as King James was concerned. Sir Bevil Skelton, the English ambassador at Paris (who had formerly served without success in Holland), had suggested of his own accord to the French King that it would be helpful if the French made a diplomatic *démarche* at The Hague. Louis XIV decided to act on his advice; on August 30 D'Avaux presented a memorial from the French King to the States-General warning them that if an attack were made on England such an action would involve them in a rupture with France. When the text of the memorial was received in London James and Sunderland were furious, for they realized at once that the implication of the memorial that a secret Anglo-French alliance already existed, was calculated to arouse and not to damp the Dutch offensive intentions. D'Albeville was ordered to deny that there were any secret treaties between England and France. Skelton was told to come home without even taking leave of the French King, and as soon as he arrived he was lodged in the Tower of London for his pains. James and Sunderland acted out of fright. Then for the time being they shut their eyes to the situation and turned over to pottering about with preparations for the promised meeting of Parliament in the autumn. Writs were to be issued on September 19. In a way they were right to do this, for a session of Parliament might have spiked the guns of the conspirators and made the position delicate for Prince

William. When Van Citters returned to London in the middle of September he was able to report that 'although the fright has somewhat subsided on my arrival, yet the King's uneasiness remains'.[21] Indeed he thought that James was anxious to be placatory. By his treatment of Skelton he had publicly repudiated D'Avaux and the idea of an Anglo-French plot against the United Netherlands, and he assured the Dutch that his fleet's movements were purely defensive.

But James did not recover his nerve for long. On September 15 Louis XIV had written to Barrillon ordering him to announce in England that the French Army was besieging Philippsburg in the Palatinate, over 200 miles from the Dutch frontiers; and that he felt himself at present in no need to make war on the Dutch. This crossed a dispatch from Barrillon to his King dated September 13/23 in which he reported that James now believed that William was planning an invasion, though he felt sure it could not succeed. James admitted that his fleet was too small to defend his kingdom, but he had a strong army, of which seven thousand men were concentrated in the London area, while reinforcements could quickly be brought over from Ireland. Those who were suspected of disaffection would, he said, be immediately put under arrest if William attempted to come over, but James was quite sure that, as with Monmouth, the expedition would fail. D'Albeville had meanwhile seen William and been unable to extract from him a satisfactory denial that he was embarking troops. Further dispatches received by Barrillon and another dispatch from D'Albeville finally convinced the English Government that invasion was imminent. On September 18 Evelyn took note of a panic in Whitehall over a report that William had already landed. The King, who had gone to Chatham to inspect the ships fitting out there, was hastily recalled to London on September 20. Later there was another panic in Whitehall over a report that the Dutch fleet was approaching the English coast and that an army of ten to twelve thousand men was ready to embark. On September 24 a letter from The Hague forecast that the invasion would take place in a fortnight. The King hastily appointed his Protestant friend Dartmouth as admiral of his fleet over the head of the Roman Catholic Strickland, and sent for the Lord Mayor and Aldermen of London to tell them of his fears. Finally on September 28 a royal proclamation gave the news to the kingdom at large, announcing that the Government had 'received notice of a great and sudden invasion from Holland purposing an absolute conquest of these kingdoms'.[22]*

Meanwhile William of Orange had his own anxieties. Ever since the death of the Elector of Cologne he had been obliged to look in two different directions and to wonder what the attitude of his own people was going to be when they knew about his plan to invade England. Although his own personal group of advisers—Fagel, Bentinck, Dijkvelt, Zuylestein, Waldeck—trusted him, timorous voices were raised on both sides of the North Sea. Halifax continued to insist that it was best to sit still and do nothing. Danby, one of the signatories of the letter of invitation, began to grow nervous and think it was wiser to postpone action until the next spring. But Fagel was firm. On August 21 William wrote to Bentinck to say that 'the Pensionary's reasons for undertaking the great affair at once are absolutely convincing'.[23] William still feared a war on two fronts, now that Louis XIV was committed to war in Germany: on August 25 the Prince confessed to Bentinck that he was afraid that their plan might fail and that in consequence they would find themselves involved in a great war. In his next letter to Bentinck, who was also obsessed by private cares, as his wife was slowly dying, William expressed concern over 'the timidity of Amsterdam and irresolution which might endanger their success'.[24] Supposing the fleet were not ready in time? Even then insufficient soldiers and sailors had been recruited. Fagel, however, was a pillar of strength, fertile in expedients; if Amsterdam would not pay for the hiring of German troops, for example, then perhaps Leiden would do so.

It is evident that from the first William hoped for a bloodless success in England. Admiral Arthur Herbert, who was the commander-elect of the invasion fleet, was told more than once that he was to avoid battle if possible and that his primary task was to escort the troop transports in safety. 'If anything happens to the fleet,' wrote William on September 6, 'all would be lost.'[25] He hoped that Herbert's personal popularity with English sailors, the dubious loyalty of the English fleet to their King, who had tried to force popery upon his naval commanders, and the general demoralization of the English people would ensure an unopposed sailing and landing. William drafted a letter addressed to the English fleet in these terms:[26]

* Appendix E.

> We have no other design but the preservation of the Protestant religion and the restoring of the laws and liberties of England, the total ruin of your religion being as much designed by the Papists in England as it is already accomplished in France and it will as certainly be effected if they are able to prevail at this time.

With an exaggerated flourish he added that the English people would be enslaved by the Popish Irish and foreigners and that their destruction would be completed unless he were allowed to rescue them.

By now William had made known his intentions to his own people. Fagel had prepared the way. On September 19 the States of Holland gave their consent to the plan and on September 28 the States-General approved the expedition. Thus on September 30/October 10 William took off the mask. He published a declaration to the people of England of a purely propagandist character.* No doubt it had been drafted for him by his English advisers: Sidney, who arrived in Holland in the middle of August, had an important hand in it; but so had others: it was rather long-winded and over-detailed after the fashion of Dr. Burnet. The declaration condemned the introduction of 'arbitrary government and slavery'; it criticized the appointment of papists to civil and military offices; it insisted that the birth of the Prince of Wales was an imposture; and it announced that William's aim was to protect the legitimate right of succession. All the blame for the attack on the laws and liberties of the English people was laid upon the 'evil counsellors' of James II who, it was implied, would be punished once a free and lawful Parliament had been called. Thus it appeared to give the English King the option, if he would accept the advice of good Protestants, instead of evil 'papists', of at least continuing to reign.

William believed that he was pushing against an open door. His intelligence services suggested that his operation would succeed because the King and his people were disunited. On September 21 the Imperial envoy in London had written to his master that James II 'had against him all the clergy, all the nobility and all the people (*das ganze Volk*) and all the army and the navy with a few exceptions . . .'.[27] On September 24 James rather pathetically asked his brother-in-law, the Earl of Clarendon, who had no reason to love him and knew the invasion was

* Appendix D.

coming, what the Church of England men would do. He answered rather sourly: 'Your majesty will see, they will behave themselves like honest men; though they have been somewhat severely used of late.'[28] The Earl of Sunderland, so long the trusted chief minister of the Crown, completely lost his nerve. He told Barrillon 'that the King could do nothing in his present state but escape the best way he could, for he had no hope of outside aid, and he might well be driven from England in a week'.[29] Lord Chancellor Jeffreys told Clarendon: 'all was nought; some rogues had changed the King's mind [about compromise]: that he would yield nothing to the bishops; that the Virgin Mary was to do all.'[30] That was recorded on September 27, the day before James published his royal proclamation appealing to the loyalty of his subjects.

In fact the King was now driven to compromise. For other measures besides naval and military precautions then announced by the King were the withdrawal of the writs then issued for the calling of a Parliament intended to repeal the Tests, the return of the forfeited Charter of the City of London, a promise to restore the ejected Fellows of Magdalen College, Oxford, and the taking off of the suspension of the Bishop of London. These concessions to public opinion were more significant of James's fears than of his generosity of spirit, and did not impress his critics. For if the mere rumour of approaching invasion by the Dutch were sufficient to bring about such a sharp reversal of his policies, might not larger benefits be expected if William actually landed? Barrillon thought so: 'many people,' he reported, 'say they are due to fear of the Prince of Orange and it is he who should be thanked for them.'[31] The Countess of Sunderland wrote: 'God direct us all for the best and grant that we may not defer our repentance until it is too late, as I fear His Majesty's good deeds are.'[32] One wonders what her husband, that recent Roman Catholic convert, thought of these high-sounding reflections by his wife.

It was at this very moment, as September drew to its close, that William learned that the King of France had declared war on the Emperor and was sending troops to the Palatinate as well as Cologne. Already William was being asked to lend Dutch assistance to Germany. But he relied upon his old friend the Prince of Waldeck to deal with the German situation. He had made up his mind to go to England and would not be held back or diverted from it. He told Waldeck that he would send him artillery and money and ordered him to strengthen the defences of Nymegen. On October 3 Dr. Gilbert Burnet wrote that the 'great design' was about to be undertaken by a prince who had been chosen by Providence to do wonders. 'If he manages the English nation as dexterously as he hath done the Dutch,' he added, 'he will be the arbiter of Europe and will very quickly bring Lewis the Great to a much humbler posture.'

But the operation had still to be carried out across the autumn seas in the teeth of King James II's fleet and army. The Royal Navy might be numerically smaller than that of the Dutch, but the army was a strong and professional one. How loyal would these soldiers and sailors be? Would the nobility and gentlemen of England in the last resort betray their anointed monarch? William might, as was generally believed, have assembled four or five hundred ships to carry over a large army of Dutch, Germans, French, English and others under the guard of the Dutch fleet. 'But we hope,' observed one loyal letter-writer in England at the same time as Dr. Burnet was pledging his faith in the adventure, 'they reckon without their host, and that England and its old renown is not yet sunk so low as to be made a prey to such mongrel invaders.'[32]

NOTES TO CHAPTER X

1. Intelligence letters to Bentinck, Misc. 19 P.W.A. 2087 *seq.* (Nottingham University).
2. D'Avaux, vi, 212.
3. Cf. K. H. D. Haley, *William of Orange and the English Opposition* (1953).
4. Egerton Mss. 2621, f. 10.
5. *Correspondentie*, i, 46–7.
6. Hoffmann to the Emperor June 4/14 in Cavelli.
7. Cavelli, ii, 259.
8. *Ibid.*, ii, 231–3.
9. Nottingham, P.A. 2171a.
10. Letter of June 18, Nottingham, P.A. 2171a.
11. *Ibid.*
12. Evelyn, v, 592 and note.
13. Foxcroft, *A Character of the Trimmer*, 248.
14. Mazure, iii, 61.
15. Durand, 199.
16. *H.M.C.* 12, v, 121.
17. Sidney, ii, 274.

18. Cavelli, 11, 255.
19. *Instructions*, XV, 405–9.
20. Durand, 203.
21. Add. Mss. 34512, f. 95 v.
22. B.M. 21 h 3 (38).
23. *Correspondentie*, i, 53.
24. *Ibid.*, 1, 55.
25. *Ibid.*, 1, 58.
26. Egerton Mss. 2621, f. 13.
27. Cavelli, 11, 266.
28. Clarendon, ii, 66.
29. Cit. Kenyon, 219.
30. Clarendon, ii, 69.
31. *Instructions*, 412.
32. Sidney, ii, 280.

CHAPTER XI

The Invasion (i)

IT was in the third week of August 1688 that King James II had at last realized that the Dutch were in earnest in preparing an invasion of England; and it was a month later in the third week of September that William of Orange pressed the button. King Louis XIV had published his manifesto against the Emperor on September 14/24 and immediately launched his troops upon Philippsburg in the Palatinate. Towns could not be conquered in a day, and although the celebrated French expert in sieges, Sebastien Vauban, was in charge, it was not until October 19/29 that Philippsburg fell. The French concentration against distant Philippsburg gave William a breathing space and the incitement to take the final steps towards the invasion of England. It is true that at the same time other French forces were operating near Cologne, much closer to Holland, in support of Cardinal Fürstenberg, but, according to Burnet, their numbers were insufficient to perturb the Dutch.[1] William relied on the veteran Prince of Waldeck to watch the French there and even help those German princes, headed by his cousin, the Elector of Brandenburg, who were ready to resist French pressure. William had notified Waldeck of the French declaration of war on September 22/ October 2 and given him his instructions. According to D'Avaux, the French ambassador at The Hague, the Dutch succeeded in hiring 25,000 German mercenaries, so that Waldeck had a useful force at his command.[2]

Meanwhile William continued to receive assurances both at home, in England, and from abroad. At home his friend Caspar Fagel had exerted his influence with the Regents of Holland and after a long campaign of lobbying this led to the approval of William's enterprise from the Dutch States.[3] William's old friend, the handsome and jovial Henry Sidney, joined him in the middle of August; so did the young Earl of Shrewsbury and Edward Russell; a fortnight earlier William had received an impressive letter promising help from John, Lord Churchill, a former

Brigadier in James's army and the personal friend of Princess Anne. In Germany, though Louis XIV could still boast some allies—such as the Elector of Mainz—most of the princes were glad to contribute to William's enterprise because it would be a genuine advantage to them if England could be swung over to the Dutch side against France. Finally, Louis XIV had alienated the Pope and thus could not pretend to official Roman Catholic backing. In early October he went so far as to occupy the papal territory of Avignon with his troops. James II was distressed by the French King's behaviour to the papacy and tried to use his good offices to patch up a long-standing quarrel; but all his efforts were in vain. William gave secret promises to his German allies that the Roman Catholics would be no worse off in England if he went there, and indeed that they would be quite as well off as they were in the United Netherlands, where they enjoyed religious freedom. Incensed with Louis XIV, the Pope was thus disinclined to interfere with William of Orange even though he was moving against a Roman Catholic monarch.

Louis XIV had ultimately decided to stake all upon his invasion of Germany. By swift and effective aggression he hoped to frighten the Emperor and the German princes into accepting his advance to the Middle Rhine, just as he had forced them four years before to assent to the truce of Ratisbon. In fact he even fancied he might turn the truce into a permanent settlement of Europe in his favour. He wanted to strike before the Emperor was in a position to organize a counter-offensive. Louis therefore tried not to provoke the Dutch. Although the reports of his ambassadors in England were far from satisfactory about the loyalty of James II's army and navy, he hoped that the King of England would put up a stubborn fight against the Dutch invading forces and that William would be bogged down for the whole of the winter. Louis was not prepared to help James except by giving him a little money. In September he placed the sum of 150,000 livre tournois (about £12,000) at his disposal in Calais. He had also contributed to the upkeep of the newly formed regiments, but, excluding debts owed to Charles II, the whole of the French financial assistance given to James II during his reign amounted to only some £30,000 as compared with a royal income of over £2,000,000 a year.[4]

So James was left to his own devices. His policy was far from being that of the hard, wise, strong man that he had painted himself to be at the outset of his reign. He reversed nearly all his domestic policies in a desperate attempt to placate his Protestant subjects; he told the Dutch that he had no intention of attacking them if they did not attack him. He claimed (not altogether accurately) to have refused all offers of French help and to have signed no secret treaties with France; and he began to look to Protestants like Lord Dartmouth, Lord Churchill and Henry, Duke of Newcastle, instead of to his old Roman Catholic favourites, to man his defences against the coming wrath of his son-in-law.

George Legge, first Baron Dartmouth, superseded the Roman Catholic Sir Roger Strickland as 'Admiral and chief commander of His Majesty's ships in the narrow seas' on September 24. According to Dartmouth, Strickland was generally disliked in the navy and had been 'very indiscreet' and 'disobliging'.[5] Dartmouth may have been more popular, but he was neither so popular nor so good a sailor as Arthur Herbert. Dartmouth had fought against the Dutch and supervised the evacuation of Tangier in the reign of Charles II, but his experience was limited. James II thought highly of his own naval knowledge, but since he himself had been a commander at sea he realized what went on, and was understandably reluctant to give detailed instructions to the man actually in charge. However, the King had a clear conception of what he thought the Dutch strategy would be. He imagined, he told Dartmouth, that William would first send over a fleet to fight or bottle up the English Navy and then bring over his land forces, protected by a few men-of-war, to make a descent on the English coast. James's belief was that the operation would begin as soon as the winds favoured the Dutch. Dartmouth was therefore counselled to get out from the sands at the Buoy of the Nore, where his ships were being concentrated, at the first westerly wind. For, the King wrote on October 8, 'expects at the first easterly wind the Dutch will look you out to engage you whilst they send their forces to land somewhere else . . . '.[6]

Where did James and his advisers expect the Dutch to land? They did not really know. That is why the admirals wanted to move the fleet from the Nore to the Buoy of Gunfleet, south of Harwich, which, being directly opposite to the main Dutch bases, would be the best vantage point for collecting information of Dutch intentions. On the other hand, when the wind and tide were unfavourable, the Gunfleet was a difficult anchorage to get out from in order to initiate a pursuit either north or south, and James himself was of the opinion that at that time of year it was 'a very ill road'. Nevertheless ultimately on October 24 Dartmouth did manage to move his ships from the Nore to the Gunfleet. In one of his first letters to Dartmouth as chief naval commander James hazarded the view that the Dutch might try to land at Chatham, possibly recalling their sensational success of 1667.[7] But Chatham was now well fortified and unlikely to be surprised. Dispatches from D'Albeville in Holland suggested that the Dutch would try to land in the north of England; it may have become known to D'Albeville's spies that William had been pressed to land in Yorkshire. On the whole, the English Government seems to have finally reached the conclusion that William would not try to disembark his troops anywhere in the south-east, but would aim to land as far from the main concentration of the royal army as possible so as to obtain time to reorganize before beginning an advance. Hence the general feeling that the landing would take place somewhere in the east or north-east of England. No one seriously envisaged the possibility of the whole Dutch armada sailing through the Channel and reaching the west of England where the Duke of Monmouth had so signally failed with his invasion three and a half years earlier.

What were the relative strengths of the opposing fleets? When Strickland was still in full command he had at his disposal twenty-two men-of-war and thirteen fireships, the torpedo boats of those days. As a result of urgent efforts by the King and his Secretary of the Admiralty, Samuel Pepys, this was brought up quickly to the size of 'a good winter guard'. On October 1 when the concentration at the Nore began Dartmouth had twenty-six ships, on October 17 he had thirty-one ships, and by the time the Dutch invasion took place he had a total of thirty-seven men-of-war and eleven fireships. The Dutch naval forces assigned for the operation were divided into three squadrons, one under Herbert, who was finally on October 17 appointed commander-in-chief with the title of Lieutenant-Admiral-General, one under Van Almonde who was to sail on the starboard side of the convoy, and one under Admiral Evertsen who was to sail on the port side: altogether it is estimated that the Dutch warships in these three squadrons numbered forty-nine men-of-war and ten fireships. But the English had more third-rates (ships of over sixty guns) than had the Dutch. The Dutch ships were built fairly light and of comparatively low draught so as to operate more easily in their creeks and harbours. Thus the Dutch ships were, on the whole, more manoeuvrable, the English more heavily gunned. Both fleets were 'winter guards', that is to say contained no first-class ships of the line, which could be safely used only during the summer. Indeed when Dartmouth contemplated the idea, which he went so far as to put to the King, of 'showing himself on the Dutch coast as near as I can in the daytime' so as to impress his enemy, he was aware that he dared do it only 'in settled fair weather', which was hardly likely in the late autumn.[8] In fact, though he gave utterance to some brave remarks, it was Dartmouth's fixed intention to 'keep his fleet in being', expecting, as he did, that the Dutch would seek him out in battle before they took the risk of dispatching a convoy of troop transports to attempt invasion.

English intelligence was not far out in its estimate of the size of the Dutch fleet—the figure of fifty or fifty-two men-of-war was usually mentioned, for example, in D'Albeville's dispatches—but the appreciation of Dutch intentions went completely astray. For from the very beginning William's instructions to Admiral Herbert were clear: his orders were to escort the transports and protect them from any interference by the English fleet, but to avoid battle if he possibly could. 'When an enemy fleet shows itself,' Admiral Herbert was told, 'the war fleet shall place itself between the enemy and the transport ships.' The fleet's duty was 'to protect and defend' these ships from any attack by the enemy.[9]

It might well have seemed incredible to English naval experts that such a hazard should be run, that William of Orange should offer a target of hundreds of slow-moving merchant ships and flat boats to a more heavily gunned enemy fleet. But two factors entered into his calculations. The first was that the operation was not going to be undertaken until the late autumn when the weather was notoriously uncertain, with winds ever changing and mists coming up, so that the whole armada might actually be able to cross the sea before being spotted until it was too late. Secondly, William counted on the dubious loyalty of James II's navy. Not only the Dutch ambassador in England but other foreign observers, like Hoffmann, the Imperial envoy, had questioned the men's willingness to fight for a popish monarch against their former admiral. Traditionally the English Navy was radical in its outlook, as it had shown during the civil wars. It had resented James's attempts to hold Masses on board ship. Not only

Herbert, but another former admiral, Edward Russell, had gone over to the Dutch side. Dartmouth himself reported on October 17 'caballing' on his ships and has written that 'hearing Mr Russell is gone for Holland . . . makes me more jealous than of any interest Herbert can have here'.[10] Dartmouth, as we have seen, could not stand Herbert. There is excellent evidence that several of Dartmouth's captains were well-wishers to the Dutch cause: one of them was George Churchill, John Churchill's brother. It is probable also that the Duke of Grafton, who, like John Churchill, was to go over early to William of Orange after his landing and who had been disappointed that he was not offered Dartmouth's command, was a means of stirring up unrest among the captains; and it was also said that 'the captains . . . infused strange notions in the seamen'. Finally William's propaganda letter written to English sailors and a manifesto published by Herbert somehow reached the cabins and forecastles of the royal fleet. The Earl of Ailesbury, a royalist, afterwards expressed the opinion in his memoirs that 'it was generally thought . . . that the fleet would not have stuck firm to the King'.[11]

English intelligence, as we have noticed, was puzzled or misled over the destination of the Dutch fleet. That was why Lord Dartmouth and his Council preferred to remain so long at the Gunfleet, in spite of its disadvantages as an anchorage. William not only had Herbert as his admiral but had some twenty pilots who knew the English coasts. Dartmouth was sceptical over D'Albeville's views about the likely destination of the Dutch fleet. At one time the English ambassador at The Hague had talked of Southwold Bay in Suffolk, at another of Yarmouth in Norfolk. The French also thought up to the very end that the objective would be Yarmouth or somewhere farther north.[12]

On land James's army outnumbered the invading force. An 'abstract of the numbers of all His Majesty's forces in England' dated October 26 gave a total of over 40,000 men, while more could be brought over from Ireland.[13] Of this number 6,000 were cavalry or dragoons. The central reserve, concentrated in London, was estimated to be about seven or eight thousand, and the ports from Portsmouth in the west (where the Duke of Berwick was in command) as far north as Bridlington in Yorkshire were adequately garrisoned. The Lords Lieutenant of the counties were also warned to call up the militia, notably in Yorkshire. Barrillon, who watched James's military preparations with eagle eyes, thought that while James's navy was smaller than that of the Dutch and not in the condition it ought to be, his army was a sizable one but might equally be disloyal. Hoffmann was of precisely the same opinion.[14] Indeed Hoffmann had little doubt that the King's army was less trustworthy than that which was to accompany the Prince of Orange.

Various estimates were made of the strength of the invasion force. D'Albeville thought that it consisted of 18–20,000 fighting men and that the ships carried supplies sufficient for 12,000 horse and 40,000 foot for fifteen days. Unquestionably this guess was an exaggeration. In an earlier dispatch D'Albeville spoke of 10–13,000 men.[15] Also the common estimate was that William had 400 or 500 transports at his command; the real figure may have been half that, though many small craft were used. It is likely that the invasion force did not consist of more than 13,000 men together with arms sufficient for 20,000.

From the end of September both James II and his principal minister panicked. Sunderland pressed the King to offer every conceivable concession to Protestant opinion and to consult the bishops. He himself made a last-minute attempt to pacify the Dutch by talking of reaffirming the Treaty of Nymegen; his wife was still in intimate touch with Prince William's friend Henry Sidney, and wrote to tell him that all she and her husband wished for now was a peaceful retirement. At the same time Sunderland himself told Barrillon that he might throw himself on the mercy of the King of France. On Sunderland's advice—curious advice perhaps—James cancelled plans to arrest suspected conspirators in England and renewed and extended a general pardon to all offenders. But even before he published his proclamation about the impending Dutch invasion James finally withdrew the writs he had issued for calling Parliament. Then he started trying to enlist the help of the bishops. The suspension of the Bishop of London (the only ecclesiastic to sign the letter of invitation to William) was at last removed; on September 30 the King saw the Archbishop of Canterbury in private; on October 3 he interviewed a group of the bishops.

Acting on the advice of Sunderland, his Protestant ministers and the bishops, the King now announced the dissolution of the Ecclesiastical Commission; he instructed the Bishop of Winchester as Royal Visitor to put back the Fellows of Magdalen College, Oxford, he restored the Charter of the City of London and finally on October 17 published a proclamation dropping the regulation of the boroughs and restoring forfeited charters everywhere. He also appointed new Lords Lieutenant and Deputies in the counties—for examples, the Duke of Newcastle in the three Yorkshire Ridings and the Earl of Oxford in Essex—and restored justices of the peace who had been dismissed because of their answers to the Three Questions. He warned the Anglican leaders that they would find the Prince of Orange 'a worse man than Cromwell'.[16] But close observers continued to feel convinced that his change of direction had come too late. It was plainly attributable to the threat of Dutch invasion and it was commonly believed that James would again reverse his policies if William failed to come or if a free Parliament was not held.

While James was busily backing away his once formidable engine of State and was beginning to harbour doubts about Sunderland who (as he told Barrillon later) had shown 'so little firmness and courage', he was also gently trying to persuade Admiral Dartmouth to play a bolder part. On October 5 he reminded Dartmouth of his view that the Dutch fleet would aim to engage him while the transports were being convoyed across; he said that the Admiral must expect them 'with the first snatch of wind' and advised him to get out of the sands as soon as he could.[17] In fact the very next day the west wind changed to east, and on October 8 James again begged Dartmouth to move out from the sands at the first westerly wind. For he expected that the Dutch would 'look him out' as soon as the wind turned east again and would engage him while their land forces were disembarking. On October 12 Dartmouth himself had plucked up sufficient courage to tell the King that if the weather were reasonable he might conceivably venture to show himself by day off the Dutch coasts, though he dared not attack their ports at that time of the year. But James now had his own doubts over the wisdom of such a move, for he was afraid that if Dartmouth sailed towards Holland Herbert might attack him while the troop transports slipped past him towards England. On October 17 the Secretary of the Admiralty tried to cheer Dartmouth with the premature news that the Dutch fleet had already been damaged by bad weather.[18]

In fact on October 14 the wind shifted to the east and William was hastening his final moves. Troops had already been embarking for over a fortnight, moving down from their main camp at

Nymegen to various ports. On October 16 William wrote to the Holy Roman Emperor assuring him that he did not intend to wrong the English King or those with the right to succeed, still less to seize the Crown for himself or extirpate the Roman Catholics in England. His object, he explained, was to procure a Parliament to safeguard the Protestant religion, but he would see that Roman Catholics were guaranteed liberty of conscience. On the same day he informed the Prince of Waldeck that the States-General had authorized him to assist Cologne if he could, for the bulk of the French Army was still occupied in the Palatinate. That day William also took his farewell of the States, thanking them for their care of him since his youth. Then he said goodbye to his wife, Princess Mary, with tears in his eyes, treating her with so much tenderness that she wrote in her diary that she would never forget it. On the afternoon of October 19 William embarked on his yacht and by evening the whole armada was at sea.

King James at this time was feeling a little more optimistic than he had been. On October 20 he told Dartmouth that he was glad that his fleet was in such good heart and so well manned. He said that on land he was growing stronger every day because Scottish and Irish troops were coming to London and several newly-raised regiments of horse and foot were nearly ready.[19] He made light of the exaggerations embodied in William's declaration and the attempts to cast doubts on the validity of the King's own recent political concessions. But really the situation had not changed. On the very date that the Dutch fleet set sail, Sir John Reresby, a loyal Yorkshire royalist, was writing in his memoirs:[20]

> It was very strange, and a certain forerunner of the mischiefs that ensued upon this invasion that neither the gentry nor the common people seemed much afeard or concerned at it, saying, the Prince comes only to maintain the Protestant religion; he will do England no harm.

Earlier old John Evelyn had noted in his diary that the people 'passionately seem to long for and desire the landing of the Prince whom they look upon as their deliverer from popish tyranny'.[21] The day before Reresby wrote, Barrillon had written to inform Louis XIV that James's fleet was not in the condition that it should be—that sailors were lacking and fishermen desperately being pressed. He agreed with Evelyn that the loyalty of the army could not be counted upon.[22] None of these three men, all giving their opinions that October, was unfriendly to the King; they recorded what they believed to be true.

But James had one reason to be cheered. Soon after the Dutch men-of-war and transports put to sea the wind shifted and a storm drove them piecemeal back into the Dutch ports. Inevitably exaggerated rumours of the immense damage done by the gales percolated to England. Though in fact all the ships got back safely, they drifted into different ports and for some hours perturbation shook the authorities at The Hague. D'Albeville reported thence that the cruel dispersal of the fleet had been deliberately kept from the Dutch people; that Prince William was the first to return; that Admiral Herbert was missing for two days; and that the shaken and sea-sick soldiers had to be appeased with fresh victuals.[23] In the end it proved that neither ships nor men had been lost—only some horses, estimated at a maximum of a thousand, who were swept overboard or stifled. From London Hoffmann wrote to his Emperor saying that the damage to the Dutch fleet would lead to the English fleet approaching the Dutch coast as soon as the weather permitted, but in truth Dartmouth was making it clear that his intention was still to keep his fleet 'together and entire' and in view of the weather and the time of year he found it was 'not advisable to venture over'.[24] William of Orange was made of sterner stuff. As soon as he realized that the extent of his losses was small, he began collecting more horses and told Waldeck that he was preparing to start again as soon as the weather was favourable. He was, he added, relying upon Providence.

Thenceforward James II's spirits fluctuated between fear and bouts of confidence. On October 22, provoked by the allegations in William's declaration about the dubiousness of his son's birth, the King summoned a Privy Council to meet in his presence at Whitehall and listen to the detailed evidence. The meeting began badly because the Earls of Clarendon and Nottingham (who were on friendly terms with the leading conspirators) made a demonstration by refusing to sit with Father Petre, James's Jesuit adviser, who was one of the councillors. Even though James tried to pacify them by saying Petre would no longer attend the Council, they were adamant. Nor did the elaborate proofs of the Prince of Wales's birth, including testimony from the midwife and laundress and others who were present at the delivery, carry conviction except with those who were already convinced. The proceedings were minuted and copies of the depositions sent to Princess Anne, who was again pregnant herself. After they were handed to her she said sarcastically: 'My Lords, this was not necessary, for I have so much duty for the King that his word must be more to me than these depositions.'[25] Four days later James dismissed Sunderland, the pilot who had failed to weather the storm. At the time the King accused him of loss of nerve, not of treachery, though James took a different view when he compiled his memoirs. The line between treachery and political reinsurance was to be a very fine one in the years that followed. Though it is always hard to gauge the precise relationship between a husband and wife, it seems not unlikely that Sunderland had allowed his Countess to take out an insurance policy on his behalf with William through her friend Henry Sidney. At any rate in later days Sunderland, who fled the kingdom before the Revolution, was allowed to return to England and become one of William's own ministers.

The King gathered courage from the news that Dartmouth had at last succeeded in reaching the Gunfleet, the station from which the Admiral thought it best to keep watch on the movements of the Dutch. Dartmouth was cock-a-hoop.

> Sire [he wrote to his King on October 24], we are now at sea before the Dutch after all their boasting, and I must confess I cannot see much sense in their attempt with the hazard of such a fleet and army at the latter end of October . . . I wonder to hear by so many letters of the frights that are ashore, though I thank God they have no effects upon us here. . . . Your statesmen may take a nap, and recover, the women sleep in their beds, and the cattle, I think, need not be drove from the shore.[26]

This chimed in with the exaggerated reports of the recent disaster to the Dutch fleet. James congratulated Dartmouth on his success and told him he must decide what was best to be done in such a blowing season; if what he said of the Dutch coming out with only a small quantity of victuals and water were true, was that not next to madness? So Dartmouth and his King whistled to each other to keep their courage up. The conscientious Samuel Pepys ventured to hint to Dartmouth on October 27 that it might not be a bad idea if his fleet went out to sea towards the Dutch coast to discover 'whether any advantage could be taken of them' while they were licking their wounds—though of course the King left it entirely to him. Dartmouth at once put a damper on that suggestion; his duty was to keep the fleet in being, not to sail out into the gales. 'The whole proceeding at this season,' he added, 'looks like the advice of land men. . . .'[27] It really would be most unprofessional of the Dutch—or 'mad', as James himself had put it—for them to try again. So why worry?

NOTES TO CHAPTER XI

1. Burnet, iii, 285 *seq.*
2. D'Avaux, vi, 207 *seq.*
3. Burnet, iii, 292; Japikse, 237 *seq.*; P. Geyl, *The Netherlands in the Seventeenth Century*, ii, 173; Ranke, *History of England*, iv; G. H. Kurtz, *Willem III en Amsterdam*.
4. Cf. Robert H. George, 'The Financial Relations of Louis XIV and James II', *Journal of Modern History* (1931).
5. Powley, 26, quoting, *H.M.C.* xi, 5, 261.
6. *H.M.C.* xi, 5, 152.
7. *Ibid.*, 144.
8. *Ibid.*, 258.
9. Powley, 43. A plan of the Dutch expeditionary fleet showing 59 warships and about 200 transport vessels is in Add. Mss. 38495, f. 58.
10. *H.M.C.* xi, 5, 259.
11. Ailesbury, 186.
12. E.g. Seignelay to Barrillon, Oct. 31/Nov. 10, 1688, in Cavelli, iii, 304.
13. *H.M.C. Dartmouth*, xi, 5, 171.
14. Cavelli, ii, 308.
15. Add. Mss. 34512, f. 104.
16. Clarendon, ii, 195.
17. *H.M.C.* xi, 5, 169.
18. *Ibid.*, 164–7.
19. *Ibid.*, 169.
20. Reresby, 522.
21. Evelyn, iv, 600.
22. *Instructions*, 412.
23. Add. Mss. 34517, f. 4.
24. Powley, 73.
25. Clarendon, ii, 81.
26. *H.M.C. Dartmouth*, xi, 5, 158; Powley, 62–6.
27. *Ibid.*, 262; Powley, 71–4.

CHAPTER XII

The Invasion (ii)

WHILE King James II and his naval commander-in-chief were congratulating themselves at the end of October 1688 on how admirably things were going from their point of view and how unprofessional it would now be of the Dutch to invade England, King Louis XIV, with many sources of information at his disposal, was not feeling so optimistic. In fact he was writing to King James II to offer him some advice and a little money. He instructed Barrillon to incite the King of England to take vigorous action, to declare war at once upon the Dutch, to pronounce guilty of treason all those Englishmen who supported the Prince of Orange, to rally both the Anglicans and the nonconformists to his side, and to put himself at the head of his army. '*Plus un Roi marque de grandeur d'âme dans le peril plus il affermit la fidelité de ses sujets.*'[1] But James's soul was not particularly grand in peril; in fact, now that Philippsburg had fallen, he was hoping that perhaps the French would help him by making some diversion in his favour which would prevent William from even thinking of leaving Holland. He also made another attempt to induce the leaders of the Church of England, whom he had invited to compose prayers against an invasion, to lend their spiritual support to his sacred cause. William had reissued his declaration in an expanded form on October 24. James now proposed that the bishops should prove that they had no complicity in the plot by signing a paper abhorring the Prince's declaration. The Archbishop of Canterbury thereupon reminded his sovereign sardonically that they had recently received a sharp lesson from him of the dangers of interfering with State affairs when seven of them had been put on trial for seditious libel. Thus James's own foolishness recoiled on his head.

Two questions are still asked about William's invasion of England. The first is what were his ultimate intentions when he undertook this dangerous military operation so late in the year; the second is where did he intend to land his forces and why. As we have seen, before William set sail for the first time he had written to the Holy Roman Emperor to assure him that it was not his intention to seize the English Crown. He also wrote a letter on October 19 in the same sense to Count Gastagaña, the Governor of the Spanish Netherlands.[2] Earlier, on September 29, a group of Dutch deputies reported to the States-General that 'His Highness had no intention of removing the King from the throne or to make himself master of England, but only to take care that by the convocation of a free parliament . . . the reformed religion be placed in security and out of danger of apprehension'.[3] After he had established himself in England and it became obvious that James was not going to help him in the calling of a free Parliament, William twice wrote to his friend, the Prince of Waldeck, saying that he was embarrassed at the thought of now being elected King, as he had no ambition for it and it was not the reason why he had come to England. But he feared that he would be forced to accept what he did not ask for, 'although I foresee that the world will judge it otherwise'.[4] There he was right.

Such is the evidence on one side; the quotations hitherto gathered upon the other are obscure and hardly carry the weight that has been attached to them. But documents are not everything. It can be argued that the great sovereigns of Europe, the Emperor, the Pope, the King of Spain (although he was half-mad) and most of the German princes were so wedded to the principle of inviolable divine right that they had necessarily to be deceived about William's real intentions. They could not be expected to accept any radical doctrines of social contracts thought up by English and Dutch political theorists (though the right to depose wicked kings went a long way back into history). If, however, William were suspected of mere personal ambition these potentates, it is said, would never have approved his mission. Nor, for that matter, would the Dutch republicans. Moreover the English conspirators—the Immortal Seven—who had invited William over in the first place, might reasonably have said that they had not called him over for any such purpose, but purely in order to protect their religion and their liberties.

But was it realistic of William of Orange to imagine that his father-in-law, habitually so stubborn, would allow his son-in-law to sit down with his troops outside London while a free Parliament met and reversed the entire policy of his reign? Statesmen are, after all, frequently unscrupulous in their methods, if not in their aims. William's behaviour to De Witt and to Monmouth was proof enough of his ruthlessness. He had certainly received suggestions, for example, from his cousin, the Elector Frederick of Brandenburg, that he had best seek the English Crown. Yet it remains possible that William was telling the truth as he saw it in his letters to Waldeck; that he had not made up his mind when he first set sail; that the end of his mission differed from what he had first intended; [5] but that, like Oliver Cromwell, he realized that no man rises so high as he who does not know where he is going.

There is one further consideration. A man's mind is shaped by his own experiences earlier in life. Whether consciously or not, William must have been influenced by his memories of the events of 1680–81. Then too he had been invited to come to England by leading English statesmen in order to exert his influence against his Roman Catholic father-in-law. Charles II had then almost promised him the regency of England when he himself died. William of Orange had been invited to show himself so as to exert pressure on the deliberations of a Protestant Parliament. [6] On that occasion he had come over far too late. But now neither cowards nor storms were to stop him coming over to secure a Parliament in England that very winter.

The second question about William's intentions derives from the first. For it has been suggested by one or two modern historians that the real reason why William in fact landed in the west, in Devon, where after what had happened to Monmouth three and a half years earlier he was least likely to find assistance, was because he did not 'want to be committed to any particular group of Englishmen' [7] or because he aimed at wresting the Crown from his father-in-law with his own soldiers. [8] Before William finally sailed French intelligence was convinced that he would land in the north of England or in Scotland. The Earl of Danby, his most active supporter in England, had urged him to come over with a large fleet and a small army and land in Yorkshire where many Englishmen would join him. The English ambassador at The Hague, who ought to have been in a good position to find out, first (on October 23) reported a story obtained from a Roman Catholic pilot that the Dutch were going to steer course to the river Humber, and D'Albeville observed astutely that 'the farther the Prince lands from the King's army the greater the opportunity to strengthen his interest and increase his own army and disperse his manifesto'.[9] After William successfully sailed D'Albeville wrote to say that he was headed towards Yarmouth and later added that he was expected to land at Yarmouth 'or somewhere in the north'.[10] Hoffmann, a little earlier, was reporting to the Emperor from London that the Dutch fleet was directed northward and that it was presumed it would make for the Scottish border near Berwick at Holy Island.[11] Dr. Burnet, who actually sailed with William as his chaplain, stated positively in his memoirs that William had resolved to land in the north and 'then to have sent the fleet to lie in the Channel'.[12]

Were all these stories rumours deliberately spread by the Dutch counter-intelligence services in order to confuse the English defences? It is possible, but even then it is not necessary to look for a political explanation: there were sound military reasons for landing in the west. The Dutch knew where the English fleet was stationed and had no wish to run into it, if the wind changed. Admiral Herbert was said to have been 'vehemently opposed' to a landing in the north at that season of the year, and it was known that James had reinforced his garrisons in Suffolk and Norfolk and ports in the north of England. On the other hand, Herbert's original instructions from William (dated October 17/27) suggested that a landing in the east or the north was intended;[13] for Herbert was told that after the landing had been effected he was to be prepared to make diversions first towards Scotland and then to the west of England. It is generally accepted that after the Dutch fleet set sail the wind blew so heavily from the east that it would have made it difficult for the fleet to turn north. On November 16, eleven days after he landed, William of Orange wrote to the Prince of Waldeck from Exeter:[14] 'It is *unfortunate* that we have been obliged *by the wind* to land here in the west, where we are so much out of the way of correspondence with Holland that we are quite out of the world.' Unless we are to believe that William habitually lied to Waldeck (and here on a matter that surely had little significance) this must be decisive.

The English Government was certainly surprised by the landing in the west. In deciding how best to distribute his army James was obviously dependent upon his intelligence of his enemy's likely movements. A military solution, which was to be practised in later times, was to keep a large mobile reserve in the London area and hope that by the time William had completed his disembarkation, marshalled his forces, and collected any needed supplies, the English army could confront him and outnumber his mixed army on a battlefield of James II's own choosing. It is not certain that the English King had any thought-out plan, though in so far as he did have one it must have been of this nature. His army, as we have seen, numbered about 40,000 men, and that was insufficient for him to guard all likely ports of disembarkation. In addition, up to the last moment he was bringing in reinforcements from Scotland and Ireland. For example, in late October Sir John Reresby, the Governor of York, reported that seven hundred Scottish cavalry and dragoons were marching south under Major-General John Graham of Claverhouse; they passed through York on October 19.[15] A rising in Yorkshire itself was rightly feared, so that the garrison of York itself had to be reinforced. According to the Dutch ambassador, writing on October 30, troops were then being sent daily to the east coast, principally to Essex, Suffolk and Norfolk; later some of these regiments were recalled and hurried to the west.[16] King James always appears to have regarded Portsmouth as the place that would give him—and, more important, his wife and child—a refuge from which they could escape to France, if the worst came to the worst, and he took care to have an adequate garrison there too, commanded by his illegitimate son, the Duke of Berwick. As soon as the news of the Dutch sailing came through, Berwick was ordered to join his garrison and additional reinforcements were dispatched thither. An unfortunate incident from the King's point of view had occurred in Portsmouth during September. It had been decided to reinforce Berwick's own regiment with Irish Roman Catholic recruits. But the officers and some of the men had violently objected to such a move, and six of the officers were cashiered. This was one of the reasons why foreign observers in England questioned the loyalty of the English army to the King.

Thus it is doubtful if there was any carefully worked-out plan behind the military dispositions of the King. Indeed an element of panic may be detected in them. It is true that the Lords Lieutenant had been ordered that horses and cattle were to be driven twenty miles inland in the event of a landing,[17] which perhaps indicates that the King did not hope to destroy his enemy on the beaches (once Admiral Dartmouth had let them through) but to lead his army to fight his son-in-law wherever he was to be found. At any rate that was what James told the bishops he intended to do. In his first proclamation about the invasion James had declared that he had refused foreign help and that he relied on the loyalty of his subjects. Londoners were told to have their muskets ready. Right up to the moment of invasion James refused to declare war on the Dutch or to demand French help. He found it hard to believe that this incredible operation at such a late season in the campaigning year could possibly be a success or that his people should fail to back him against foreigners. The trouble was, as the Marquis of Halifax remarked afterwards in his 'maxims of State': 'That a people may let a King fall, yet still remain a people; but if a King let his people slip from him, he is no longer King.' The tragedy of James II was that, with all his high-mindedness about liberty of conscience for all Christians, he had managed so to undermine the loyalty of the majority of his people that neither his navy nor his army was trustworthy when the crux came.

·   ·   ·   ·   ·

It had taken a week to reassemble the Dutch expeditionary force after its earlier mishap. On October 27 William Bentinck wrote from Helvoetsluys that 'all our vessels that should come from Rotterdam and the Texel' had not yet joined up.[18] After their battering at sea some of the English exiles, who were accompanying the expedition, grew nervous. According to Dr. Burnet: 'they went so far as to propose to the Prince that Herbert should be ordered to go over to the coast of England and either fight the English fleet or force them in: and in that case the transport fleet might venture over; which otherwise they thought could not be safely done'.[19] That was what James II had all along expected to happen. But William would have none of it: he knew that to try out such tactics so late in the season might easily mean abandoning the operation altogether until after the winter was over. By October 28 the weather had calmed and the fleet was ready. But another two days of east wind were wasted before all the transport vessels were in place and the expedition was again ready to sail.

The land forces were divided into three squadrons, Red, White and Blue: the English and Scots commanded by Major-General Mackay, the Prince's Dutch Guards and the Brandenburgers under Count Solms, and the rest of the Dutch forces and the French Protestants under Count Nassau. At ten o'clock on the morning of Thursday, November 1, William signalled to Admiral Herbert that his intention was to put to sea as soon as the wind permitted. Herbert and his naval squadron went ahead and the two other naval squadrons carefully picked up their positions on either side of the fleet of transports. It was a mixed collection of ships and boats of all sizes: the little Scheveling vessels, invaluable for landing purposes, had to be made fast with ropes to the merchantmen to cross the high seas. The armada sailed on the evening tide and at dark set out their lights 'which was very pleasant to see'. Herbert steered north in very good weather. But on the afternoon of November 2 the fleet turned south-west because of the ferocity of the east wind, causing the ships to roll and lurch, and possibly also—it has been suggested—because Herbert now knew the exact whereabouts of the English fleet, still at the Gunfleet, and did not wish to pass near it. During the night the Dutch ships shortened sail and on Saturday morning were protected from view from the land by fog, but when the mists lifted they could see the Thames estuary. A council of war was held, the decision was taken, and before noon the armada had abandoned the east coast and was entering the Dover strait.

It must have been an extraordinary, a unique sight. The passage took seven hours, from ten in the morning until five in the evening. No attempt was made, or could be made, to conceal the movement of this huge concourse of ships upon that bright autumn day. The Prince of Orange set up his standards 'For the Protestant Religion and Liberty' and *'Je Maintiendrai'*. The men-of-war hoisted their flags: 'the whole fleet,' wrote one who was there, 'was resolved to make a bravado'.[20] It looked, it was reported in London, 'like a thick forest'.[21] Each vessel kept its proper distance from the next and the Channel was bespangled with gaily coloured sailing ships. As Dover and Calais were passed, the Dutch Navy fired its cannon in salute. Crowds watched the procession from the white cliffs. For three hours drums and trumpets played, though the soldiers on board did not feel too comfortable after the previous rough night. When darkness fell again, the ships were once more lit up; from the land were seen the fires of beacons. Next day, Sunday, November 4, Prince William's birthday and the anniversary of his marriage, the ships were still strung out in good order along the Channel, and it was expected that a landing would be made on the Isle of Wight or at Portsmouth. But William signified from his yacht that, by the advice of the pilots, he intended to disembark his forces at Dartmouth and Torbay in Devon.

One who sailed with the expedition wrote how on the evening before the Monday when the landing was intended 'many delighted to be above deck, it was so exceedingly pleasant between the stars of the firmament and our stars'.[22] But owing to a mistake of the chief pilot the leading vessels overshot their objective. Suddenly, however, the sea was becalmed and four hours later the whole fleet drew into Torbay. The men-of-war then positioned themselves to protect the disembarkation of the troops, but no resistance was encountered. The surprise had been complete. The English fleet, after several vain efforts to get out from the Gunfleet, at last succeeded in sailing as far as Beachy Head, but had there been compelled by adverse winds to give up the pursuit. A council of war was held off Beachy Head and some of the captains of the English fleet who were there decided that if they caught up with the Dutch they would go over to the enemy. At any rate Admiral Dartmouth decided at that time to do no more than send scouting frigates westward and prepared to turn back to the Downs.

The afternoon of November 5, the anniversary of the Gunpowder Plot, a famous day in English Protestant history, passed in clear sunshine and was followed by a warm night. Two thousand men of the invading army were landed that day; the landings continued by torchlight through the night, but it took another two days before the disembarkation was completed. By the evening of November 9 William had set up his headquarters at Exeter, whence he wrote to Admiral Herbert to tell him that he had received a great acclamation from the people, although no gentry nor clergy had yet come to him. He announced his intention of sending the transport vessels back to Holland, and asked for Herbert to arrange an escort, a mark of confidence in himself and his mission.[23] He also ordered Herbert to keep watch on the English fleet, but added that some men-of-war should be detached to watch the French. Little did he know that the French Minister of Marine was about to write to say that he was doubtful if he could help the King of England at all that year.[24]

In the United Netherlands the rejoicing was sober as the news of Prince William's achievement was received. 'There was never such praying in these countries,' wrote D'Albeville, now virtually a prisoner in his own embassy, 'as is now daily for the success of the Prince's enterprise; all the preachers thank God for the late tempest which changed the weather and caused the happy landing in the west.'[25] In Whitehall, on the day after the Court had learned of the Prince's safe arrival in Torbay, Samuel Pepys, the naval administrator who had worked himself to death to bring Dartmouth's fleet up to scratch, was writing to the English Admiral:[26]

> Though all that know your Lordship and above all the King, is abundantly assured that no part of your disappointment in relation to the Dutch fleet can be charged upon any thing in your power to have prevented yet the consequences of it in the said fleet's passing without the least interruption to the port they were bound for with their whole fleet, are too visible.

NOTES TO CHAPTER XII

1. Mazure, iii, 166.
2. Cf. Japikse, ii, 241.
3. Add. Mss. 34512, f. 11 v.
4. Müller, ii, 125–7.
5. Cf. Japikse, ii, 241.
6. Cf. chap. III above.
7. J. P. Kenyon, *The Nobility in the Revolution of 1688*, 12.
8. Pinkham, chap. 5.
9. *H.M.C. Dartmouth*, xi, 5, 180.
10. Add. Mss. 34512, f. 6.
11. Cavelli, ii, 310.
12. Burnet, iii, 291.
13. Powley, 43.
14. Müller, ii, 118.
15. Reresby, 518.
16. Add. Mss. 34512, f. 160: Oct. 30/Nov. 9, 1688.
17. *Ibid.*, f. 158 v: Oct. 23/Nov. 2, 1688.
18. Grew, 132.
19. Burnet, iii, 308.
20. *Exact Diary*, 30–1.
21. Cavelli, ii, 315–16.
22. *Exact Diary*, 33. Cf. Add. Mss. 33970.
23. Egerton Mss. 2621, ff. 41, 43.
24. Cavelli, ii, 300, 320.
25. Add. Mss. 34516, f. 13 *seq.*
26. *H.M.C.* ii, v, 184.

CHAPTER XIII

The Revolution

NOT long after William of Orange disembarked in Torbay on November 5, 1688, with his motley expeditionary force only about one third of the size of that of the royal army, he had ordered his hired transport ships back home to Holland, for he was confident that his coming would be welcomed by the majority of the English and Scottish people and that even James's soldiers would not fight for him. When William's unfortunate predecessor, the Duke of Monmouth, had landed in the west with a handful of men and weapons, although local recruits had rallied to his cause in an astonishing way, he had been betrayed by his supporters in London, who sent him neither arms nor money. William was not going to take any such military risks. He had sufficient men and resources to buy himself time. Having established his bridgehead, he waited to see what would happen. He did not, like Monmouth, declare himself King, but, like George Monck, promised the people of England a free Parliament. Moreover he had already paved his way by the publication of his declaration, which was widely distributed throughout England, while by his dramatic sailing along the English Channel he had proclaimed that his mission was not for conquest but was an open Protestant crusade.

Whether it was an accident borne on the wind or deliberate, William's landing in the west had created a strategic surprise. Had he succeeded in reaching Yorkshire, his army might conceivably have been caught between royal forces coming south from Scotland and north from London and the eastern counties. At Exeter, it is true, he had the garrisons of Bristol and Plymouth lying on his flank, but 100 miles stretched between him and James's main concentration. Moreover, if the King brought all his forces south that would open up the north to rebellion. Of the Immortal Seven, who had signed the invitation to William to come over, three had considerable influence in the north: Danby in Yorkshire, the Earl of Devonshire in Nottinghamshire and Derbyshire and Lord Lumley in Northumberland and Durham. The Earl of Shrewsbury, Henry Sidney and Edward Russell had accompanied the Prince from Holland in his invasion fleet. Henry Compton, Bishop of London, the seventh signatory, after earlier visiting Yorkshire, returned to the capital where his influence was exerted to paralyse the King by inciting his fellow-bishops to refuse to abhor the invasion and by helping to induce Princess Anne to flee from her father's Court.

These remained the most active conspirators. When the letter. of invitation had been discussed by Russell in April, he had told William that he thought it was best to keep the secret to as few persons as possible. Nevertheless others were let into it. Halifax and Nottingham had, for example, been approached; so later had been the Earl of Chesterfield and the Earl of Ailesbury. According to Dr. Burnet, many thousands of persons altogether became aware that a conspiracy was on foot. And of course ever since the middle of September it had been common knowledge, not only in Whitehall, that the Dutch expedition was being prepared.

It is sometimes said that this was 'a respectable revolution', that only a small percentage of the nobility was involved and that not the most powerful. But it is at least clear that for some time many important men had been disposed to force the King radically to change his measures. An estimate made for Dutch intelligence in May 1687 indicated that over half of the adult nobility were opposed to James II's policies.[1] As soon as William committed himself, their sympathies inclined them to join him. To name a few examples: the Earl of Clarendon's son, Lord Cornbury, was one of the first officers to desert James II. Lord Delamere, who had earlier been luckily acquitted of conspiracy with the Duke of Monmouth, was obviously a leader of the rising in the north; indeed he was the first to move. The Duke of Grafton aimed to pervert or betray the fleet. Lord Churchill was ready to lead over the army. (Both Grafton and Churchill, it is true, had been refused high-ranking appointments for which they sought.) The Earl of Stamford, the Earl of Northampton and the Earl of Derby were all committed or half-committed. The list could be extended. Naturally men already in exalted positions with vast hereditary wealth were anxious to avoid being arrested for treason and deprived of their properties or offices if William failed to establish himself. But that did not mean they had no revolutionary sympathies.

A typical case was the Marquis of Halifax. Halifax had written two devastating pamphlets, his *Letter to a Dissenter* and his *Anatomy of an Equivalent* (the equivalent being James's offers of assurances to the Church of England in return for the abolition of the penal laws and the Tests) which contributed to the undermining of loyalty to the King. Both pamphlets, naturally, were published anonymously; and Halifax kept near the King and his Court, and true to his policy of 'trimming', waited to see what was going to happen. In fact he sat still to the bitter end. But other less philosophical members of the nobility like the Duke of Ormonde, the Earl of Nottingham, the Earl of Bristol, the Duke of Beaufort and the Earl of Bath proved ready enough to join the opposition to the King as soon as a promising opportunity presented itself. One can count at least twenty-five peers who were actively or secretly committed to the Prince of Orange soon after he landed. Of those loyal to the King who were not Roman Catholics not a few—like Lord Chancellor Jeffreys and the Duke of Newcastle—were too stunned or too lethargic to be of much help to him.

As to the mass of the gentry, it is well established that the Three Questions put to them by the Lords Lieutenant at the beginning of the year, far from inducing them to promise in advance of a Parliament to agree to the repeal of the penal laws and the Tests as the King demanded, had united them against the Government.[2] It may not be exact to say that they were 'alienated', but they had certainly been displeased and dismayed by the pressures brought to bear on them, pressures which they regarded as unconstitutional. When they realized that all their friends and neighbours had equally refused to be intimidated into approving the King's policies, it gave them a sense of strength and abiding confidence. In the boroughs also even the elaborate tampering with the charters had not effectively helped the royal policies but had rather engendered discontent.

Of the common people, it is probably right to say that they preferred to watch political revolutions go by without being disturbed in their daily tasks and even, as during the civil wars, derived a silent pleasure from observing their masters quarrelling with each other. But the testimony of diarists like Evelyn and Reresby can reasonably be relied upon as evidence that they welcomed William of Orange in a passive kind of way. Reports of mob riots and demonstrations against popery were pretty numerous throughout the reign, outside as well as inside London, where the behaviour of the rabble after the acquittal of the bishops in June was typical and bore witness to an irrational prejudice against Roman Catholicism which could be traced back to the days of the Popish Plot and beyond.[3] This feeling was particularly strong in the Lowlands of Scotland: as early as April 1687 William of Orange had been begged to exert his influence with his father-in-law against the great encouragement given there to papists.[4] Naturally the most intransigent of the revolutionaries were those who had been exiled abroad and now accompanied William on his invasion. But these Englishmen and Scots, some of whom had republican views, were only extreme examples —more courageous or more foolhardy than others—of many thousands who honestly believed that James's policies and methods carried the seeds of arbitrary government and the papal domination of England.

While William and his army were sailing to England and establishing themselves at Exeter, James II was still closeted with leading Anglicans trying desperately to erase memories of his favouritism for dissenters and arbitrary pressures for toleration and hoping to revive the loyalty of the Church towards the Crown. William's declaration had claimed that his mission to England was supported by several spiritual and temporal lords. James invited the Archbishop of Canterbury, the Bishop of London (who *had* in fact invited William over) and the rest to comment on this claim. They all protested to the King that they had had nothing to do with it. So did the Earl of Clarendon and his brother, the Earl of Rochester: treason was anathema to them. Next day (November 4) the King went down to Colchester to review his troops and was there assured by the Earl of Nottingham and the Marquis of Halifax that they too were innocent of treason. While Halifax averred 'as a gentleman on his honour' that he had not invited the Prince to come over, 'no one of the Lords to whom the King spoke deigned to offer his service or assistance, but only observed how distressed they were to see His Majesty's affairs had reached so unhappy a condition'.[5] The lay peers and the bishops, on one excuse or another, significantly refused to do what the King asked them by publicly repudiating William's declaration. The King was still busily arguing with the bishops when the news reached Whitehall on November 6 of the landing at Torbay.

But it was extraordinary how few military steps the King and his advisers took after they learned of William's arrival. Portsmouth, James's escape hatch, was reinforced. Yet the King still appeared to be pinning his hopes on Dartmouth's fleet boldly sailing along the Channel and attacking the Dutch transports as they lay at anchor. Perhaps the King was at first overconfident in his belief that his army so outnumbered that of his son-in-law as to enable him to come to terms with him without fighting. For in spite of continued pressure from France James refused to declare war on the Dutch. The Imperial envoy in London reported on November 9 that more reinforcements were expected from Scotland and Ireland and that the King could not hide his feeling that he was safe and secure, and indeed that his earlier anxieties had fallen away from him.[6] For the moment James was convinced that the only backing William had from Englishmen was from the exiles who had come over with him.

In fact the middle party at Whitehall, Rochester and Clarendon, in particular, and some of the bishops were planning formally to ask the King to call a Parliament at once. This, they thought, might form a genuine basis for a compromise between William and James. After all, in the final version of his declaration, framed on English advice, William had asked for a free Parliament that autumn. The proposal therefore was a possible means to avoid bloodshed. Indeed there was a remarkable lull during the first fortnight after the invasion fleet had anchored. William remained at Exeter from November 9 to November 21. Bentinck, who was there, felt that the neighbouring gentry and clergy were becoming a little warmer towards the invaders, but the majority were afraid of the gibbet.[7] Meanwhile James was still angling for the Church's assistance and was hesitating to leave London. He did not in fact do so until November 17. It was felt by the Dutch ambassador that if the King left his capital there might be a rising against him, though equally if he did not join his soldiers soon and lead them against his enemy, the army might mutiny.[8] A succession of blows now fell thunderously upon him. The first was that his officers began to desert him. Lord Lovelace, the first to try to join William, was stopped by the Gloucestershire militia on November 11 and ignominiously taken back to the army headquarters in Salisbury. But the next officer to do so was no less a person than James's nephew by his first wife, Lord Cornbury, son of Clarendon. Clarendon denied all knowledge of his son's intentions, but his desertion on November 14 was a straw in the wind. On the next day Lord Delamere started a rising in the north by calling out two hundred or more of his tenants in Cheshire. That produced a chain reaction. A week later the Earl of Danby seized the city of York (the Duke of Newcastle, whom James had put in charge as Lord Lieutenant of the three Ridings, having failed to stop the obvious preparations made there); the previous day the city of Nottingham was occupied by the Earl of Devonshire on behalf of the revolutionaries. By the first week of December almost the whole of Yorkshire was in the hands of Orangists.

It was symptomatic of the way in which the nobility behaved that the Earl of Derby was equally remiss in Lancashire. Derby had been told by the King in the middle of October that he was to take over the Lord Lieutenancy of Lancashire and Cheshire from Lord Molyneux, a Roman Catholic, who had previously been given this post when the Lords Lieutenant were being changed about earlier in the year. Derby had assured the King that he was a Stanley and the Stanleys had always been loyal to the throne.[9] But the leading figures in Lancashire had refused to obey the Earl until he received his commission in writing and on November 1, just before William of Orange set sail, Derby had met Lord Delamere and held a secret discussion with him, with the results of which Delamere expressed deep satisfaction. It appears that Delamere warned Derby that a rebellion might take place in the north and that Derby had promised him that his home at Altrincham in Cheshire should in that event be protected by the militia. Lord Delamere afterwards maintained that the Earl of Derby had broken his word to him. But in any case the Earl of Derby, like the Duke of Newcastle, had behaved extremely sluggishly; the rebellion spread from Chester to Derby and Nottingham and by November 21 the Governor of Chester Castle was writing mournfully that he expected the rebels would soon form 'a very great body' and start marching on London.[10] Derby appears to have been ready to prevent disorder but to help neither the King nor the rebels. By December 10 Delamere was telling him sharply, 'God be praised, we need none of your help'.[11]

The northern rising began on November 15. On November 16 Admiral Dartmouth sailed back along the Channel to Spithead to await a friendlier wind. On November 17 James II, having shown his annoyance with the petition with which he had been presented asking him to call a Parliament, at last left London to join his army at Salisbury. James said, not unreasonably, that he could not be expected to call a free Parliament while foreign troops were camping upon English soil. Before he went from London he had informed Barrillon that he did not want open help from France for fear of further provoking the Dutch who, after all, had not yet actually attacked him.[12] Louis XIV himself also felt cautious. He said that he did not intend to send his fleet or his troops to James's aid unless he felt that to do so would be a positive advantage to the King of England.[13] The situation was fraught with delicacy. Everyone was still manoeuvring for position. No one wanted to strike the fatal blow.

Presumably before William departed from Exeter he must have received news of the rebellion in the north. But Danby complained that he was ignored, that all his letters were disregarded: they may however have merely gone astray. But it is likely that the Prince wanted to keep control of events in his own hands. At any rate the situation in the south of England had now cleared sufficiently for him to begin moving east and to bring pressure on the King. Edward Russell had visited Plymouth and persuaded the Earl of Bath that he could safely declare himself a rebel. At the same time as Lord Cornbury deserted, other royal soldiers were beginning to trickle in groups across the lines. Edward Seymour, a powerful figure in the west of England, had joined the Prince at Exeter, which more than compensated for the flight of the Bishop from that city, to be at once rewarded on his arrival in London with the vacant archbishopric of York bestowed upon him by his grateful King. On November 25 William reached Sherborne, where he stayed at the house of the Earl of Bristol. Thence he dispatched the Earl of Shrewsbury with two regiments to see what was happening in the city of Bristol. There he found that the Duke of Beaufort, the Lord Lieutenant of Gloucestershire and neighbouring counties, had already yielded to panic. Bristol was handed over. For both sides it had been a decisive week.

James II arrived at Salisbury on November 19. In his absence the Earl of Clarendon paid a call upon his niece, James's younger daughter, Princess Anne. The Princess asked her uncle why he had not visited her before. Clarendon explained that 'truly he was ashamed to appear anywhere since the villainy his son [Cornbury] had committed'. Anne replied that people were so apprehensive of popery that she believed many more of the army would do the same thing.[14] She knew what she was talking about. For it had already been arranged between her, Bishop Compton and the Churchills that she should secretly leave London at the same time that Lord Churchill and others were deserting the army.

James was in a highly nervous condition while he was at Salisbury. During the five days that he was there, two of them (November 20 and 21) he was perpetually bleeding at the nose. Next day his nose stopped bleeding and he held a council of war. His commander-in-chief, Lord Feversham, was for retreating; his second-in-command, Lord Churchill, was for making a stand: his descendant, Sir Winston Churchill, argued that 'he gave the right advice either because he knew the opposite course would be adopted, or because, if he had been taken at his word, that would have been convenient to his resolves'—since an advance westward would make it easier for his wife and Princess Anne to escape from London and for himself to join William of Orange.[15] At any rate Churchill's advice was disregarded and the following night, accompanied by the Duke of Grafton and other officers and with some four hundred cavalry, he rode over to join Prince William who had now reached Axminster in Devon. By a concerted movement the next night Princess Anne and Lady Churchill secretly left London, in the charge of Bishop Compton, armed with sword and pistols—'a veritable embodiment of the Church militant here on earth'[16]—and after various adventures the party reached Nottingham to be welcomed there by the Earl of Devonshire. At the same time Princess Anne's husband, Prince George of Denmark, nicknamed by Charles II 'est-il possible?', also left the King.

The desertion of his second-in-command, of his nephew and other officers was a severe blow to the King. But the northern risings and the failure of his fleet had made the decisive impact on his mind. All accounts agree that a state of confusion prevailed at the camp while he was there. Barrillon, who went with the King to Salisbury, was not at all surprised by the turn of events. In fact on November 20 he had already warned King Louis XIV that Churchill and Grafton were not to be trusted: that they were unlikely to fight with a good heart 'and the whole army knew it'.[17] Vainly Barrillon conveyed inspiriting messages to James from his

167

master. Far from showing himself willing in time of peril to lead his troops against the foe, James arranged defensive dispositions—his army was to be strung out along the Thames from Marlow eastwards—and toyed with the idea of playing for time and awaiting French help. On November 23 Barrillon reported that the King had decided to retire to London 'as has been his intention from the first'.[18] His object, James informed the French ambassador, was to keep his army intact (like his navy!) and his capital obedient. Now at last he confessed that he would be glad of French troops to prevent the Prince of Orange from becoming master of England. Before the King left Salisbury he gave orders for the arrest of Lady Churchill and the seizure of Churchill's goods and furniture. That was a pathetic effort to shut the stable door after the horses had escaped. As soon as he got back to London on November 26 the King learned with horror that even his own children had forsaken him.

On the face of it James II now decided to try to come to an agreement with his son-in-law. Before he left London for Salisbury he had brusquely rejected the petition concerted by Clarendon and others for the immediate calling of a Parliament. But once James had seen the divided and unreliable condition of his army, he realized that he could not fight or frighten away the Prince of Orange. First he consulted his Privy Council; then he summoned a large meeting of peers, lay and spiritual, and after a prolonged discussion it was decided on November 28 to call a Parliament for January 15, the earliest possible time when this could be done if the normal electoral procedures were followed. Rochester, Clarendon, Jeffreys and Godolphin all favoured that course. Halifax and Nottingham, the famous pair of sitters-on-the-fence, thought it was 'very impractical'. The two Secretaries of State, Middleton and Preston (who had replaced the frightened Sunderland), and some of the King's Roman Catholic advisers, who now hovered in the background, appear to have preferred the idea of the King going to France and collecting help. On the surface at any rate James agreed with those who wanted him to summon a Parliament and to negotiate with William of Orange about its meeting. But all along, at the back of his mind, he was postponing the evil hour of real decision. He explained that if it had not been for his nose bleeding he believed that Lord Churchill would have kidnapped him when he was proposing to inspect his troops at Warminster, fifteen miles from Salisbury, on November 21, and have taken him a prisoner to William. He said that 'it would appear that the Prince of Orange came for the Crown, whatever he pretended; that he would not see himself deposed; that he had read the story of King Richard II'.[19] Earlier James had accused the Earl of Sunderland of losing his nerve; now plainly the King had lost his.

Before James returned to London he had tried to arrange for his son, the baby Prince of Wales, to be smuggled out of the country. He had placed the child in the care of the Roman Catholic Lord Dover, recently named acting Governor of Portsmouth in the place of the Duke of Berwick, who had been summoned to Salisbury. On November 24 Lord Dartmouth—who five days earlier at Torbay had actually sighted the Dutch fleet, which William had ordered to winter in England, but had then withdrawn on account of 'much wind'—landed from the Spithead at Portsmouth in order personally to welcome the royal infant, while his fleet fired a twenty-one gun salute. A week later Dover gave Dartmouth letters from the King containing sealed orders to help him carry the Prince by yacht 'to the first port they can get to in France'. Dartmouth demurred at these instructions and proceeded to write a long letter to the King explaining his downright refusal to obey them.[20] Dartmouth was now rapidly coming round to the point of view of the other leading Protestants. Five days earlier (on November 28) he had warned the King of the growing disloyalty of the naval officers—Captain George Churchill, a younger brother of the Baron, had already gone over to the Dutch, pretending his ship had sprung a leak and added, 'for God's sake, Sire, let a parliament be called'.[21]

James was occupied in sending up smoke screens. On November 29 he saw Barrillon and told him that he could see no remedy but to call a Parliament; and explained that this 'would give him time to take his measures to guarantee himself against utter ruin'.[22] Next day it became known that Halifax, Nottingham and Godolphin, three men of the middle, who had been on friendly but not on treasonable terms with William of Orange, had been appointed commissioners to conclude a treaty on James II's behalf with his son-in-law. None of the commissioners was enthusiastic about his duties. Halifax refused to serve if Rochester were appointed to the commission; Godolphin complained that they had little power; and they all believed that their mission would be a failure before they even started. Moreover, they did not think that prolonged negotiations were in the least possible. 'The affairs of the Prince,' wrote one of them, were 'such as will admit little delay, especially since the King of France's troops have already advanced to Bois-le-duc and burnt twelve villages thereabouts.'

The commissioners' instructions were to inform William that Parliament was to be called on January 15, to which all differences and causes of complaint alleged by William would be referred, and to adjust with him 'all things necessary' for the freedom of elections and an undisturbed session.[23] Additional instructions stated that 'in case the Prince of Orange should object that there can be no security for the sitting of parliament while our forces remain near the Town you are allowed to say our forces shall be halted some reasonable time before the sitting of parliament at the same distance from the Town as the Prince's army', except for the necessary complement of guards.

The commissioners did not meet William until a week later, at Hungerford, eight days march from London. Meanwhile Princess Anne's uncle, the Earl of Clarendon, having searched his conscience long enough, decided to follow in the footsteps of his son and niece. When he met the Prince of Orange on December 3 near Salisbury William inquired about the commissioners and expressed surprise that Halifax and Godolphin had come on such an errand. Their passports were delayed and their guide got dead drunk, but the embassy eventually began business on the evening of December 7. On December 8 the commissioners handed in a written statement. When they asked to speak to the Prince privately William declined to let them, 'for he said he was come on the business of the nation and that he had no private concern of his own'.[24] William appointed his friend William Bentinck and the Earls of Oxford and Shrewsbury to convey his answers the next day. His terms were not altogether unreasonable. He required the disarming and removal of all papists from offices, while all proclamations against him were to be called in, the Tower of London and the fort at Tilbury were to be placed in the hands of the City authorities, both armies were to stay thirty miles from London, Portsmouth was to be guarded against the landing of French or other troops, and revenues were to be assigned for the maintenance of William's forces until Parliament met.

The commissioners were not empowered to discuss these terms, merely to convey them back to the King. But Halifax had taken advantage of the opportunity for a word with the garrulous Dr. Burnet, who was in the Prince's entourage. Halifax asked whether William really wanted to get the King into his power (the so-called kidnapping episode has to be remembered). Burnet retorted that there was no wish to harm him. 'And if he were to go away?' Halifax asked. 'There is nothing,' replied Burnet, 'so much to be wished.'[25] On the afternoon of December 11 the commissioners returned to London, having sent in advance two dispatches to James telling him of the result of their negotiations. The first reaction in Whitehall was that William's terms held out hopes of a satisfactory settlement and that evening James had told his Council that he had no intention of leaving the country. If that was the truth, the King changed his mind later that night. Presumably James had the time to study William's terms and decided they were too much for him. After all, his whole reign had been devoted to the protection of his fellow religionists. Could he now so humiliatingly abandon them, throwing them out of all positions of trust? That would be to stultify his whole career.

So James II came to his final decision that December night. Admiral Dartmouth having refused to send the Prince of Wales from Portsmouth to France, James had him brought back to London, and he sent his Queen and his son across from Gravesend. He gave this news to Lord Feversham, his commander-in-chief, on December 10 and added:[26]

I hope you will still have the same fidelity to me and though I do not expect you should expose yourselves by resisting a foreign army and a poisoned nation, yet I hope your former principles are so rooted in you that you will keep yourselves free from associations and such pernicious things.

Feversham later forwarded this letter to William of Orange saying that 'he had given notice of it in the army to prevent the effusion of Christian blood'. What James may have meant by 'a poisoned nation' was illustrated by a sentence from a letter written by Edward Russell to Arthur Herbert on the same day: 'All the counties we have come through have received us with great joy; great numbers of gentry and nobility have come in.'[27]

James left Whitehall Palace by a secret door in the early hours of December 12, twenty-four hours after his wife and son, taking the Great Seal with him in order, he said, to prevent a Parliament being called in his name. But as he crossed the Thames he threw the seal overboard, whence it was later recovered by a fisherman. As soon as Dartmouth at Spithead heard the news of the King's withdrawal, he handed over his fleet to the 'gracious protection' of Prince William of Orange: complicated underhand negotiations had prepared the way for this surrender. Thus five weeks after the Dutch fleet had anchored in Torbay the bloodless—and therefore glorious—Revolution appeared to have been completed.

These were the determining events. But now came an anti-climax. As soon as the King's departure was confirmed, the Archbishop of Canterbury presided over a meeting at the Guild-hall of such peers as were in London and endeavoured to provide for the maintenance of law and order in view of the precipitate disbandment of the royal army. Inevitably that night was one of riot and terror; Roman Catholics' houses and chapels were attacked by the mob, the residence of the Spanish ambassador being a particular object of wrath; but less damage was done than might have been feared. The news spread and other houses belonging to Roman Catholics outside London—such as Lord Dover's house near Cambridge and various chapels—drew the attention of the rabble. William learned of his father-in-law's escape from London with considerable relief. The Prince had now reached Wallingford on the Thames in his slow progress towards the capital. The Earl of Clarendon noted that when the Prince had dinner at Marshal Schomberg's headquarters 'he was very cheerful and could not conceal his satisfaction at the King's being gone'.[28] All his doubts, hesitations, inhibitions about the future were calmed. He did not, however, press on to London. Next day he moved to Henley where he expressed in no uncertain terms his anger that the King's commander-in-chief had so promptly obeyed James's order to disband and that 'the soldiers were all running up and down not knowing what course to take'.[29]

Meanwhile the unfortunate James II had failed to make good his escape. On December 12, relays of horses having been arranged, he, in the company of Sir Edward Hales, the Roman Catholic Lieutenant of the Tower of London, had covered fifty miles in seven hours. But the boat that was to carry them to France, which lay near Sheerness, was not yet ready to sail. Crowds of people were all over the place engaged in 'hunting papists' or 'priest-codding'. Obadiah Walker, the Roman Catholic Master of University College, Oxford, who had also been trying to escape abroad, learning of his danger, turned his coach back from Kent towards London. Hales, not a popular figure in those parts, was soon recognized, and he and the King were seized just before midnight by a party of armed sailors or fishermen, who boarded their boat. They were carried as prisoners to Faversham, where the King was also recognized, and was reduced to writing letters, including one to Prince William, demanding rescue from his rough hosts.

The Archbishop of Canterbury was a stickler for loyalty and the letter of divine right. No sooner did he hear that the King was still in England than he resigned his presidency of the *ad hoc* council of regency in London and handed it over to the Marquis of Halifax, who took the chair. The Lords ordered the London trained bands to fire on the mob if necessary. After another night of rioting, when wild rumours arose of the Irish marching on the capital, the Lords again met under Halifax's presidency. They received a message from the King in Faversham. Peers, coaches and guards were sent out to collect their wandering King. James, ever volatile, cheered up when he was told that a welcome awaited him in the City. He got back from Kent on Sunday, December 16. A crowd spontaneously acclaimed him, which induced the King to believe that their previous anger had not been with his person but with his religion. Elated, he ate a good supper, related his adventures with gusto, and slept that night once again in his palace.

Needless to say, William of Orange, who had now reached Windsor, was not pleased at the news of James's unexpected return. It had been thought in William's entourage that he had been extremely slow to act. The King by withdrawing himself had, it was said, in effect abdicated; the Prince should at once have advanced on the capital at the head of his army, declared himself King, and issued warrants for the calling of a Parliament 'according to Cromwell's model'.[30] But William was never given to sudden or unconsidered decisions. His first move, after he had received the message from King James, was to order Count Zuylestein to go to Kent and tell James to stay where he was. But it was too late for that. The King was already back in London. On December 17 while James was telling Barrillon that he had no doubt William would seize the throne by force (though rather childishly he added that without the Great Seal he would have difficulty in calling Parliament), the Prince resolved to send a suitable deputation to London ordering the King to remove himself 'for the quiet of the City and the safety of his person' to the house of the Duchess of Lauderdale at Ham in Surrey. Count Solms, one of William's generals, was dispatched with a detachment of Dutch guards to ensure that the order was carried out. The deputation, consisting of the Earl of Shrewsbury, Lord Delamere and the inevitable Halifax, found the King in bed at two in the morning. James said that he would rather go to Rochester than to Ham; it was evident that his intention was to get away to France. The three lords sent to William of Orange, now at Sion House in Middlesex, near London, to ask his permission. The Prince raised no objection, and by the evening of December 19 James was in Rochester. On the day before William himself came quietly into London. Evelyn noted that he was 'very stately, serious and reserved'. 'It happened to be a very rainy day,' wrote Dr. Burnet, 'and yet great numbers came to see him. After they had stood long in the wet, he disappointed them: for he, who neither loved shows nor shoutings, went through the park. And even this trifle helped to set people's minds on edge.'[31]

At ten o'clock on the morning of December 20 William met the peers in St. James's Palace. Next day he announced to them that while he must be responsible for the maintenance of order, he would leave to them the responsibility for the civil administration and for making arrangements for the holding of a free Parliament. A day later James II silently vanished from Rochester during the night; no efforts were exerted to impede his final escape. And while over Christmas loyal addresses were flowing into London inviting William to take over the Government of the kingdom, James crossed the sea, starting his journey in a yacht and ending it upon one of Louis XIV's frigates, to arrive safely upon the soil of France.

The late Sir Winston Churchill called the Revolution 'a national conspiracy'. That is a pardonable exaggeration. All revolutions are headed by a few dedicated men. Others will make up their minds at the latest possible moment. But in the England of 1688 a revolutionary atmosphere had been created. It was shown by the state of unrest among officers and men both in the army and navy; in the anti-Catholic riots and demonstrations that took place throughout the reign of James II in different parts of the kingdom; in the passive resistance of leading men everywhere to the pressures from the King's representatives or agents; in the scepticism generally expressed even before the birth of the Prince of Wales as to the genuineness of the event; in the attitude of the London mob to the trial of the seven bishops; even in their acquittal by a jury against the advice of the Lord Chief Justice.

Leaders of revolutions are rarely attractive figures; often they are dedicated fanatics: Cromwell, Robespierre, Lenin. Certainly the men of 1688 were more 'respectable': who would have died at the stake or in the front line for the corrupt Earl of Danby or the hypochondriac Earl of Shrewsbury, say, among the revolutionary conspirators? Modern historians tend to assign less importance to individual leaders than their predecessors did; they are inclined to examine revolutions in terms of class structure and social or economic change. Emphasis is laid upon the relationship between the concept of liberty and the possession of private property. Locke's justification of the Revolution is analysed in terms of a possessive class afraid for its possessions. The Revolution of 1688 will in future be exhaustively examined in this kind of way. And there can be no doubt that men were then afraid that James II's policies had endangered their property rights, freeholds, or franchises, whether they were Fellowships at Magdalen College, Oxford, or valuable offices of State, removed from men like Halifax or Rochester or Herbert when they refused to accept James II's pressures on behalf of his own religion. Many men also unquestionably believed that the logic of James's views about religious equality ultimately meant submission to the papacy. Had not the King said in his declaration of indulgence: 'We cannot but heartily wish that all the people of our dominions were members of the Catholic Church'?

If historical analysis requires that the origins of the Revolution be traced back far into the past, on a shorter-term basis it was clearly linked with the Popish Plot and the exclusionist agitation a decade before when men first began to question the wisdom of accepting the rule of a Roman Catholic king. It was then that William of Orange who, by his marriage, had become closely involved in English affairs, started slowly to emerge as a possible focus of a revolutionary movement. In so far as any one man was the author of the Revolution it was William, who had been feeling his way towards intervention in England at least since 1681. His invasion had been the signal that aroused many potential revolutionaries to action; yet there still might have been a revolution if he had never come. The Revolution of 1642–49 had set a precedent. James II remembered that only too clearly: hence his reluctance to call a Parliament or to leave London. But William of Orange remembered it too and came over in part at least because he did not want to run the risk of a fresh outburst of republicanism. He came indeed, it might be said, to stop a revolution; in fact, he started one.

Once the signal was given by William's landing in Torbay, men examined their consciences as well as their private concerns. If history teaches us that the causes of revolutions are complex, life tells us that men and women are always capable in a crisis of preferring their duty to their interest. Some men are born impulsive revolutionaries like Henry Booth, Lord Delamere or Bishop Henry Compton. Others are unprepared to take risks. After the Revolution the Marquis of Halifax, that balanced intellectual, once said to Reresby: 'Come, Sir John, we have wives and children and we must . . . not venture too far.'[32] Others again, like Archbishop Sancroft, dared not for conscience's sake betray the oaths of loyalty they had taken, however much they disapproved of existing policies. What all agreed upon was that Parliament should be the forum where the opinions of the ruling classes could best be expressed. James's prolonged efforts to fashion a Parliament to achieve his purposes—not, in themselves, ignoble—had failed. Now William had conquered it was time for it to meet and take its decisions.

NOTES TO CHAPTER XIII

1. 'A List of English Peers, c. May, 1687', *English Historical Review*, No. 69, p. 304.
2. Cf. Nottingham, P.A. 2110c: letter of Oct. 8, 1687.
3. Cf. William L. Sachse, 'The Mob and the Revolution of 1688', *Journal of British Studies*, Nov. 1964.
4. *Correspondentie*, ii, 16.
5. Foxcroft, *A Character of the Trimmer*, 253.
6. Klopp, 4, 214.
7. Egerton Mss. 2621, f. 46.
8. Add. Mss. 34510, f. 171 v.
9. *H.M.C. Kenyon*, 199.
10. Add. Mss. 38695, f. 86–7 v.

11. *H.M.C. Kenyon*, 206.
12. Mazure, iii, 180–1.
13. *Ibid.*, 178–80.
14. Clarendon, ii, 90–1.
15. *Marlborough*, i, 298.
16. *Ibid.*, 303.
17. Mazure, iii, 202.
18. *Ibid.*, 204.
19. Clarendon, ii, 96.
20. Powley, 134–6.
21. *Ibid.*, 125.
22. Mazure, ii, 218.
23. All Souls Mss. 273: cf. Tresham Lever, *Godolphin*, chap. v.
24. Egerton Mss. 2621, f. 69.
25. Tresham Lever, *op. cit.*, 73.
26. Turner, 442.
27. Russell to Herbert, Dec. 10, 1688, in Egerton Mss. 2621.
28. Clarendon, ii, 113.
29. *Ibid.*, 114.
30. *Ibid.*, 115.
31. Burnet, ii, 339.
32. Reresby, 566.

CHAPTER XIV

The Consequences

'THE people,' observed the Marquis of Halifax sagely, 'can seldom agree to move together against a government, but they can sit still and see it undone.' That is what many Englishmen, though not all, did in the crucial months of November and December 1688. Respect was still felt for the person of the King, but long pent-up emotions were released and anti-papist rioting took place not merely in London but in many other parts of England. A story survives that before James finally left Whitehall 'he looked out of the window and saw the violence and fierceness of the rabble' and said, 'I cannot help or hinder it, God alone can do it'.[1] While awaiting the arrival of William of Orange at St. James's Palace, a Londoner was writing, 'we all pray [he] may come quickly that a stop may be put to the fury of the rabble who have done great mischief'.[2] Lack of an adequate police force and the rapid dispersal of the royal army were enough to make respectable people tremble for their goods and their lives. The council that met under Halifax and the City authorities did their utmost to keep order: Halifax tried to pacify the mob by ordering a general arrest of papists (an idea not at all pleasing to William who had no wish to upset his Roman Catholic allies abroad) and by telling the militia to shoot if need be; but what was wanted was the presence of William's soldiers and the prospect of a swift constitutional settlement, heralding an effective Government.

On the day before Christmas the Lords met in their own House still under the chairmanship of the Marquis of Halifax—the Archbishop of Canterbury having again declined to appear—and warmly debated the future. They refused to receive letters sent to them by the King and it was urged that James's second withdrawal meant that the Government had fallen and was 'a demise at law'. The Earl of Clarendon then moved that they should inquire into the birth of the Prince of Wales. To this Lord Wharton retorted: 'My lords, I did not expect, at this time of day, to hear anybody mention that child, who was called the

178

Prince of Wales. Indeed I did not; and I hope we shall hear no more of him.'[3] Such was the force of past propaganda, overriding the conclusive proofs deposed in Chancery. It was resolved to invite the Prince of Orange to take over the civil administration and to send out circular letters so that a Convention should meet as soon as possible in January and decide about the future of the monarchy.

On Christmas day the two addresses were presented by the Lords to Prince William. He replied that he had already invited all the gentlemen who had sat in the House of Commons during the reign of Charles II and also the Lord Mayor, Aldermen and Common Council of the City of London to meet him on the following day as he wished to consult their opinions. The former Members of Parliament, after being addressed by the Prince adjourned to the House of Commons, where they accepted the proposals of the Lords. Two days later William agreed to take over the Government and to arrange for an election of a 'convention'.

Views were divided about what should be done when the Convention met. Some—a Tory party, John Evelyn called them[4]—advocated the proposal for a regency, which had first been adumbrated by Charles II eight years earlier. Others argued that Princess Mary should unquestionably by heredity succeed to the throne which her father had deserted (it being taken for granted that the Prince of Wales was suppositious). Quite a number of people at the centre of affairs were anxious to discover any solution that would avert the danger of a republic. Sir Edward Seymour, for example, expressed perturbation over the 'countenance' that William was giving to dissenters: if they were supported, he said, 'we should run into a commonwealth, and all would be ruined'. Princess Anne also informed her uncle that 'the commonwealth party was very busy'.[5] John Wildman, who came over with William's invasion force, warmed by memories of his youth, was busy writing republican pamphlets.[6] Prince William himself told Halifax that he had received the impression that the Commonwealth party was the strongest in England; but observed that he had not come over to establish a Commonwealth or be a Duke of Venice.[7]

It was plain enough that before the year was out William himself had finally decided that the only practical solution was for him to become King. He had hinted as much in his letters

179

to the Prince of Waldeck. He said so to Halifax on December 30. He then emphasised that he would not stay in England any longer if the Convention decided to bring back King James, that he expected to be asked to occupy the throne, along with his wife, and that the claims of Princess Anne to succeed would have to be postponed until his own death. Princess Mary had long before made it known privately that she would defer to her husband, while he, as he later indicated, would not contemplate being his wife's 'gentleman usher'. It is clear that during the three weeks that were to pass before the Convention met William's friends were lobbying to obtain the Crown for him. William, for instance, had confided to Halifax that he regarded the two Hydes, Rochester and Clarendon, as 'knaves'. Nevertheless both Bentinck and Dijkvelt, who had accompanied the King to London, did their best to bring them round to the Prince's interest. When Clarendon hinted that the religion of the Church of England did not allow its members to depose kings, Dijkvelt showed himself very alarmed indeed. In fact as subsequent events proved, a large number of peers were extremely reluctant to accept the clear-cut solution of replacing King James by King William. As at the time of the civil wars, there was a strong undercurrent of feeling that if the institution of monarchy were not treated as sacrosanct, other hereditary institutions—such as the peerage itself—might be in peril. That was why honourable men like the Earl of Nottingham hesitated before committing themselves.

Writing of the elections to the Convention, Dr. Burnet observed in his memoirs: [8] 'All men were forming their schemes, and fortifying their party all they could. The elections were managed fairly all England over. The Prince did in no sort interpose in any recommendation, directly or indirectly.' William had promised free elections, and it would have ill become him to attempt to apply the elaborate and blatant pressures that had been employed by the Earl of Sunderland (now fled to—of all places—Holland) on King James II's behalf. In considering seventeenth-century elections one has to empty one's mind of the idea of electioneering in modern terms: most members were chosen by local influence or over local issues; even the use of the labels Whig and Tory was hardly appropriate to the elections to the Convention. When Burnet spoke of 'party' he was obviously thinking about the various groupings of opinion which did not, however, emerge at all clearly until the two Houses actually met.

The complicated tampering with the parliamentary borough charters had left a state of confusion and resentment behind. There is some reason to suppose that in electoral areas where James II's campaign on behalf of the repeal of the penal laws and Tests had been especially disliked, candidates closely connected with his Government were not welcome. Samuel Pepys, for example, faithful to the King until the last, was defeated at Harwich. In Kent a candidate who had not associated himself with the welcome to William of Orange was rejected. Some candidates were rejected because they were accused of having connived at popish practices. Yet nearly 200 (out of 513 members) of those elected to the Convention had sat in the ultra-royalist House of Commons of 1685. The general impression is that the majority of members were enthusiastic Anglicans; that is also indicated by the fact that when an attempt was made later to comprehend the nonconformists within the Church (as in 1660) the proposal was rejected.[9]

But the most curious fact of all about this election to the Convention is that little evidence exists that what would be regarded in modern times as its main issue was discussed or debated—that is to say, the future shape of the Government of the kingdom, the question of who was to mount the throne and what his powers were to be. William and William's adherents were naturally eager that men should be elected who would fulfil his wish to become King. A letter that William wrote to Danby as early as December 12 advising the Yorkshiremen who had actively engaged on his behalf in the northern rebellion 'to go back to their respective dwellings and stand to be chosen parliamentmen in their counties, and keeping their inclinations for me . . .' has been quoted as evidence of William's realism.[10] But just as in answer to James II's Three Questions potential parliamentary candidates had refused to commit themselves to any specific line of policy until Parliament actually met at Westminster, so it is safe to say that the gentlemen of England who were anxious to acquire the prestige of membership did not intend to make up their minds until they had gathered together and thrashed things out. That the climate of opinion was unfavourable to the self-exiled James II and his former ministers is plain enough: but the election was not fought on party lines or over specific questions.

When the Convention met on January 22, 1689, William of

Orange sent a message giving an account of his administration during the interregnum of the past six weeks, recommending members to take the entire political situation into consideration in a spirit of unity and with the rapidity that the state of affairs in Ireland (still under the military control of King James's adherents) and on the continental mainland required. He also expressed the hope that as the United Netherlands and France were now officially at war, England would see fit to declare war on France too, if only in gratitude for the assistance lent him by the States-General in rescuing the kingdom from popery and arbitrary power. But neither House of Parliament was prepared to be rushed. The Commons set about its business in a leisurely manner, and the Lords deliberately waited upon the Commons.

The first critical debate took place on January 28. The Commons then voted that 'King James II, having endeavoured to subvert the constitution of this kingdom by breaking the original contract between King and people, and, by the advice of Jesuits, and other wicked persons, having violated the fundamental laws; and having withdrawn himself out of his kingdom, had abdicated the government, and that the throne is thereby vacant'. On the next day the Commons resolved that a popish prince was 'inconsistent with a Protestant state', and furthermore agreed in principle that before the throne were filled they ought to 'secure the rights, laws, and liberties of the nation'. Here indeed were the seeds of a genuinely revolutionary settlement. The throne was vacant, but the new incumbent must accept conditions laid down by Parliament before he was placed upon the throne; and if it were to be William alone, then the hereditary principle in the strictest sense was being abandoned. An elected king who was required to accept parliamentary conditions for his succession, if not a complete novelty (one can instance medieval precedents), was at least startling to old Tory loyalists.

The House of Lords, inevitably more conservative in its outlook than the Commons, did not care for this approach at all. The Archbishop of Canterbury and a large number of the bishops, still wedded to notions of divine right and passive obedience, were not prepared to admit that the throne was vacant, and wanted a regency. So did Nottingham, Rochester and Clarendon. But Halifax and Danby, rivals for William's favours, joined forces. There were some significant abstentions (such as that of Lord Churchill who pleaded 'indisposition'), and the regency proposal was defeated in the Lords by two or three votes. As to the question of whether the King had broken 'the original contract' between him and his people, the Lords consulted their 'legal assistants' who obviously thought that there was no such contract, that it was a mirage of the philosophers. They and the majority of the Lords, however, decided to swallow the concept. But on January 30 the House voted that the throne had been 'deserted' not 'abdicated', and on January 31 rejected by fifty-five votes to forty-one the deduction that 'the throne is thereby vacant'.

It might have seemed that a deadlock had arisen between the two Houses, since the Commons promptly reaffirmed their original vote. But the matter was really decided outside Parliament. The regency proposal, though suggested by Charles II in 1681 and considered by William himself before he set sail, was never a practical proposition. Nor was the idea that Mary should become queen, with William as her prince consort. When Danby, the chief advocate of the latter plan, sounded Mary herself upon it, he received 'a very sharp answer' in which she declared that 'she would take it extremely unkindly, if any, under pretence of their care of her, would set up a divided interest between her and the Prince'. She sent Danby's letter and a copy of her own reply to her husband.[11] But even before he sailed for England, William was aware of his wife's attitude. He now thought it time to intervene himself. He asked Halifax, Danby, Shrewsbury and others to see him on February 5 and told them firmly that he would neither be regent nor prince consort, and that if he were not appointed king for life he would go back to Holland. Danby thereupon abandoned his original plan and came round to the solution that was finally adopted, that William and Mary should be jointly declared King and Queen. Halifax, who believed in the subjection of women, was even inclined to make Mary into a queen consort. That indeed would have been to throw overboard the hereditary principle and to lend substance to the view of some of Halifax's critics that he was a republican at heart.

The committee that had been appointed by the House of Commons on January 29 to frame conditions 'for the better securing our religion, laws, and liberties' which were to be imposed on the new occupants of the throne, a committee which had Sir George Treby as its rapporteur and in which John Somers, a future Lord Chancellor, took an important part, ranged over very wide ground including the independence of the judges and the future of the court of Chancery.[12] But in fact the final draft of the Declaration of Rights, which was sent up to the House of Lords for its concurrence on February 8, and finally agreed between the two Houses on February 12, was limited to practical and empirical questions.* The Declaration began by outlining the grievances felt against James II, notably his exercise of power to dispense with or suspend the laws, his appointment of the commission for ecclesiastical causes, his maintenance of a standing army in time of peace, and his violations of the freedom of election for Members of Parliament. The Declaration then vindicated and asserted what it called 'ancient rights and liberties' by asserting that the suspending power was illegal without the consent of Parliament, that the dispensing power was illegal 'as it has been assumed and exercised of late', that the Ecclesiastical Commission was illegal, the standing army was illegal, the prosecution of subjects for petitioning (as the seven bishops had been) was illegal, and so on. It was also stated that the election of Members of Parliament ought to be free, that the freedom of speech and of debate of Members in Parliament ought not to be questioned outside Parliament, and that excessive bails and fines should not be imposed. Some of the wording of the Declaration was vague, but the tenor was clear: it was a sharp condemnation of the behaviour of King James II.

On the same day that the Declaration was agreed by the two Houses, Princess Mary arrived in England from Holland to join her husband. Next day they were waited upon in the Palace of Westminster by members of both Houses. Since a Lord Chancellor had not (and could not) yet be appointed, Halifax was still the leader or Speaker of the House of Lords; so it was he who read the Declaration of Rights to William and Mary and then offered them the Crown. The Crown and the royal dignity were to belong to them both during their lives and the life of the survivor. But 'the sole and full exercise of the regal power' was to be only in and executed by the Prince of Orange in the name of them both during their joint lives. If William and Mary had children, they were to succeed to the throne; if not, it was to go to Princess Anne and her heirs. On no account was a popish prince to succeed or any king or queen marrying a papist. The Declaration expressed an 'entire confidence' that the Prince of Orange

* Appendix F.

184

would 'perfect the deliverance so far advanced by him and still preserve them from the violation of their rights and from all other attempts upon their religion, rights and liberties'.

So the new King and Queen were acclaimed with bonfires, bells and cannon. John Evelyn noted that the King was 'morose', but Queen Mary came into Whitehall laughing and jolly, 'as to a wedding'. She 'smiled upon and talked to everybody' so that no change seemed to have taken place at Court since her last going away, 'save that the infinite crowds of people thronged to see her, and that she went to our prayers'.[13] It was largely an act. But the censorious thought it improper in one occupying a father's throne. However Mary became popular and offset the reserved nature of her Dutch husband, always 'wonderful serious and silent'.

The offer of the Crown was made in England on February 13; it was not until three months later, on May 11, that a similar offer arrived at Whitehall from Scotland. A Convention had met in Edinburgh in the middle of March and various solutions to the constitutional problem had been explored. It was suggested that the new settlement might be made conditional upon an agreed union between the two kingdoms, but it was decided that negotiations for that would take too long. The deliberations in Edinburgh, which were boycotted by the highlanders, were influenced by the Declaration of Rights in England: a Scottish 'Claim of Right' was put forward including a clause condemning episcopacy. The Scottish episcopalian clergy and the highlanders remained loyal to King James and thus for the Scots the Revolution meant the final triumph of Presbyterianism as the religion of their official Church. The Claim of Right also asserted that James had attempted to convert 'a legal, limited monarchy to an absolute, despotic power'. In effect the Scots deposed King James II and elected William and Mary in his place. Thus the Scottish revolution was more radical than the English; for it enshrined the idea of an elective, constitutional monarchy. As in England, the offer of the throne to the new monarchs was made dependent upon their agreement to conditions, and afterwards the Convention that made the offer was transformed into a legal Parliament.

The English Convention had done the same thing. By a procedure that only a constitutional lawyer could justify or fathom it voted itself into becoming a normal Parliament and later (in December) embodied the Declaration of Rights into a Bill. The constitutional clauses thus enacted were added to by a number of other measures passed during the reign of William and Mary and, after Mary died in 1694, of William alone. These Acts included a Mutiny Act, a Toleration Act, a Triennial Act, a Civil List Act, and an Act of Settlement. The Mutiny Act (1689) was evidently intended, as its preamble indicated, to prevent the keeping of a standing army in time of peace without the consent of Parliament, but it was also meant to control the powers of the Crown over the army in time of war. It was, however, the dependence of the King on Parliament for money which continued to be the most effective method of control. The Toleration Act (1689) or, more strictly, Act of Indulgence, was by no means as far-reaching as James's two declarations of liberty of conscience. Nonconformists were still excluded from public offices (much against the wishes of King William) and from the universities, and had to obtain licences from the local Church authorities or quarter sessions to meet in their chapels. The penal laws were not abolished, and nonconformist clergy were expected to take an oath against transubstantiation, to subscribe to most of the Thirty-Nine Articles of the Church of England, and to take oaths of fidelity to William and Mary. Roman Catholics were less fortunate; in fact two new Acts were passed against them, one excluding them from London and Westminster, the other forbidding them to possess arms. But there was no persecution. Unitarians were left outside the law.

The Triennial Act (1694) provided for the holding of a Parliament every three years and for no Parliament to sit longer than three years. The Civil List Act voted King William an annual sum of money to cover the costs of his household and family. Other money votes were increasingly appropriated to specific uses, so as to reduce the royal power. The Act of Settlement (1701), a wide-ranging measure, not only provided for the ultimate succession of the Protestant Hanoverians, descended from King James I, but secured the independence of the judiciary—which William III in any case perforce accepted in practice—insisted that future monarchs must be members of the Church of England, forbade them to leave the country without the consent of Parliament or to make war on behalf of territories not belonging to the British Crown, and laid it down that no person holding an office or place of profit under the King should be allowed to serve as a Member of Parliament. The Act also aimed clearly to confine all political decisions to the Privy Council, so that blame for policies of which Parliament did not approve could be duly apportioned. But both these last clauses proved impractical. If they had been maintained and enforced, ministers would not have been allowed to sit in Parliament and cabinet government could not have evolved. Thus it may be said that most of the constitutional changes which arose out of the Revolution of 1688 were practical criticisms of the behaviour of King James II, though in the Act of Settlement they were also criticisms of William III, whose single-minded devotion to foreign policy was not liked. But changes of a more fundamental character which might have altered the course of subsequent British history became dead letters.

William of Orange was not deeply interested in all this constitutionalism. As we have seen, even at the time of the exclusionist agitation, he had argued that nothing ought to be agreed by King Charles II which would reduce the future rights of the monarchy. Most of the controversies that split the English Parliament were of no importance to him, though in general he resented restrictions on his effective rights. He sought as ministers men like Halifax, Nottingham, Shrewsbury and later even Sunderland who he believed to be capable of advising Queen Mary when he was abroad fighting the war against France. He had tried to commit the English at once against Louis XIV, but it was only when it was realized that the French were helping James II to regain his throne by sending an expeditionary force to Ireland that support was willingly given to King William's war effort. It was not until after the Dutch and the Emperor had joined together in an alliance against the French that William was able to accede to the alliance on behalf of England.

Halifax noted early in 1689 that William was conscious of being an inexperienced king who 'really shrank at the burden' when he first put on the Crown and 'fancied he was like a king in a play'.[14] He wrote to his friend, Waldeck, that 'the glitter of a Crown did not blind him' and Dutch friends like Witsen who saw him in England found him sombre, melancholy and indisposed, a very different person from what he had been in Holland.[15] Though he had made up his mind to become king as soon as the Hungerford negotiations collapsed, to obtain the supreme authority had not, one believes, been his original

187

intention, and it was something of a surprise and certainly a load of worry to him. He regarded it as a necessity, just as Oliver Cromwell once fancied it had been destined for him by an inscrutable Providence. But William's heart was in Holland and his thoughts in the renewed world war against France.

Thus King William's chief desire was to manipulate the English political machine in such a way as to make it work for his international ends and allow him to return to the continental mainland as soon as he decently could. To avoid personal difficulties he put both the Chancery and the Treasury in the hands of commissioners. Though the Treasury commission was presided over by Lord Mordaunt, now created Earl of Monmouth, who was one of the first advocates of the Revolution, its ablest member was Sidney Godolphin, who had been among James II's more efficient servants. The Secretaries of State were the Earl of Nottingham, a man of the middle who had long been dubious of the wisdom of making William king, and the Earl of Shrewsbury, one of the Immortal Seven. Halifax the Trimmer became Lord Privy Seal and Danby, leader of the northern rebels, Lord President of the Council. The King, noted David Ogg, 'disliked the complaints of one as much as the dissertations of the other'. He found English politicians, on the whole, tiresome; he much preferred to rely on old and trusted colleagues like Bentinck and Dijkvelt. Nevertheless his was a pretty capable group of ministers, and in John Churchill, whom he created Earl of Marlborough, and Arthur Herbert, whom he made Earl of Torrington, he had a general and an admiral of outstanding capacities.

Historians in recent times have tended to argue that the rights of the English monarchy were not in fact much restricted as a result of the Revolution. 'It has long been realized,' says Professor Kenyon, 'that the Revolution did not inaugurate a period of constitutional monarchy or parliamentary government, and that George II for instance was in many respects a much more powerful monarch than Charles II.'[16] The offer of the Crown, observed the late Professor Pinkham, was at no time made 'directly or implicitly contingent upon the acceptance of the Declaration of Rights by William and Mary' and in fact it did not contain any limitations that were not already in existence.[17] The late Professor Richard Pares, on the other hand, wrote[18] that while Parliament deliberately refrained from making new law, 'under the form of a declaration of existing law, it made important changes that limited the prerogative. Moreover the circumstances in which the Declaration was presented to the new sovereigns surely had some significance: only after they had (it is true in general terms) accepted the statement of the nation's rights, were they declared king and queen'. Sir David Keir has written that 'the new sovereigns . . . were armed on their accession with a panoply of undoubted legal powers as ample as that borne by their immediate successors' and that 'with a title based on popular consent and not on Divine Right' William succeeded 'in substance to the position of the last two kings'.[19] Mr. Derek Jarrett has recently observed: 'The Declaration of Rights made it clear that the King must rule through Parliament, but it also left intact the means of his doing so.' It was in fact by the deft use of patronage that the Hanoverian kings were able to influence the structure of governments. Still, this was a step forward in parliamentary history.

As to the question of divine right, here again is a matter for infinite and complicated historical argument. The clergy of the Church of England were required to take oaths of allegiance to the new monarchs by September 1, 1689. Eight bishops altogether, five of them those who had been put on trial by James II for seditious libel, and 400 clergy refused to take the oaths as being contrary to their religion and their consciences. Thus they became known as Non-Jurors. It was not until 1691 that Archbishop Sancroft, whose conscience had been delicate from the first and who had shut himself up in Lambeth, was replaced by Archbishop Tillotson. The Non-Jurors tended to be High Church. Most of the bishops created by William were Broad Churchmen or Latitudinarians. The Non-Jurors and Jacobites, as the dyed-in-the-wool adherents of King James II were called, argued that it was blasphemous to accept the new monarchy and that 'the happiness of England depends upon a rightful king'. To this, other learned clerics, such as William Lloyd, Bishop of St. Asaph, and William Sherlock, Dean of St. Paul's, retorted that a Christian must obey the existing Caesar. 'The transferring of this [the sovereign] power from one to another is the Act of God,' said Lloyd. Sherlock, who at first sympathized with the Non-Jurors, eventually concluded that Christians might submit to the King *de facto* once his Government 'was thoroughly settled'.[20] Thus in religious as in constitutional development it was argued: *'plus ça change plus c'est la même chose'*.

The Revolution had a profound effect on the general social and ethical atmosphere in England.[21] Both Queen Mary and her sister Princess Anne had disapproved alike of their uncle's moral laxity and their father's sexual exuberance. King William, though he had a mistress in Elizabeth Villiers, was a man of austerity and reserve, whose Court was expected to set an example of moral behaviour to the masses. On February 13 William ordered the clergy to preach against 'blasphemy, swearing, drunkenness and the profanation of the Lord's Day'. 'If acts of parliament and orders of the justices of the peace could have created a moral paradise,' writes Mr. Dudley Bahlman, 'England would have been one by 1700.' The Societies for the Promotion of Christian Knowledge and for the Propagation of the Gospel came into being during William's reign. So did the Society for the Reformation of Manners. So too did the charity school movement, 'animated' as it had recently been said,[22] 'by a genuine sense of pity and compassion'. In their sermons the Broad Churchmen stressed the value of ethical codes and high standards of public and private behaviour. In general, the clergy of this epoch were better educated and more tolerant than their predecessors. The final recognition of the legitimacy of nonconformity, which perhaps owes as much to James II as to the Revolution, played its part in forming the more puritanical climate of opinion that survived into the reign of Queen Anne. A spirit of genuine Christian charity, which often took concrete forms, is characteristic of the reigns of the last Stuart monarchs. It can hardly be wrong to attribute this change of atmosphere in part to the rulers themselves.

But of course the first ten years of William III's reign were dominated by war. William's friend, the Prince of Waldeck, had succeeded, while the Prince of Orange was invading and establishing himself in England, in protecting the United Netherlands from a French assault. By the early spring of 1689, 100,000 Germans and Dutchmen were in arms along the Rhine. In February the States-General had declared war on France, justly confident in the help coming from England. An Anglo-Dutch naval treaty was concluded in April, a preliminary to the English Government joining in the Grand Alliance against France. War was declared on May 7, and before it ended not only was the English Navy fully committed but a force of British troops or troops in British pay numbering nearly 90,000 had been engaged in the war against France. Thus William achieved the main objective of his invasion of England. In 1697 Louis XIV was compelled to make peace, and before he died in 1702 William III was able to hand on the torch to John Churchill, Earl of Marlborough, who completed the defeat of Louis XIV's prolonged attempt to become the master of Europe. William accepted the predestined hour of his death with resignation, but he confessed he would have liked to live a little longer to see the great new prospect opening up at the end of his reign as King of England.[23]

What of the other leading character in the story? It is an oversimplification to say that James II was a bully who proved himself a coward. But certainly he lost his nerve not only at Salisbury and during his last hours in Whitehall Palace. When under French pressure he returned to confront William III in Ireland his nose again started bleeding and he did not distinguish himself at the battle of the Boyne where he was defeated on July 1, 1690. His latest biographer writes that 'he was merely a puppet in the hands of men who had possession of his person and of what remained of his mind'.[24] It is likely that his final paralysis of mind was caused by his obsession with his sexual sins. As late as December 1687 Bonrepaus had reported that, much to the jealousy of the Queen, James still saw his mistress, the Countess of Dorchester, and that other obscure women visited him by way of the back stairs at the palace.[25] Even during his Irish campaign he still could not shake off the habits of a lifetime. Later he wrote how he 'abhorred' and 'detested himself' for having 'lived so many years in almost a perpetual course of sin'.[26] That surely was 'the black thing' under which, some thought, he 'could not support himself'.[27] In his sixties when all this was over and he dwelt at St. Germain Palace surrounded by Jesuits and confessors, he wrote papers of devotion warning his son of the dire consequences of his 'predominant sin'. But also in his last years before he died in 1701 he reiterated his unshaken belief in the policy of religious toleration for which he had sacrificed his throne.

NOTES TO CHAPTER XIV

1. Add. Mss. 32095, f. 306.
2. H.M.C. Portland, iii, 420.

3. Clarendon, ii, 126–7.
4. Evelyn, iv, 614.
5. Clarendon, ii, 133 *seq.*
6. Ashley, *John Wildman*, chap. XX.
7. Foxcroft, ii, 203.
8. Burnet, iii, 352.
9. Cf. J. H. Plumb, 'The Elections to the Convention Parliament in 1689', in *Cambridge Historical Journal*, V, No. 3 (1937). Through the courtesy of Professor Basil Henning, I have also read Dr. Alan Simpson's doctoral thesis on the Convention Parliament (Bodleian Ms. D. Phil. d. 339, Oxford, 1939) which criticizes Dr. Plumb.
10. *Cambridge Historical Journal*, V, 107–8.
11. A. Browning, *Thomas, Earl of Danby*, i, 430.
12. Cf. Ogg, 226.
13. Evelyn, iv, 624 *seq.*
14. Foxcroft, *A Character of the Trimmer*, 279.
15. Japikse, ii, 278.
16. J. P. Kenyon, *The Nobility in the Revolution of 1688*, 4.
17. Pinkham, 234.
18. R. Pares, *Limited Monarchy in Great Britain in the Eighteenth Century* (1957), 8–9.
19. D. L. Keir, *Constitutional History of Modern Britain* (1960), 269.
20. Gerald M. Straka, *Anglican Reaction to the Revolution of 1688* (1962), *passim.*
21. Cf. Dudley Bahlman, *Moral Revolution of 1688* (1957).
22. Charles Wilson, *England's Apprenticeship* (1965), 234.
23. Burnet, iv, 547.
24. Turner, 456.
25. Baschet, 'Memoir of the State of England', 1687.
26. *Papers of Devotion of James II* (ed. Davies), 314.
27. Burnet, iii, 236.

CHAPTER XV

Summary and Conclusion

THOUGH the ultimate causes of the events of 1688 in England may be traced back to the Protestant Reformation or even earlier —whenever the secular and religious movement against the supremacy of the Roman Catholic Church gathered momentum— the origins of the 'Glorious Revolution' are to be connected most clearly with the period 1678–81. The majority of the members of the House of Commons then believed that since the heir presumptive to the throne, James, Duke of York, was a Roman Catholic convert, and married to a Roman Catholic princess, he should be excluded by statute from all right of succession. This move was supported by a number of influential statesmen and peers, some of whom pressed Prince William of Orange, a Protestant hero in Europe, married to the Princess Mary, who was next in the line of succession to the English Crown, to come over to England and exert his influence in favour of James's exclusion.

As a compromise, in order to avert the threat of civil war, King Charles II actually suggested that William and Mary should after his own death act as Regents for James who would be allowed to reign but not to rule. William himself preferred any political solution that would not reduce the authority of the English Crown, which his wife might one day wear, and would enable him to bring the English Government over into the anti-French camp; but he hesitated about exerting his own influence in England or going there while Parliament was still sitting; and by the time he did go over the exclusionist movement had been defeated and the King of England was committed to an alliance with France. Thus William learned a profound lesson that was to guide his actions and decisions in 1688. He realized that his hesitation had been fatal and had played into the hands of the French King.

During the last years of Charles II's reign suspicion and antagonism between James and William increased. William met with opposition also in the United Netherlands to his policy of resisting French aggression all the time and by all the means at his disposal. But when James peacefully succeeded his brother on the thrones of England and Scotland there was a temporary improvement in Anglo-Dutch relations. William, who had no wish to see his father-in-law overthrown by his illegitimate nephew, the Duke of Monmouth, sent over six British regiments in Dutch service to the help of King James II and offered to come over himself with Dutch troops to help suppress Monmouth's rebellion. After Monmouth's defeat and death, Anglo-Dutch treaties were renewed and James refused to become a client of the French King, as his brother had been.

Encouraged by his defeat of Monmouth, James II tried to push through a policy of genuine civic equality for all his Christian subjects, but he openly favoured his Roman Catholic co-religionists. He insisted that his leading ministers must be sympathetic to Roman Catholicism, even if they were not Roman Catholics themselves, and he introduced Roman Catholic officers into his army and navy, using his royal authority, sustained by the law courts, to override the Test Act, passed in his brother's reign, forbidding Roman Catholics to hold public offices. This created fear and resentment among his leading Protestant subjects and even provoked anti-papal riots and demonstrations. Unfortunately for James, the cruel and ruthless methods employed at this very time by the French monarchy to destroy Protestantism in France caused Englishmen to wonder whether it was their King's ultimate intention to follow in the footsteps of Louis XIV. There is no reason at all to suppose that James intended any such thing; he always asserted that he did not wish to interfere with any man's liberty of conscience—though he was not above trying hard to convert everyone around him to his own religious beliefs.

James's defiance of the Church of England and of Parliament by his policies and methods of enforcing them caused William to be concerned lest the King of England might be driven into dependence upon France in order to secure protection against his own subjects. In fact James was relying upon his own resources —his army and navy—to maintain his position. But James's naval rearmament, on which he now began, was again a source of suspicion and concern to William and the Dutch. William at this time was perturbed over the likelihood of a renewal of French aggression in northern Europe and therefore he did not want his father-in-law to be forced into a French alliance by his own necessities and the English fleet placed at the service of France.

Early in 1687 England and the United Netherlands exchanged ambassadors and an attempt was made to resolve differences and misunderstandings. James wanted William's support for his policy of liberty of conscience for all. William wished to discover if James's naval preparations were aimed at the United Netherlands in alliance with France. Dijkvelt, the special Dutch ambassador, reported to William that James's naval preparations were not directed against them nor was there any likelihood of an Anglo-French alliance. But at the same time he reported rising discontent among many influential Englishmen over James II's methods of rule and his favouritism for Roman Catholics. William was secretly asked both in England and Scotland to use his influence to restrain his father-in-law, but he was given reason to fear either that a Parliament would be packed to fulfil James's wishes or a civil war provoked. Remembering the lessons of 1681, the idea grew in William's mind that he might be obliged to intervene in England to prevent James from being forced into becoming a dependent of France or, alternatively, to stop the English again being driven into a civil war that might destroy the Stuart monarchy and re-establish a Commonwealth, of which the Dutch had unpleasant memories. Possibly by the turn of the year and certainly by the spring of 1688 William had resolved to intervene forcibly in England, at any rate if he received positive promises of moral support from leading Englishmen.

The birth of the Prince of Wales on June 10, holding out the possibility of a permanent Roman Catholic dynasty in England, and the trial at the same time of seven Anglican bishops for protesting against the King's use of his royal prerogative powers to impose his policy of religious liberty and equality on his kingdom stimulated a group of English Protestant leaders to write to William, asking him to intervene against James II and promising a rising on his behalf as soon as he landed. On receipt of the letter of invitation William intensified his preparations for a military expedition. Three months later he was ready, and published a declaration condemning arbitrary rule and the conspiracy of James II's 'evil counsellors' against Protestantism in England and Scotland. It was not until just after this declaration was published that James finally realized the fate that was going to befall him.

Nevertheless James hoped and believed that the invasion would fail. Even if William succeeded in landing so late in the year, James expected that his subjeḟts would remain loyal to him and that his superior army would destroy his son-in-law. He therefore refused French offers of help until Louis XIV was so completely committed in Germany that it was too late for him to give it.

When on November 1, 1688, William of Orange set out for England his announced intention was to oblige James II to call a free and lawful Parliament. For William wanted to prevent and not to provoke a civil war. He feared that a Parliament facing the King unaided by outside support would either capitulate or revolt. But a 'free parliament' might compel the King to abandon his unpopular policies and commit him to joining a coalition against France. Possibly William also thought that such a Parliament would invite him and his wife to become Regents, as Charles II had suggested they should do in 1681; then they could ensure that James did what was best for England and for Europe. But after William's unopposed landing and his completely abortive negotiations with James about the holding of such a free Parliament, it became obvious to the Prince that if he was to make sure that a republic were not established in England again, he himself must become the effective ruler of the kingdom.

The free Parliament (which was known first as the Convention) that now met, after King James had fled the country, drew up a Declaration of Rights aimed at defining and in reality restricting the future authority of the monarchy and then offered the throne to William and Mary, with William as the executive authority, on those terms. Soon after their acceptance, war was declared on France.

Such is a summary of the political events set out in this book. The question remains why this should be called a Glorious Revolution. Was not what happened merely a *coup d'état* or an enforced change of succession to the throne comparable with Henry IV's overthrow of Richard II or Henry VII's defeat of Richard III? Would not William have been able to impose his authority on his father-in-law by force of arms without any active help at all from the English people in general, help which, it has even been suggested, he spurned? Secondly, when William came to the throne did he not in fact succeed to virtually all the royal power possessed by earlier Stuart monarchs—the right to make war and peace, to choose his own ministers, to call and dissolve and fashion his own Parliaments, to preside over his cabinets and enforce his own wishes and policies? Finally, may it not be argued that looking at the story from a long view of history it was James II with his ideas of liberty of conscience for all Christians—ideas that had been foreshadowed by Oliver Cromwell and Charles II—whose mind was attuned to the future, rather than William whose declaration before his invasion was coloured by distortion and prejudice?

In answer to the first question, can it be doubted that William would never have won his almost bloodless victory if James II's army and navy had not been riddled by disaffection? William would never have ventured to undertake this highly dangerous military operation in the first place if he had not been encouraged by Dijkvelt's and Zuylestein's reports of active discontent in England, by his belief that James's army and navy would not fight, by his knowledge of divisions even among James's own advisers and inside the Church of England and by the letter of invitation from the Immortal Seven which he believed (rightly or wrongly) to represent influential members of the spiritual and lay nobility who had not signed it. All revolutions are initiated by relatively small groups who count upon an underlying sense of unrest within a nation. The French, Russian and Chinese peasants were not revolutionaries by nature. Understandably the ordinary English people in the late seventeenth century hesitated to take part in another civil war. But they looked for leadership and accepted it when it was offered.

As to the question whether a revolution was in fact achieved, it is perfectly true that there was no such complete destruction of a form of government or of society in 1688 as there was to be during the French, Russian, Chinese or Cuban revolutions of later times: for that matter no seventeenth-century revolution could compare with these. The outward form of government remained unchanged: it could still be called a 'mixed monarchy'. But one must distinguish between rights and powers. The Whig interpreters of history from Locke to Macaulay argued that the rights of the monarchy remained what they had always been: that James II or his predecessors had infringed them. The power of the monarch was, however, in fact reduced. The restrictions and conditions that William III was compelled to accept, such as the regular meeting of Parliaments (which he did not like) and the independence of the judiciary, which he accepted, meant that the 'mixed monarchy', which up till his time had been largely a form of words bandied about by political theorists, was in the process of becoming a constitutional and political reality. The power of Parliament, asserted by the trial and execution of King Charles I, was thus confirmed for another three centuries, and became a real check on the executive, when James II fled rather than face a 'free parliament'.

As to the question whether James rather than William spoke for the future, we come here to the difficult problem of the relationship betw.:en character and policy. James was a stupid, prejudiced and cowardly ruler; William was courageous and realistic. He reluctantly appreciated that the time was not ripe for any revolutionary change in the attitude to liberty of conscience in England. Cromwell had discovered that too, to his cost. In that sense, however, it was certainly James II, like Cromwell, who was the true revolutionary. But what determines the immediate course of events is not theories or good intentions, but the character of the men in authority. James was incapable of pushing through his policies; William did so. Thus we return to the chapter with which this book opened, describing the differences in character between William and James.

Do mass movements really alter the shape of history? Cannot it be manipulated? It is the exceptional men who are not afraid of taking risks, of fighting for what they believe to be right or desirable, of sacrificing their own personal interests for a cause, that bring about revolutions. It may well be that James's ideals were as noble as those of William; perhaps they were nobler. William took over the Government from James not because he was the more dedicated man but because he was the stronger character. The price that he paid for his victory was in effect to accept restrictions on the authority of the executive and to acknowledge the power of Parliament. Whether that was to make this historic episode into a Glorious Revolution is a question of opinion or of definition. It undoubtedly contributed to the evolution of parliamentary democracy in England and of a balanced constitution in the United States of America.

Documentation

A. James II's Declaration for Liberty of Conscience

April 4, 1687

It having pleased Almighty God not only to bring us to the imperial crown of these kingdoms through the greatest difficulties but to preserve us by a more than ordinary providence upon the throne of our royal ancestors, there is nothing now that we so earnestly desire as to establish our government on such a foundation as may make our subjects happy, and unite them to us by inclination as well as duty; which we think can be done by no means so effectually as by granting to them the free exercise of their religion for the time to come, and add that to the perfect enjoyment of their property, which has never been in any case invaded by us since our coming to the Crown; which, being two things men value most, shall ever be preserved in these kingdoms during our reign over them as the truest methods of their peace and glory.

We cannot but heartily wish, as it will easily be believed, that all the people of our dominions were members of the Catholic Church. Yet we humbly thank God it is, and hath of long time been, our constant sense and opinion (which upon divers occasions we have declared) that conscience ought not to be constrained, nor people forced in matters of mere religion; it has ever been directly contrary to our inclination, as we think it is to the interest of government, which it destroys by spoiling trade, depopulating countries and discouraging strangers; and finally, that it never obtained the end for which it was employed . . .

We therefore, out of our princely care and affection for all our loving subjects, that they may live at ease and quiet, and for the increase of trade and encouragement of strangers, have thought fit by virtue of our royal prerogative to issue forth this our declaration of indulgence, making no doubt of the concurrence of our two Houses of Parliament when we shall think it convenient for them to meet.

In the first place we do declare that we will protect and maintain our archbishops, bishops and clergy, and all other our subjects of the Church of England in the free exercise of their religion as by law established, and in the quiet and full enjoyment of all their possessions, without any molestation or disturbance whatsoever.

We do likewise declare that it is our royal will and pleasure that from henceforth the execution of all and all manner of penal laws in matters ecclesiastical, for not coming to Church, or not receiving the sacrament, or for any other nonconformity to the religion established, or for by reason of the exercise of religion in any manner whatsoever, be immediately suspended; and the further execution of the said penal laws . . . is hereby suspended.

And to the end that by the liberty hereby granted the peace and security of our government in the practice thereof may not be endangered, we have thought fit, and do hereby straitly charge and command all our loving subjects, that we do freely give them leave to meet and serve God after their own way and manner, be it in private houses or places purposely hired or built for that use, so that they take especial care that nothing be preached or taught amongst them which may any ways tend to alienate the hearts of our people from us or our government; and that their meetings and assemblies be peaceable, openly and publicly held, and all persons freely admitted to them; and that they do signify and make known to some one or more of the next justices of the peace what place or places they set apart for those uses . . .

And forasmuch as we are desirous to have the benefit of the service of all our loving subjects, which by the law of nature is inseparably annexed to and inherent in our royal person, and that none of our subjects may for the future be under any discouragement or disability (who are otherwise well inclined and fit to serve us) by reason of some oaths or tests that have been usually administered on such occasions, we do hereby further declare that it is our royal will and pleasure that the oaths commonly called the oaths of supremacy and allegiance, and also the several tests and declarations mentioned in the acts of parliament made in the 25th and 30th years of the reign of our late royal brother King Charles II [i.e. the Test Acts of 1673 and 1678] shall not at any time hereafter be required to be taken, declared or subscribed by any person or persons whatsoever, who is or shall be employed in any office or place of trust, either civil or military, under us or in our government. And we do further declare it to be our pleasure and intention from time to time hereafter to grant our royal dispensation under our great seal to all our loving subjects so to be employed, who shall not take the said oaths, or subscribe or declare the said tests or declarations, in the above-mentioned acts and every of them . . .

B. The Petition of the Seven Bishops

May 18, 1688

The humble petition of William archbishop of Canterbury [Sancroft] and of divers suffragan bishops of that province [St. Asaph, Bath and Wells, Bristol, Chichester, Ely, and Peterborough] now present with him, in behalf of themselves and others of their absent brethren, and of the clergy of their respective dioceses,

Humbly sheweth,

That the great averseness they find in themselves to the distributing and publishing in all their churches your Majesty's late declaration for liberty of conscience proceedeth neither from any want of duty and obedience to your Majesty, our Holy Mother, the Church of England, being both in her principles and constant practice unquestionably loyal nor yet from any want or due tenderness to dissenters, in relation to whom they are willing to come to such a temper as shall be thought fit when that matter shall be considered and settled in parliament and Convocation, but among many other considerations from this especially, because that declaration is founded upon such a dispensing power as hath often been declared illegal in parliament, and particularly in the years 1662, 1672, and in the beginning of your Majesty's reign, and is a matter of so great moment and consequence to the whole nation, both in Church and State, that your petitioners cannot in prudence, honour or conscience so far make themselves parties to it as the distribution of it all over the nations, and the solemn publication of it once and again even in God's house and in the time of His divine service, must amount to in common and reasonable construction.

Your petitioners therefore most humbly and earnestly beseech your Majesty that you will be graciously pleased not to insist upon their distributing and reading your Majesty's said declaration.

C. The Letter of Invitation from the Immortal Seven

June 30, 1688

We have great satisfaction to find by Russell and since by M. Zuylestein that your Highness is so ready and willing to give us such assistance as they have related to us. We have great reason to believe we shall be every day in a worse condition than we are, and less able to defend ourselves, and therefore we do earnestly wish we might be so happy as to find a remedy before it be too late for us to contribute to our own deliverance; but although these be our wishes, yet we will by no means put your Highness into any expectations which might misguide your own councils in this matter; so that the best advice we can give is to inform your Highness truly both of the state of things here at this time and of the difficulties which appear to us.

As to the first, the people are so generally dissatisfied with the present conduct of the Government in relation to their religion, liberties and properties (all which have been greatly invaded), and they are in such expectation of their prospects being daily worse, that your Highness may be assured there are nineteen parts of twenty of the people throughout the kingdom who are desirous of a change and who, we believe, would willingly contribute to it, if they had such a protection to countenance their rising as would secure them from being destroyed before they could get to be in a posture to defend themselves.

It is no less certain that much the greatest part of the nobility and gentry are as much dissatisfied, although it is not safe to speak to many of them beforehand; and there is no doubt but that some of the most considerable of them would venture themselves with your Highness at your first landing, whose interests would be able to draw great numbers to them whenever they could protect them and the raising and drawing of men together. And if such a strength could be landed as were able to defend itself and them till they could be got together into some order, we make no question but that strength would quickly be increased to a number double to the army here, although their army should remain firm to them; whereas we do upon very good grounds believe that their army then would be very much divided among themselves, many of the officers being so discontented that they continue in their service only for a subsistence (besides that some of their minds are known already) and very many of the common soldiers do daily show such an aversion to the popish religion that there is the greatest probability imaginable of great number of deserters which would come from them should there be such an occasion; and amongst the seamen it is almost certain there is not one in ten who would do them any service in such a war.

Besides all this, we do much doubt whether the present state of things will not yet be much changed to the worse before another year . . .

These considerations make us of the opinion that this is a season in which we may more probably contribute to our own safeties than hereafter. . . . We who subscribe this will not fail to attend your Highness upon your landing and to do all that lies in our power to prepare others to be in as much readiness as such an action is capable of, where there is so much danger in communicating an affair of such a nature till it be near the time of its being made public. But, as we have already told your Highness, we must also lay our difficulties before your Highness, which are chiefly that we know not what alarm your preparations for this expedition may give, or what notice it will be necessary for you to give the States beforehand, by either of which means their intelligence or suspicions here may be such as may cause us to be secure before your landing. And we must presume to inform your Highness that your compliment upon the birth of the child (which not one in a thousand here believes to be the Queen's) hath done you some injury . . .

If upon due consideration of all these circumstances your Highness shall think fit to adventure upon the attempt, or at least to make such preparations for it as are necessary (which we wish you may), there must be no more time lost in letting us know your resolution concerning it, and in what time we may depend that all the preparations can be so managed as not to give them warning here . . .

signed by Shrewsbury, Devonshire, Danby, Lumley, the Bishop of London, Edward Russell and Henry Sidney.

September 30, 1688

... We cannot any longer forbear to declare that, to our great regret, we see that those counsellors who have now the chief credit with the King have overturned the religion, laws, and liberties of those realms and subjected them in all things relating to their consciences, liberties and properties to arbitrary government ...

Those evil counsellors for the advancing and colouring this with some plausible pretexts did invent and set on foot the King's dispensing, power by virtue of which they pretend that, according to the law, he can suspend and dispense with the execution of the laws that have been enacted by the authority of the king and parliament for the security and happiness of the subject and so have rendered those laws of no effect ...

Those evil counsellors, in order to the giving some credit to this strange and execrable maxim, have so conducted the matter, that they have obtained a sentence from the judges declaring that this dispensing power is a right belonging to the Crown; as if it were in the power of the twelve judges to offer up the laws, rights and liberties of the whole nation to the King, to be disposed of by him arbitrarily and at his pleasure ...

It is likewise certain that there have been, at divers and sundry times, several laws enacted for the preservation of those rights and liberties, and of the Protestant religion; and, among other securities, it has been enacted that all persons whatsoever that are advanced to any ecclesiastical dignity, or to bear office in either university, as likewise all others that should be put into any employment civil or military should declare that they were not papists, but were of the Protestant religion, and that, by their taking of the oaths of allegiance and Supremacy, and the Test: yet those evil counsellors have, in effect, annulled and abolished all those laws, both with relation to ecclesiastical and civil employments ...

[those evil counsellors] have not only without any colour of law, but against the express laws to the contrary, set up a commission of a certain number of persons, to whom they have committed the cognizance and direction of all ecclesiastical matters; in the which commission there has been, and still is, one of his Majesty's ministers of state, who makes now public profession of the Popish religion [Sunderland] ... and those evil counsellors take care to raise none to any ecclesiastical dignities but persons that have no zeal for the Protestant religion, and that now hide their unconcernedness for it under the specious pretence of moderation ...

The Declaration then instances the favouritism of papists, the pressures on the clergy and local government, the forfeiture of the charters and the trial of the seven bishops as grievances against the 'evil counsellors' of James II and continues:

Both We ourselves and our dearest and most entirely beloved Consort the Princess have endeavoured to signify in terms full of respect to the King the just and deep regret which all these proceedings have given us . . .

The last and great remedy for all those evils is the calling of a parliament, for securing the nation against the evil practices of those wicked counsellors; but this could not be yet compassed, nor can it be easily brought about: for those men apprehending that a lawful parliament being once assembled, they would be brought to an account for all their open violations of law, and for their plots and conspiracies against the Protestant religion, and the lives and liberties of the subjects, they have endeavoured, under the specious pretence of liberty of conscience, first to sow divisions amongst Protestants, between those of the Church of England and the dissenters. . . . They have also required all the persons in the several counties of England that either were in any employment, or were in any considerable esteem, to declare beforehand that they would concur in the repeal of the Test and penal laws; and that they would give their voices in the elections to parliament only for such as would concur in it . . .

But, to crown all, there are great and violent presumptions inducing us to believe that those evil counsellors, in order to the carrying on of their evil designs, and to the gaining to themselves the more time for effecting of them, for the encouraging of their complices, and for the discouraging of all good subjects, have published that the Queen hath brought forth a son; though there hath appeared both during the Queen's pretended bigness, and in the manner in which the birth was managed, so many just and visible grounds of suspicion that not only we ourselves, but all the good subjects of those kingdoms, do vehemently suspect that the pretended Prince of Wales was not born by the Queen . . .

And since our dearest and most entirely beloved Consort the Princess, and likewise ourselves, have so great an interest in this matter, and such a right, as all the world knows, to the succession to the Crown . . . and since the English nation has ever testified a most particular affection and esteem both to our dearest Consort the Princess and to ourselves, we cannot excuse ourselves from espousing their interests in a matter of such high consequences; and from contributing all that lies in us for the maintaining both of the Protestant religion and of the laws and liberties of those kingdoms; and for the securing to them the continual enjoyments of all their just rights: to the doing of which we are most earnestly solicited by a great many lords, both spiritual and temporal and by many gentlemen and other subjects of all ranks.

Therefore it is that we have thought fit to go over to England and to carry with us a force sufficient, by the blessing of God, to defend us from the violence of those evil counsellors; and we, being desirous that our intention in this may be rightly understood, have, for this end, prepared this declaration, in which we have hitherto given a true account of the reasons inducing us to it; so we now think fit to declare that this our expedition is intended for no other design but to have a free and lawful parliament assembled as soon as possible . . .

We do, in the last place, invite and require all persons whatsoever, all the peers of the realm, both spiritual and temporal, all lords lieutenants, deputy lieutenants, and all gentlemen, citizens, and other commons of all ranks, to come and assist us, in order to the executing of this our design, against all such as shall endeavour to oppose us, that so we may prevent all those miseries which must needs follow upon the nation's being kept under arbitrary government and slavery, and that all violences and disorders, which may have overturned the whole Constitution of the English government, may be fully redressed in a free and legal parliament . . .

E. KING JAMES II's PROCLAMATION
September 28, 1688

We have received undoubted advice that a great and sudden invasion from Holland, with an armed force of foreigners and strangers, will speedily be made in a hostile manner upon this our kingdom; and although some false pretences relating to liberty, property, and religion, contrived or worded with art and subtlety may be given out (as shall be thought useful upon such an attempt) it is manifest however (considering the great preparations that are making) that no less matter by this invasion is proposed and purposed than an absolute conquest of our kingdoms and the utter subduing and subjecting us and our people to a foreign power, which is promoted (as we understand, although it may seem almost incredible) by some of our subjects, being persons of wicked and restless spirits, implacable malice, and desperate designs, who having no sense of former intestine distractions, the memory and misery whereof should endear and put a value upon that peace and happiness which hath long been enjoyed; nor being moved by our reiterated acts of grace and mercy, wherein we have studied and delighted to abound towards our subjects, and even towards those who were once our avowed and open enemies, do again endeavour to embroil this kingdom in blood and ruin, to gratify their own ambition and malice, proposing to themselves a prey and booty in such a public confusion.

We cannot omit to make it known that although we had notice some time since that a foreign force was preparing against us, yet we have always declined any foreign succours, but rather have chosen (next under God) to rely upon the true and ancient courage, faith, and allegiance of our own people, with whom we have often ventured our life for the honour of this nation and in whose defence against our enemies we are firmly resolved to live and die. And therefore we solemnly conjure our subjects to lay aside all manner of animosities, jealousies and prejudices, and heartily and cheerfully to unite together in the defence of us and their native country, which they alone will (under God) defeat and frustrate the principal hope and design of our enemies, who expect to find a people divided, and by publishing perhaps some plausible reasons for their coming hither, as the specious, though false, pretences of maintaining the Protestant religion, or asserting the liberties and properties of our people, do hope thereby to conquer the great and renowned kingdom. But albeit the design hath been carried on with all imaginable secrecy and endeavours to surprise and deceive us, we have not been wanting on our part to make such provision as did become us and by God's blessing we make no doubt of being found in so good a posture that our enemies may have cause to repent such their rash and unjust attempt.

We did intend (as we lately declared) to have our parliament in November next and the writs are issued forth accordingly, proposing to ourselves, amongst other things, that we might be able to quiet the minds of all our people in matters of religion, pursuant to our several declarations we have published to that effect, but in regard of this strange and unreasonable attempt from our neighbouring country (without any manner of provocation) designed to divert our said gracious purposes, we find it necessary to recall our said writs . . . And forasmuch as the approaching danger now is at hand we call on all our subjects (whose ready concurrence, valour, and courage as true Englishmen we no way doubt in so just a cause) to be prepared to defend their country; And we do hereby command and require all Lords Lieutenants and Deputy Lieutenants to use their best and utmost endeavours to resist, repel, and suppress our enemies who come with such confidence and quiet preparations to invade and conquer these our kingdoms. And lastly we do most expressly and strictly enjoin and prohibit all and every of our subjects of what degree and condition soever from giving any manner of aid, assistance, countenances or succour, or from having or holding any correspondence with these our enemies or any of their accomplices upon pain of high treason, and being prosecuted and proceeded against with the utmost severity.

F. THE DECLARATION OF RIGHTS
February 13, 1689

Whereas the late King James the Second, by the assistance of divers evil counsellors, judges, and ministers employed by him, did endeavour to subvert and extirpate the Protestant religion and the laws and liberties of the kingdom.

1. By assuming and exercising a power of dispensing with and suspending of laws, and the execution of laws, without the consent of parliament.
2. By committing and prosecuting divers worthy prelates for humbly petitioning to be excused concurring to the said assumed power.
3. By issuing and causing to be executed a commission under the Great Seal for erecting a court called the Court of Commissioners for Ecclesiastical Causes.
4. By levying money for and to the use of the Crown by pretence of prerogative, for other time and in other manner than the same was granted by parliament.
5. By raising and keeping a standing army within this kingdom in time of peace without the consent of parliament and quartering soldiers contrary to the law.
6. By causing several good subjects, being Protestants, to be disarmed at the same time when papists were both armed and employed contrary to the law.
7. By violating the freedom of election by members to serve in parliament.
8. By prosecutions in the Court of King's Bench for matters and causes cognizable only in parliament; and by divers other arbitrary and illegal courses.
9. And whereas of late years, partial, corrupt, and unqualified persons have been returned and served on juries in trials, and particularly divers jurors in trials for high treason, which were not freeholders.
10. Excessive bail hath been required of persons committed in criminal cases, to elude the benefit of laws made for the liberty of the subjects.
11. And excessive fines have been imposed; and illegal and cruel punishments inflicted.
12. And several grants and promises made of fines and forfeitures, before any conviction or judgment against the persons, upon whom the same were to be levied.

All which are utterly and directly contrary to the known laws and statutes and freedom of this realm.

And whereas the said late King James the Second having abdicated the government, and the throne being thereby vacant, his Highness the Prince of Orange (whom it hath pleased Almighty God to make the glorious instrument of delivering this kingdom from popery and arbitrary power) did (by the advice of the lords spiritual and temporal, and divers principal persons of the Commons) cause letters to be written to the lords spiritual and temporal, being Protestants; and other letters to the several counties, cities, universities, boroughs, and Cinque

Ports, for the choosing of such persons to represent them, as were of right to be sent to parliament, to meet and sit at Westminster upon January 22, 1689 . . .

And thereupon the said lords spiritual and temporal and Commons . . . do in the first place (as their ancestors in like case have usually done) for the vindicating and asserting their ancient rights and liberties, declare:

1. That the pretended power of suspending of laws, or the execution of laws, by regal authority, without consent of parliament, is illegal.
2. That the pretended power of dispensing with laws, or the execution of laws, by regal authority, as it hath been assumed and exercised of late, is illegal.
3. That the commission for erecting the late Courts of Commissioners for Ecclesiastical Causes and courts of like nature are illegal and pernicious.
4. That levying money for or to the use of the Crown, by pretence of prerogative, without grant of parliament, for longer time, or in other manner than the same is, or shall be granted, is illegal.
5. That it is the right of the subjects to petition the King, and all commitments and prosecutions for such petitioning are illegal.
6. That the raising or keeping a standing army within the kingdom in time of peace, unless it be with consent of parliament, is against law.
7. That the subjects which are Protestants may have arms for their defence suitable to their conditions and as allowed by law.
8. That election of members of parliament ought to be free.
9. That the freedom of speech and debates or proceedings in parliament ought not to be impeached or questioned in any court or place out of parliament.
10. That excessive bail ought not to be required, nor excessive fines imposed; nor cruel and unusual punishments inflicted.
11. That jurors ought to be duly impanelled and returned, and jurors which pass upon men in trials for high treason ought to be freeholders.
12. That all grants and promises of fines and forfeitures of particular persons before conviction are illegal and void.
13. And that for redress of all grievances, and for the amending, strengthening and preserving of the laws, parliaments ought to be frequently held.

And they do claim, demand, and insist upon all and singular the premises, as their undoubted rights and liberties; and that no declaration, judgments, doings or proceedings, to the prejudice of the people in any of the said premises, ought in any wise to be drawn hereafter into consequence of example.

To which demands of their rights they are particularly encouraged by the declaration of His Highness the Prince of Orange, as being the only means for obtaining a full redress and remedy therein.

Having therefore an entire confidence that his said Highness the Prince of Orange will perfect the deliverance so far advanced by him, and will still preserve them from the violation of their rights, which they have here asserted, and from all other attempts upon their religion, rights, and liberties.

The said Lords Spiritual and Temporal, and Commons, assembled at Westminster do resolve that William and Mary, Prince and Princess of Orange be, and be declared, King and Queen of England, France, and Ireland, and the dominions thereunto belonging, to hold the Crown and royal dignity of the said kingdoms and dominions to them the said Prince and Princess during their lives, and the life of the survivor of them; and that the sole and full exercise of regal power be only in, and executed by the said Prince of Orange, in the names of the said Prince and Princess, during their joint lives; and after their deceases, the said Crown and royal dignity of the said Kingdoms and dominions to be to the heirs of the body of the said Princess; and for default of such issue to the Princess Anne of Denmark and the heirs of her body; and for default of such issue to the heirs of the body of the said Prince of Orange. And the Lords Spiritual and Temporal and the Commons do pray the said Prince and Princess to accept the same accordingly.

Select Bibliography

1. *Manuscript Sources*

British Museum

Add. Mss. 22876	Ellis letters
Add. Mss. 34507–17	Mackintosh transcripts
Add. Mss. 32681	Sidney papers
Add. Mss. 33923	Sir John Knatchbull's diary
Add. Mss. 32095	Accounts of King James II in 1688
Add. Mss. 33970	Account of invasion and the march to London in 1688
Add. Mss. 34487	Newsletters of 1688
Add. Mss. 38294–5	Reports of the Polish ambassador at The Hague, 1687–8
Add. Mss. 38695	War Office correspondence
Add. Mss. 41814	D'Albeville dispatches
Egerton Mss. 1705	Bentinck letters
Egerton Mss. 2621	Herbert correspondence

Public Record Office

A. Baschet's transcripts of correspondence of French ambassadors in London [Baschet]
State Papers (Holland) S.P. 84
State Papers (Domestic) S.P. 18

Bodleian Library, Oxford

Ballard Mss. 21
Ms. D. Phil. d. 339 (Dr. Alan Simpson on the Convention)

Codrington Library, Oxford

All Souls Mss. 273

Nottingham University Library

Portland Mss. Miscellaneous 19

2. *Printed Sources*

Ailesbury, Thomas, Earl of, *Memoirs* (1890) [Ailesbury]
Bentinck, M. von, *Lettres et mémoires de Marie, reine d'Angleterre* (1880)
Bramston, Sir John, *Autobiography* (1845)
Burnet, Gilbert, *History of His Own Times* (1823) [Burnet]

Cavelli, Campana de, *Les derniers Stuarts à Saint Germain-en-Laye* (1871) [Cavelli]

Chesterfield, 2nd Earl of, *Letters* (1837) [Chesterfield]

Clarendon, Henry Hyde, 2nd Earl of, *State letters, etc.* (1828) [Clarendon]

Clarke, J. S., *Life of James II* (1816) [Clarke]

Dalrymple, Sir John, *Memoirs of Great Britain and Ireland* (1753) [Dalrymple]

Danby, Thomas, Earl of, *Letters* (ed. A. Browning, 1944)

D'Avaux, Comte de, *Négociations en Holland* (1753) [D'Avaux]

Ellis, H., *Original Letters Illustrative of English History* (1846)

Evelyn, John, *Diary* (ed. E. de Beer, 1955) [Evelyn]

Expedition of the Prince of Orange to England: Somers Tracts, IX

Fox, C. J., *A History of the Early Part of the Reign of James the Second* (1808) [Fox]

Foxcroft, H. C. ed., *Life and Letters of Sir George Savile* (1898) [Foxcroft]

Foxcroft, H. C. ed., *A Supplement to Burnet's History of My Own Times* (1902)

Histoire des evènements tragiques d'Angleterre et des derniers troubles d'Ecosse (1686)

Japikse, N. ed., *Correspondentie van Willem II an van Bentinck* (1927–28) [*Correspondentie*]

Jusserand, J. J. ed., *Recueil des instructions diplomatiques donneés aux ambassadeurs: Angleterre* (1929) [*Instructions*] |

Krämer, F. J. L., *Archives ou correspondence inédite de la Maison d'Orange Nassau 1689–1702* 3rd series (1909) [Krämer]

Middlebush, F. A. ed., *The Dispatches of Thomas Plott and Thomas Chudleigh: English Envoys at The Hague* (1926)

Müller, P. L., *Wilhelm II von Oranien und Georg Friederich von Waldeck* (1873) [Müller]

Prinsterer, G. Groen van, *Archives ou correspondance inédite de la Maison d'Orange Nassau* 2nd series (1862) [Prinsterer]

Reresby, Sir John, *Memoirs* (ed. A. Browning, 1936) [Reresby]

Temple, Sir William, *Works* (1770) [Works]

Thoresby, Ralph, *Diary* (1830)

Whittle, John, *Exact Diary of the Late Expedition* (1689) [*Exact diary*]

3. *Historical Manuscript Commission Reports* [H.M.C.]

Beaufort	Graham (Report VII)	Portland
Dartmouth	Kenyon	Rutland
Downshire	Lindsey	Savile Foljambe

4 *Secondary Authorities*

Ashley, Maurice, *John Wildman: Plotter and Postmaster* (1947)

Bahlman, Dudley, *Moral Revolution of 1688* (1957)

Baxter, Stephen, *William III* (1966)
Bell, H. E. and Ollard, R. L., *Historical Essays 1600–1750 Presented to David Ogg* (1963)
Blok, P., *History of the People of the Netherlands* (1907)
Browning, Andrew, *Thomas, Earl of Danby: Life* (1953)
Bryant, Arthur, *Pepys: the Saviour of the Navy* (1938)
Carpenter, Edward, *The Protestant Bishop . . . Henry Compton, 1632–1713* (1956)
Chapman, Hester, *Mary II Queen of England* (1953)
Churchill, W. S., *Marlborough: his Life and Times,* I (1933)
Ehrman, John, *The Navy in the War of William III* (1953)
Emerson, W. R., *Monmouth's Rebellion* (1951)
Feiling, K. G., *A History of the Tory Party* (1924)
Firth, C. H., *Commentary on Macaulay's History of England* (1938)
Foxcroft, H. C., *A Character of the Trimmer* (1946)
Geyl, P., *The Netherlands in the Seventeenth Century, 1648–1715* (1964)
  History of the Low Countries (1964)
Grew, M. E., *William Bentinck and William III* (1924) [Grew]
Jacobsen, G., *William Blathwayt* (1932)
Japikse, N., *Prins Willem III de Stadhouder Koning* (1930) [Japikse]
Jones, J. R., *The First Whigs* (1961)
Keeton, G. W., *Lord Chancellor Jeffreys and the Stuart Cause* (1964)
Kenyon, J. P., *Robert Spencer, Earl of Sunderland 1641–1702* (1958) [Kenyon]
Kenyon, J. P., *The Nobility in the Revolution of 1688* (1963)
Klopp, Onno, *Der Fall des Hauses Stuart* (1876) [Klopp]
Kurtz, G. H., *Willem III en Amsterdam* (1928)
Lever, Tresham, *Godolphin: his Life and Times* (1952)
Macaulay, T. B., *History of England* (ed. C. H. Firth, 1915)
Mackintosh, James, *History of the Revolution in England in 1688* (1834) [Mackintosh]
Mazure, F. A. J., *Histoire de la revolution de 1688* (1825) [Mazure]
Muilenberg, James, *The Embassy of Everaard van Weede* (1920)
Ogg, David, *England in the Reign of Charles II* (1955)
  England in the Reigns of James II and William III (1955) [Ogg]
Oudendijk, J. K., *Willem III* (1954)
Pinkham, Lucile, *William III and the Respectable Revolution* (1954) [Pinkham]
Powley, E. B., *The English Navy in the Revolution of 1688* (1928) [Powley]
Ranke, L. von, *History of England* (1875)
Robb, Nesca, *William of Orange 1650–1673* (1962)
Ronalds, Francis S., *The Attempted Whig Revolution of 1678–1681* (1937)
Somerville, Dorothea H., *The King of Hearts* (1962)
Straka, Gerald M., *Anglican Reaction to the Revolution of 1688* (1962)
  The Revolution of 1688: Whig Triumph or Palace Revolution? (1963)

Tindal Hart, A., *William Lloyd* (1952)
Trevelyan, G. M., *The English Revolution* (1938)
Turner, F. C., *James II* (1948) [Turner]
Wolf, J. B., *The Emergence of the Great Powers* (1951)

5. *Articles*

Cherry, George L., 'The Legal and Philosophical Problems of the Jacobites 1688–1689', in *Journal of Modern History*, XXII (1950)

Durand, R., 'Louis XIV et Jacques II à la veille de la revolution de 1688', in *Revue d'histoire moderne et contemporaine*, X (1908)

Evans, A. M., 'Yorkshire and the Revolution of 1688', in *Yorkshire Archaeological Journal* (1929)

Furley, O. W., 'The Whig Exclusionists', in *Cambridge Historical Journal*, XIII (1957)

George, R. H., 'The Financial Relations of Louis XIV and James II', in *Journal of Modern History*, III (1931)

George, R. H., 'Parliamentary Elections and Electioneering in 1685', in *Royal Historical Society Transactions*, 4th series, XIX (1936)

George, R. H., 'The Charters Granted to the English Parliamentary Corporations in 1688', in *English Historical Review*, LV (1940)

Haley, K. H. D., 'A List of English Peers c. May, 1687', in *English Historical Review*, LXIX (1954)

Kenyon, J. P., 'The Earl of Sunderland and the Revolution of 1688', in *Cambridge Historical Journal*, XI (1955)

Kenyon, J. P., 'The Reign of Charles II', in *Cambridge Historical Journal*, XIII (1957)

Kenyon, J. P., 'The Birth of the Old Pretender', in *History Today* (June 1963)

Kenyon, J. P., 'The Exclusion Crisis 1678–1681', in *History Today* (April, May, 1964)

Laslett, Peter, 'The English Revolution and Locke's *Two Treatises of Government*', in *Cambridge Historical Journal*, XII (1956)

Mitchell, A. A., 'The Revolution of 1688 and the Flight of James II', in *History Today* (July 1965)

Plumb, J. H., 'The Election to the Convention Parliament in 1689', in *Cambridge Historical Journal*, V (1937)

Sachse, W. L., 'The Mob and the Revolution of 1688', in *Journal of British Studies*, IV (1964)

Tanner, J. R., 'Naval Preparations of James II in 1688', in *English Historical Review*, VIII (1893)

Thompson, E. M., 'Correspondence of Admiral Herbert during the Revolution', in *English Historical Review*, I (1886)

INDEX

Index

Lords Lieutenant, 88, 89, 112, 115, 146, 155, 162
Lorraine, 35, 48
Louis XIV, King of France, 10, 12, 13, 21, 24, 25, 35, 38, 39, 42, 45, 46, 47, 48, 49, 50, 51, 52, 53, 54, 58, 62, 64, 73, 78, 79, 87, 100, 107, 113, 114, 130, 131, 132, 133, 136, 139, 140, 151, 187, 191, 194, 196; quoted, 151
Lovelace, Lord, 164
Lumley, Lord, 121, 122, 123, 161
Luttrell, Nicholas, 84
Luxembourg, 39, 48, 53
Lyme, 60

Mackay, Major-General, 156
Macpherson, Professor C. B., 104
Madrid, 49, 50
Magdalen College, Oxford, 68, 89, 93, 116, 117, 136, 145, 175
Magna Carta, 97, 102, 106
Maintenon, Madame de, 48, 62
Mainz, Elector of, 140
Maria Teresa, Queen, wife of Louis XIV, 45, 46, 48
Marlow, 168
Mary Beatrice, Queen, formerly Princess of Modena, 20, 91, 92, 110 seq., 171
Mary, Princess, mother of King William III, 10, 11, 16, 74
Mary II, Queen, wife of King William III, 13, 20, 21, 31, 37, 40, 41, 81, 84, 85, 92, 118, 129, 147, 179 seq., 190, 193
Mary, Queen of Scots, 23
Mediterranean sea, 123
Middleton, Lord, 168
Milton, John, 99, 100, 102, 105; quoted, 98
'Mixed monarchy', 97, 99, 100, 106, 107, 197
Molyneux, Lord, 112, 165
Monck, General George, 61, 160
Monmouth, James Scott, Duke of, 27, 28, 29, 30, 31, 33, 38, 40, 41, 60 seq., 71 seq., 110, 129, 131, 142, 153, 160, 161, 194

Montecuccoli, Raimundo, 50, 51
Mordaunt, Charles, Viscount, later Earl of Monmouth, 61, 75, 80, 91, 122, 188; quoted, 62
Moulin, Peter du, 127
Mutiny Act (1689), 186

Nantes, Edict of, revocation of, 62, 64, 78, 125
Nassau, 10
Nassau, Count, 156
Nassau-Ouwerkerk, Hendrick van, 70, 71
Navy, Dutch, 125, 128, 133, 142, 143, 146, 147, 148, 156 seq., 172
Navy, English, 42, 114, 123, 131, 137, 142, 143, 145, 148, 157, 190
Navy, French, 131
Netherlands, Spanish, 39, 45, 46, 51, 54, 152
Netherlands, United, 23, 24, 28, 29, 37, 38, 40, 41, 42, 45, 54, 61, 71, 73, 77, 78, 79, 84, 94, 96, 113, 114, 125, 126, 133, 134, 139, 140, 141, 146, 159, 164, 166, 182, 187, 190, 193, 194, 195
Nevile, Henry, 106, 107, 108
Newcastle, Henry Cavendish, Duke of, 141, 146, 162, 165
Newton, Isaac, 105
Nobility, English, 161
Nonconformists, 83, 84, 130
Non-Jurors, 189
Nore, Buoy of the, 130, 141, 142
Norfolk, 90, 154, 155
Northampton, George Compton, 4th Earl of, 161
Northumberland, 161
Nottingham, 165, 168
Nottingham, Daniel Finch, 2nd Earl of, 85, 122, 123, 129, 148, 161, 162, 163, 168, 169, 180, 182, 187, 188
Nottinghamshire, 160
Nymegen, 126, 147
Nymegen, Treaty of, 25, 47, 48, 145

Oates, Titus, 26, 60

221

222

England and the United Netherlands in 1688

Berwick

York
Hull

R Boyne
Dublin

IRELAND

R Shannon

WALES

ENGLAND

Hungerford
Bristol

Salisbury
Ports

Exeter
Spithea

Plymouth
Torbay
Dartmouth

I. of
Wight

ATLANTIC

OCEAN